Advance praise from family law experts across the globe for *The Family Law Professional's Field Guide to High-Conflict Litigation*

In this book, the authors have captured complex dynamics of high-conflict families and their boundary problems, explaining them in readable terms with sensitivity and warmth and forcing the reader to give up either/or, binary thinking. This book is a must-have resource for lawyers, judges, and all who work in the family court system.
—Philip M. Stahl, PhD, ABPP (Forensic)

Whether you are new to the practice of family law, board certified, or a member of the Academy, psychologist Ben Garber and colleagues provide in one easy-reading volume the knowledge base not offered in law school or at advanced seminars. Writing in nontechnical language, the authors offer a thoroughly researched, amply referenced "field guide" to understanding a divorcing family's dynamics as a system (not individuals) in the process of divorce. This book is THE essential (and first) guide for lawyers providing an understanding of the impact of child development and family dynamics on divorcing families. Whether you litigate, mediate, or collaborate, the information the authors deliver can only make you better at what you do.
—Jerome Poliacoff, PhD

An excellent book for family law attorneys who wish to gain new and important perspectives on their clients who are part of high-conflict families. The authors' central focus, understanding clients not as purely autonomous individuals but as part of a dynamic family system, is well presented. The field-guide approach makes it easy to see how family dynamics impact healthy child development and how the legal system is then used (properly or improperly) to address the resulting challenges. It also contains valuable advice about avoiding the burnout that so many family law practitioners experience. I highly recommend it.

—Professor Mary Kay Kisthardt
Tiera M. Farrow Faculty Scholar and Emerita Professor of Law, University of Missouri–Kansas City School of Law
Executive Editor, Journal of the American Academy of Matrimonial Lawyers

The Family Law Professional's Field Guide to High-Conflict Litigation: Dynamics, Not Diagnoses *was a pleasure to read. The authors mapped out, in detailed and comprehensive chapters, a list of current topics that starts with a description of healthy children and family development and ends with a cogent argument for self-care of therapists and other professionals who work with high-conflict families. As the subtitle "Dynamics, Not Diagnoses" illustrates, the book is designed to provide the reader with a systemic lens that is ever changing and not static. This book covers the current topics related to working with high-conflict family systems in a manner that is entertaining and informative. I would recommend this book to anyone, novice or experienced, who comes in contact with these families as they struggle to make sense out of their challenges.*

—Ralph Fretz, PhD, ABPP

This book should be required reading for judicial officers and lawyers who handle cases involving children and their parents.

The authors set out to present, in readable form, the current state of the literature on family relationships. The emphasis is on understanding not only the complexity of these relationships, which extend beyond the parents who are parties to litigation and their children to grandparents and other family members, but also that relationships are dynamic and change constantly. For this reason a diagnosis, which is by definition given at a fixed point in time and deals usually with one individual, is at best a minor factor in making decisions that look to the future of the children and their families.

The authors systematically explain the terminology used by mental health professionals and others for the types of dislocations of relationships, including the difficulties caused by controversies about specific terms. In connection with each of the situations described, the authors recommend how to respond to and help all those involved in the case.

They rightly point to the inappropriateness of the adversarial system in most family cases, not least because it encourages the parents to see victory over the other parent, rather than the needs of the individual child, as the objective. They demonstrate the need for the professionals involved in the case to collaborate in tailoring the arrangements for the children to the needs of each child and the abilities of the parents and others to supply those needs.

Their recommendations, especially for training of judicial officers, are to be applauded.

—Philip Marcus
Judge (Retired) of the Jerusalem Family Court
Jurist
Consultant on Family Courts, Family Law, and Procedure
Researcher, Author, and Lecturer on Child Law, Elder Law, Professional Ethics, and Jurisprudence
Recent articles: "Innovative Programs in Israel for Prevention & Responding to Parental Alienation: Education, Early Identification and Timely, Effective Intervention" in *Family Court Review*, vol. 58, issue 2 (April 2020)
"The Israel Family Court—Therapeutic Jurisprudence and Jurisprudential Therapy from the Start" in *International Journal of Law and Psychiatry*, vol. 63 (2019), pp. 68–75
"The Role of the Social Worker in Preventing Child-Parent Contact Failure" in *Contemporary Family Magazine*, Spring 2021, pp. 18–19

THE FAMILY LAW PROFESSIONAL'S FIELD GUIDE TO HIGH-CONFLICT LITIGATION

Dynamics, Not Diagnoses

BENJAMIN D. GARBER, PH.D.
DANA PRESCOTT, J.D., L.M.S.W., PH.D.
CHRIS MULCHAY, PH.D.

AMERICAN BAR ASSOCIATION
Family Law Section

Cover design by Amanda Fry/ABA Design

Printed in the United States of America.

25 24 23 22 5 4 3 2

A catalog record for this book is available from the Library of Congress.

Dedications

Writing as a team, we collectively dedicate this book to the children whom we serve, their families, and to you, the professionals who are routinely charged with understanding their needs. May you each have the good fortune to enjoy the support of caring and brilliant friends that we three enjoy in one another.

To Edgar I. Landerman, the man who trusted me thirty-five years ago with one of his two most precious possessions. "Egger" you are a model of humility, wisdom, kindness, empathy, and generosity that I am proud to emulate.

BDG

To my mom, Lois Prescott, who reminds me that we gain much from the wisdom and life experiences of prior generations and to never forget those lessons, and to my granddaughter, Charlotte, whose joy and laughter pours forth so freely to all around her because she lives in a world of parents and grandparents who cherish her.

DEP

To my father, Michael V. Mulchay, JD, your stories and your reverence for your time on the bench (as a Judge Pro Tempore) inspired me as I worked on this field guide. As a father and an attorney, you role modeled the art of listening as well as the art of (Irish) storytelling, qualities that I have tried to emulate in understanding families and in sharing their stories.

CM

We are indebted to Kate Vetrano and Jeffrey Salyards and the American Bar Association for guidance, patience, and skill as we collectively worked to bring "dynamics, not diagnoses" into your hands.

"Who is more humble? The scientist who looks at the universe with an open mind and accepts whatever the universe has to teach us, or somebody who says everything in this book must be considered the literal truth and never mind the fallibility of all the human beings involved?"

— Carl Sagan

Contents

SECTION I
Setting the Stage

SECTION II
Taxonomy: The Dynamics of the Conflicted Family System

SECTION III
At the Intersection Where the Family System Meets the Legal System

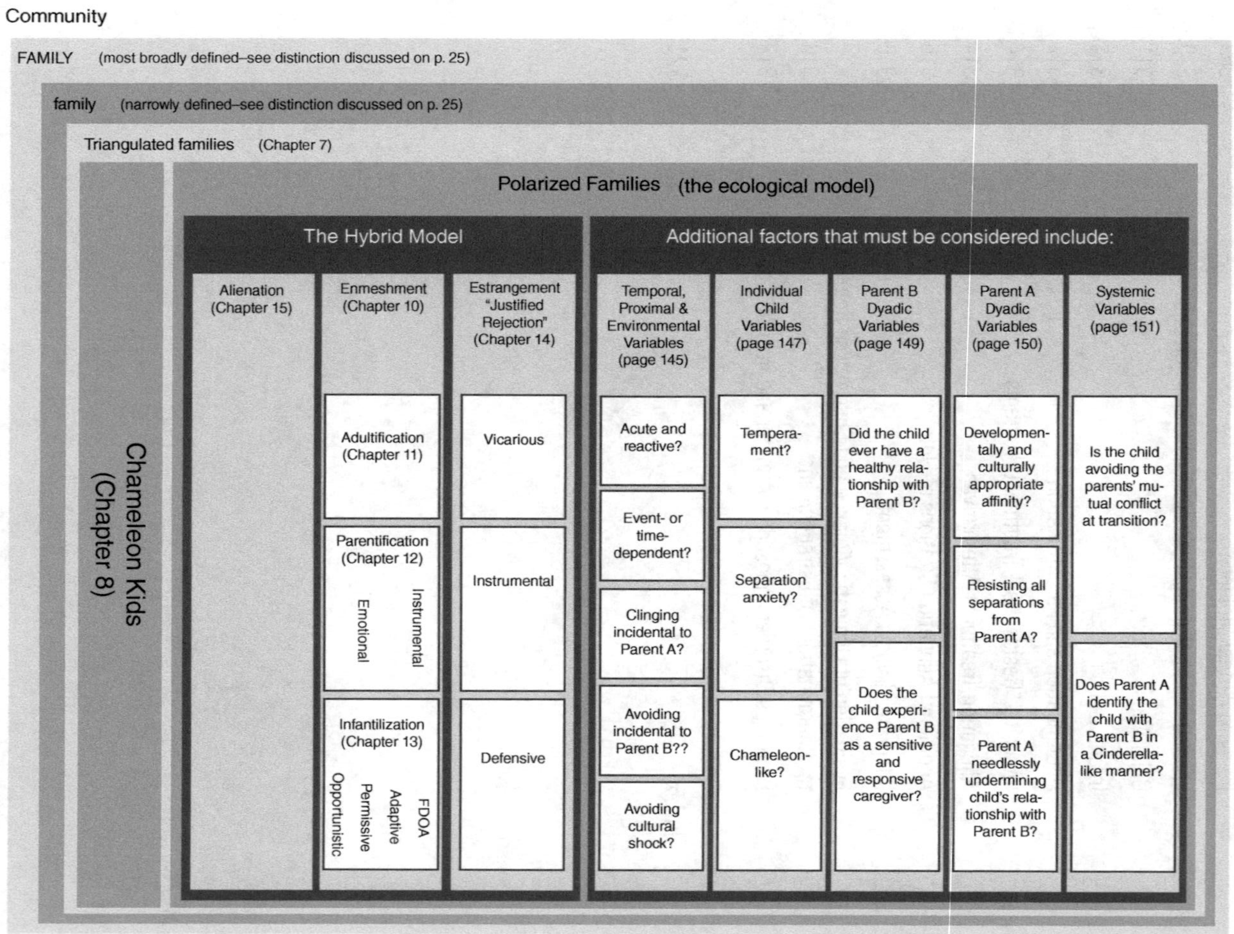

Community
FAMILY (most broadly defined–see distinction discussed on p. 25)
family (narrowly defined–see distinction discussed on p. 25)
Triangulated families (Chapter 7)
Chameleon Kids (Chapter 8)
Polarized Families (the ecological model)
The Hybrid Model
Alienation (Chapter 15)
Enmeshment (Chapter 10)
Adultification (Chapter 11)
Parentification (Chapter 12)
Instrumental
Emotional
Infantilization (Chapter 13)
FDOA
Adaptive
Permissive
Opportunistic
Estrangement "Justified Rejection" (Chapter 14)
Vicarious
Instrumental
Defensive
Additional factors that must be considered include:
Temporal, Proximal & Environmental Variables (page 145)
Acute and reactive?
Event- or time-dependent?
Clinging incidental to Parent A?
Avoiding incidental to Parent B??
Avoiding cultural shock?
Individual Child Variables (page 147)
Tempera-ment?
Separation anxiety?
Chameleon-like?
Parent B Dyadic Variables (page 149)
Did the child ever have a healthy rela-tionship with Parent B?
Does the child experi-ence Parent B as a sensitive and responsive caregiver?
Parent A Dyadic Variables (page 150)
Developmen-tally and culturally appropriate affinity?
Resisting all separations from Parent A?
Parent A needlessly undermining child's rela-tionship with Parent B?
Systemic Variables (page 151)
Is the child avoiding the parents' mu-tual conflict at transition?
Does Parent A identify the child with Parent B in a Cinderella-like manner?

SECTION I
Setting the Stage

Chapter 1
Introduction

"At one level of analysis, the human body is comprised of a variety of systems (e.g., the circulatory system, the digestive system, etc.). At a broader level of analysis, individual humans are a part of a variety of interpersonal systems, the most central of which typically is one family form or another."[1]

At issue is a question of focus.

Imagine that you're viewing Earth through the lens of an infinitely powerful telescope orbiting the planet. You can narrow the lens to view a single blade of grass or widen it to view all of humanity in a single frame. You can choose to capture an entire continent, a single country, an individual state, a specific county, a favorite neighborhood, a particular family, a particular couple, or a unique individual. Where you should focus most productively—how you define *the level of inquiry*—will depend upon the question that you're trying to answer.

Curious about global warming? Broaden the frame to take in Earth's poles.

Interested in urban traffic patterns? Focus on New York City or Mumbai or Paris or Moscow.

Intrigued by teenage high school attendance? Narrow the frame further to examine particular school districts.

Tasked to investigate and make recommendations about the best interests of a child caught up in family conflict and transition? Some choose to focus on the individual child and each individual parent in the belief that the sum of Mom's drinking and Dad's depression and their daughter's attention disorder is sufficient to capture the nature of

1. Robert E. Emery, *Families as Systems: Some Thoughts on Methods and Theory, in* Emerging Methods in Family Research 109, 124 (Susan M. McHale et al. eds., 2014) (volume 4 of the National Symposium on Family Issues book series).

the family's functioning. It is not. But this common mistake is easily understood. Psychology, and many of its allied mental health professions (MHPs) such as social work, counseling, and marriage and family therapy, are built on the medical model of individual assessment, diagnosis, and treatment.[2]

Some of these licensed clinical professionals will argue differently based upon codes of ethics or training programs, but when confronted with child custody conflict, much of what judges and lawyers will read in reports and hear in testimony will be about individuals. There may be historical context or labels-by-diagnosis and even subtle shading to add depth to why an individual thinks and behaves as she does when engaged with the other parent or a child. But most of the time the explanation in writing or under oath will be about the "client" or the "patient."

We're trained, from classrooms to post-grad programs to continuing education seminars, to focus on the individual. As one obvious result, the development, sale, administration, and interpretation of individual psychometric assessment instruments has become a multibillion-dollar business that implicitly contributes to unfounded stereotypes, biases, a false equivalence between diagnosed psychopathology and the best interests of the child, and profound negative consequences for vulnerable groups in our society.[3]

This book is about pulling the lens back, shifting the focus of family law assessments and interventions and legal representation from the individual to relationships. It's about redefining the level of inquiry and resetting the frame so as to capture the social and emotional ecology—the system—within which the child exists rather than the characteristics of the individuals who engage in those relationships. Our title "dynamics, not diagnoses" is meant to telegraph that shift.

---

2. *See* John Gunderson, *Borderline Personality Disorder: An Overview*, 6 Soc. Work Mental Health 5 (2008); Steven C. Hayes et al., *A Process-Based Approach to Psychological Diagnosis and Treatment: The Conceptual and Treatment Utility of an Extended Evolutionary Meta Model*, 82 Clinical Psych. Rev. 101908 (2020); Steven J. Kingsbury, *Cognitive Differences between Clinical Psychologists and Psychiatrists*, 42 Am. Psych. 152 (1987).

3. Chris Chambers, The Seven Deadly Sins of Psychology: A Manifesto for Reforming the Culture of Scientific Practice (2019); 10 Ronald Samuda, Psychological Testing of American Minorities: Issues and Consequences (1998).

Diagnosis is familiar. In medicine, diagnosis is presumed to answer the question, "what's wrong with me?" Diagnosis is a label that communicates how one person's particular pattern of distress and/or dysfunction resembles patterns observed in other individuals so as to invite prognosis and predict the most effective remedy.

Diagnosis is little different in mental health practice. In psychology, for example, diagnosis communicates the recognition of a consensually defined pattern of thoughts, feelings, and/or behaviors *within* the individual that has been determined to constitute an illness. MHPs collect and periodically update formal lists of diagnoses in the form of the Diagnostic and Statistical Manual (DSM; American Psychiatric Association 2013) and the International Classification of Diseases (ICD; World Health Organization 2019). The goal of these nosologies is to create a common language, a task that most recently required 15 to 20 years and $25,000,000. The strength of the DSM is that it produces a relatively reliable method of diagnosing an individual. The manual helps MHPs to use the same labels in the same ways, even if questions persist about the inter-rater and test-retest reliabilities and the associated validity of many DSM diagnoses.[4]

Our reference to the *consensual definition* of diagnoses deserves special attention. Whereas diagnosis in medicine is generally based on an objective determination of quantifiable pathology, diagnosis in psychology and its allied mental health practices is generally based on a subjective and culture-based determination of dysfunction. Thus, physicians can reliably measure liver enzymes associated with cirrhosis, the degree and severity of bone fractures, and white blood cell counts, and thereby reliably predict associated functional deficits up to and including death. By contrast, MHPs are generally left to identify pathology based upon consensually determined labels handed down by a select and highly privileged few.

(continued on next page)

4. *See* Michael Chmielewski et al., *Method Matters: Understanding Diagnostic Reliability in DSM-IV and DSM-5*, 124 J. Abnormal Psych. 764 (2015).

> The most familiar example of the cultural specificity of the determination of psychopathology concerns sexual preference. The first and second editions of the DSM (DSM-I and -II) identified homosexuality as a mental illness. It wasn't until 1973 that the diagnosis was removed from the diagnostic manual.[5] Today, the idea that homosexuality is a form of pathology is abhorrent within medicine.[6] It wasn't until 20 years later that the fourth edition of the DSM acknowledged the cultural variability not only of many specific diagnoses but of the concept of psychopathology in general. This nod to diversity was subsequently elaborated in the form of the Cultural Formulation Interview introduced in 2013 in the DSM-5.[7] We view this evolution as promising, even if it occurs at a glacial pace. Perhaps the lens is slowly being pulled back. Perhaps MHPs across guild affiliations are beginning to move from a consensually derived and culturally biased focus on individual psychopathology toward a contextual sense of relational adaptation.

There can be no doubt that individual diagnoses have their place in contemporary mental health practice. They can be reliable and valid and have distinct practical value for some types of individual treatment planning and medication management, for occupational screenings, and for safety determinations. Even allowing for problems associated with sample sizes, lack of sampling diversity, the weakness of statistical analyses, poor test-retest reliability in field trials, and the biases of contributing clinicians, the diagnoses catalogued in the DSM-5, and its more highly respected alternate, the ICD Tenth Edition (ICD-10), do have a place in mental health evaluation and treatment.[8]

---

5. Jack Drescher, *Out of DSM; Depathologizing Homosexuality*, 5 Behav. Sci. 565 (2015).

6. Gender bias in psychiatric diagnosis more generally has been and remains a serious concern. *See, e.g.*, Janet B. Williams & Robert L. Spitzer, *The Issue of Sex Bias in DSM-III: A Critique of "A Woman's View of DSM-III" by Marcie Kaplan*, 38 Am. Psych. 793 (1983).

7. Roberto Lewis-Fernández et al., *Culture and Psychiatric Evaluation: Operationalizing Cultural Formulation for DSM5*, 77 Psychiatry 130 (2014).

8. K. Dayle Jones, *A Critique of the DSM-5 Field Trials*, 200 J. Nervous & Mental Disease 517 (2012).

Not so in family law where the questions that must be answered are inevitably about relationships, not individuals. Both clinicians and the courts are slowly beginning to recognize the need to understand individual functioning in the context of its social ecology. If we hope to genuinely understand and serve the best interests of any particular child, we must first learn how to adjust the level of inquiry—to pull back that infinitely powerful telescope's lens—so as to focus on relationship dynamics.

Unless you're a student of sociology or social work, dynamics are likely far less familiar than diagnoses. The concept challenges professionals who are trained to look *within* the individual to look instead for patterns of thoughts, feelings, and/or expressed emotions that occur *between* individuals. The difference amounts to a paradigm shift, a redefinition of the subject of study. Dynamics weave the social and emotional fabric within which individuals function. They are the constituent elements of every family system's relational ecology. Dynamics are the social and emotional stage upon which the actors engage. As such, dynamics capture the relationship environment or ecology within which forensic best-interest questions are most effectively and efficiently addressed.

Perhaps you're thinking that this is a false dichotomy, a strawman argument meant to sell books or stir controversy pitting within-individual diagnoses against between-individual dynamics as if family law professionals have to choose between the two. Aren't we needlessly ignoring the chicken-egg reality that individual functioning creates relationship dynamics and vice versa? Indeed, shouldn't the conscientious professional tasked with conducting a forensic family system evaluation or intervention address *both* diagnoses and dynamics?

Yes, of course the conscientious clinician and astute family law professional must have one eye on every level of inquiry from individual diagnosis to relationship dynamics, to family system functioning, and up the fractal chain even to understand how the family system fits into its community. Yes, extremes at any level of inquiry including the level of individual psychopathology will always be relevant. We are not arguing against the relevance of these extremes. We are arguing, instead, that the whole is always greater than the sum of its parts. Relationship questions cannot and must never be answered by sequential evaluations of their constituent members. At the same time, we recognize the practical reality of finite resources. Given the limited time, effort, and money, we wholeheartedly believe that the professional tasked with conducting a best-interests evaluation, intervention, or judgment more wisely invests in understanding dynamics rather than diagnoses.

Case in point: Mom and Dad are involved in contentious custody litigation. Their acrimony has been amplified by their respective zealous advocates working in the conventional guilt-versus-innocence courts.[9] You've been charged with conducting an evaluation so as to advise the court about the future allocation of parenting rights and responsibilities (i.e., custody). Six-year-old Sally lives with Mom and refuses to have any contact with Dad. Mom alleges that Dad is abusive. Dad alleges that Mom is alienating.

Individual assessment might reliably and validly diagnose Dad with narcissistic personality disorder and Mom with major depression and borderline personality disorder. Sally is known to have attention-deficit/hyperactivity disorder (ADHD) and is being treated for anxiety. These labels may be extremely useful for a clinician's evidence-based treatment planning, medication management, and prognosis. The school might rely on Sally's ADHD diagnosis to accommodate her unique learning needs under the Individuals with Disabilities Education Act (IDEA).[10] For all these practical values, generating and/or relying upon these diagnoses as dispositive in the context of a forensic family evaluation generates far more heat than light.[11] Family law questions are about relationships, not individuals, and must therefore focus first and foremost on understanding dynamics, not diagnoses.

---

9. "[T]here is reason to question whether a zealous mindset is an unmitigated good. Zeal might cloud the mind of the advocate, undermining their sensitivity to the sensibilities of their audience and blinding them to the weaknesses of their argument." Dan Simon et al., *The Adversarial Mindset*, 26 Psych. Pub. Pol'y & L. 353, 372 (2020).

10. Individuals with Disabilities Education Act, Pub. L. No. 101-476, 104 Stat. 1103 (1990).

11. The model standards of the Association of Family and Conciliation Courts (AFCC), like similar publications issued by numerous mental health guild associations, clarify that "[e]valuators recognize that the use of diagnostic labels can divert attention from the focus of the evaluation (namely, the functional abilities of the litigants whose disputes are before the court) and that such labels are often more prejudicial than probative." AFCC, Model Standards of Practice for Child Custody Evaluation 4.6(c) (2006).

So, the answer is no. We are not arguing for a false dichotomy or neglecting the chicken-egg circularity inherent in the individual's contribution to relationships. Instead, we are arguing for efficiency and focus in a field that is widely criticized as often overstepping its bounds at a crippling cost to the families it purports to serve.

And then there's the question of validity—that is, the degree to which a reliable measurement is relevant and meaningful to the question being asked. By analogy, your bathroom scale is likely a very reliable (if often depressing) means of measuring your weight. Your weight, in turn, is a valid and meaningful predictor of many other variables including whether you're likely to fit into your summer wardrobe or suffer from cardiac disease. Your weight does not, however, have a valid or meaningful relationship with the weather or the price of milk in Boise. This means that investing finite resources to measure an individual's weight is an excellent choice in some contexts and irrelevant, if not simply silly and wasteful, in others.

Child custody evaluators struggle with the validity dilemma constantly. Trained in the art and science of assessing and labeling individual psychopathology, burdened and biased by a shelf full of very expensive and impressive individual psychometric instruments (tests), they commonly fall victim to the bathroom scale dilemma. Their measures are reliable but seldom valid for this use. The best among them acknowledge these limitations in their reports and on the stand. Many leap the gap from reliability to validity with their eyes closed and their fingers crossed, hoping that no one knows the difference.

Given the paucity of data bridging this gap between individual diagnosis-based instruments and relationship (e.g., parent-child, sibling, co-parenting, family) functioning, we contend that the use of these instruments in the context of forensic family evaluations risks introducing unnecessary, inflammatory, and prejudicial data into the legal process.[12]

12. "More recent case law has emphasized that courts need to make custody judgments on the basis of an evaluation of parental competency and child risk, not by the mere presence of mental illness alone," and studies have found that "mental health professionals are biased in interpreting the behavior of diagnostically labeled individuals." Corina Benjet et al., *Evaluating the Parental Fitness of Psychiatrically Diagnosed Individuals: Advocating a Functional-Contextual Analysis of Parenting*, 17 J. Fam. Psych. 238, 238, 240 (2003).

The counterargument is, of course, that individual adult psychometric tools administered in the context of forensic family evaluations can generate hypotheses that might otherwise be missed and, in turn, encourage more precise systemic inquiry or develop, in the language of forensics, multiple hypotheses to be explicitly accepted or rejected.[13] The scientific method, after all, calls for a successive process of observation, hypothesis generation, and hypothesis testing.

However much the scientific method is necessary and appropriate to physics and chemistry and similarly objective and empirically driven sciences, it poses a number of often-neglected problems when it is applied to relationship questions. Chief among these are the subjective and putative meanings of data collected and discarded but that remain vulnerable to disclosure via the legal process of discovery. Much as the evaluator who collects individual-focused assessment data for the purpose of hypothesis generation may wisely choose not to discuss resulting DSM and ICD diagnoses in his summary report, these potentially stigmatizing labels lay dormant in the evaluator's record awaiting an astute lawyer and his hired experts to uncover and exploit on cross-examination.[14]

Thus, the physicist who argues that more data is better stands on solid ground with everyone except perhaps her funding agency. The family law professional who makes the same argument risks doing harm.

13. *See* Sol R. Rappaport et al., *Psychological Testing Can Be of Significant Value in Child Custody Evaluations: Don't Buy the Anti-Testing, Anti-Individual, Pro-Family Systems Woozle*, 30 J. Am. Acad. Matrimonial Law. 405 (2017).

14. There have been revisions to the rules related to disclosures of privileged or work-product information, which may differ in rule and practice between federal courts and between each state family court system. *See* Republic of Ecuador v. Hinchee, 741 F.3d 1185, 1192 (6th Cir. 2013) ("Unlike an 'attorney, consultant, surety, indemnitor, insurer, or agent,' *see* Fed.R.Civ.P. 26(b)(3)(A), a testifying expert's role is to provide independent, impartial, qualified opinion testimony helpful to the trier of fact. Given that testifying experts offer evidence in court, the opposing side must have the opportunity to challenge the opinions of a testifying expert, including how and why the expert formed a particular opinion. *See* Fed.R.Civ.P. 26, advisory committee notes (1970) (Subdivision (b)(4)). Cloaking all materials prepared by or for a testifying expert under the work-product doctrine inhibits the thorough and sharp cross examination that is vital to our adversary system. *Id.*"); *see also* Milfred D. Dale & Jonathan W. Gould, *Science, Mental Health Consultants, and Attorney-Expert Relationships in Child Custody*, 48 Fam. L.Q. 1 (2014); Micaiah Zwartz, *Report Writing in the Forensic Context: Recurring Problems and the Use of a Checklist to Address Them*, 25 Psychiatry Psych. & L. 578 (2018).

Family law inquiry and litigation must take into account the data relevant to the question before the court and risk becoming sidetracked and failing the child's needs when data with little validity (no matter how strong its reliability) is introduced. Recognizing the risks and deficits of an individual-focused, diagnosis-focused process, we must commit instead to developing and relying on reliable methods to assess the variables that have a valid bearing on the relationship questions at hand—that is, the quality of relationship dynamics.

This is the conceptual foundation upon which we have built this book, a field guide intended to assist family law professionals to better understand and communicate about the dynamics of the conflicted family system. Think of this the way that a football coach thinks of the playbook that turns a disparate group of powerful players into a single team capable of winning a game, or the way that a conductor thinks of the composer's score as elegantly integrating a roomful of skilled musicians and their instruments into a single, complex tapestry of sound, or even the way that the cardiologist understands each heart valve and blood vessel as serving the entire muscle. Our goal in writing this book is to broaden the lens of your thinking so as to consider relationships as the unit of inquiry and thus to begin to ask how relationships—not individuals—fit together as the relevant and valid question addressed by the family law process.

Please note that throughout this discussion, we have not yet used the word "divorce." Although everything that follows is relevant to divorce, the legal status of the adult relationship is irrelevant. These dynamics commonly arise in the context of divorce because divorce is a very public process and because people who enter the legal system are more easily counted and studied than others. In fact, the high-conflict, systemic dynamics described throughout this book are just as relevant to understanding never-married, still-married, intergenerational, and other, less conventional family systems. We contend, as well, that the dynamics described here are likely to be more or less common to particular cultures and communities but are generally blind to race, religion, gender identity, sexual preference, and differences of genetic, biological, gestational, legal, and emotional parent-child bonds. Thus, please understand our recurrent references to generic mothers and fathers as nothing more than ease of expression never intended to communicate gender-specificity or to exclude any type of caregiver or relationship status.

"High Conflict"?

Although the divorcing families who consume the vast majority of family law professionals' time are often described by this phrase, it is seldom adequately defined. Certainly, many families manage what might be described as low or moderate levels of conflict without obvious harm or the need for professional intervention. Indeed, a child's experience of low or moderate conflict and the resolution of these conflicts within the context of loving relationships builds resilience. The social and emotional damage associated with high-conflict relationships is thought to be due to the chronic, explicitly damaging, and unresolved nature of this experience. Being raised in the midst of parents' high conflict can be like being raised in a war zone. Among the many dysfunctional and damaging lessons learned in this relationship ecology is that anger and love are incompatible.

In a seminal article on this subject, Janet Johnston explains:

> Divorce conflict has at least three important dimensions which should be considered when assessing incidence and its effects on children. First, conflict has a *domain dimension*, which can refer to disagreements over a series of divorce issues such as financial support, property division, custody, and access to the children, or to values and methods of child rearing. Second, conflict has a *tactics dimension*, which can refer to the manner in which divorcing couples informally try to resolve disagreements either by avoiding each other and the issues, or by verbal reasoning, verbal aggression, physical coercion and physical aggression; or it can refer to ways in which divorce disputes are formally resolved by the use of attorney negotiation, mediation, litigation, or arbitration by a judge. Third, conflict has an *attitudinal dimension*, referring to the degree of negative emotional feeling or hostility directed by divorcing parties toward each other, which may be covertly or overtly expressed.[15]

15. Janet R. Johnston, *High-Conflict Divorce*, 4 Future Child. 165, 165–66 (1994).

Our thesis is quite simple: family law questions are about relationships, not individuals. In an admitted effort to shift the thinking among family law professionals from individual diagnoses to relationship-level functioning, we offer this field guide as a means of better identifying, communicating, and responding to the dynamics of the conflicted family system. In pursuit of this lofty ambition, we must first establish a number of critical caveats:

1. Like any field guide, the family-level natural phenomena we are endeavoring to catalog must always be understood to be evolving within the larger contexts of community, culture, and the law. For example, we write in the midst of a pandemic that is certainly reshaping how we communicate and connect with others in ways likely to affect interpersonal dynamics long after the crisis has passed. Thus, we take this book as a first edition that will necessarily need to be updated and revised as our understanding of family systems grows within the context of our ever-changing physical, social, and political environments.
2. Variation cannot be understood without first understanding norms. Thus, we begin with a broad overview of healthy family development circa the second decade of the 21st century in the United States. We fully recognize and respect that concepts of "health" and the definition of "norms" is very culture- and era-specific.[16] With this in mind, we preach cultural humility and contextual sensitivity throughout this volume and endeavor to acknowledge these critical variables whenever possible.
3. We hope to give practical value and empirically based consensual meaning to concepts and terms that are often conflated, misunderstood, and passed off as arcane psychobabble. In so doing, we have made every effort to acknowledge continuing areas of controversy, ambiguity, and the need for further research. Toward this end, we present each concept in a uniform format set forth

---

16. Dana E. Prescott, *Bending the Light of Social Science in Family Court: Epistemic Injustice and Epistemic Exceptionalism Matter*, 33 J. Am. Acad. Matrimonial Law. 99 (2020).

under clear headers: definition, research foundation, case law illustrations and precedents, areas in need of further exploration, and practical implications in the context of forensic family evaluation and intervention.

4. Finally, recognizing the controversies surrounding many of the concepts discussed here, how these concepts change across cultures, over time, with experience, and as our empirical foundations grow, we welcome your feedback at any time. It is only by accommodating others' thinking that we humans can begin to see around our own biases and limitations to better grasp the full experience of human relationships. Please reach us at any time at DynamicsNotDiagnoses@gmail.com.

Chapter 2
Why a Field Guide?

"[L]anguage is not merely a reproducing instrument for voicing ideas but rather is itself the shaper of ideas, the program and guide for the individual's mental activity. . . ."[1]

John James Audubon (1785–1851) is credited with organizing our understanding of birds by phyla, class, species, and subspecies. His field guide not only remains valuable in the present but was an instrumental model to his most notable student, Charles Darwin.

Today, Audubon's field guides are portable, practical, and beautiful means of helping observers to make critical distinctions among naturally occurring events. Among his many contributions to ornithology are hundreds of stunning, photograph-like illustrations of the birds he described.

As authors, we have no artistic skills and no pretension that a book seeking to clarify, operationalize, and organize the dynamics of the high-conflict family system has even a fraction of the historical significance or scientific impact of Audubon's work. In writing this book, we do, however, aspire to similar goals: to introduce a more uniform means of recognizing, communicating, and responding to the varieties of these natural and universal phenomena. Toward that end, we offer this very brief overview of all that follows.

Fractals and Nested Hierarchies

"Fractal" is the word used in mathematics and borrowed by biology to describe the repetition of patterns across hierarchical levels of analysis. It refers to the fact that if you look carefully, you'll recognize that the same

1. Language, Thought, and Reality: Selected Writings of Benjamin Lee Whorf 212 (J.B. Carroll ed., 1956).

patterns recur in the same relationships to one another at every level of inquiry, from the microscopic to the interplanetary. We find this type of unfolding or regressive symmetry, for example, in the topography of the Earth, cloud formations, snowflakes, and Saturn's rings.

We contend that interpersonal dynamics recur in the same manner at every level of relationships, from the dyad to the family to the community and up the ladder of social organization at least to the level of species. We find, for example, that relationships are defined at every level of inquiry by stronger alliances within the group than alliances between the group and others outside the group, that relationships are more or less bounded and thereby more or less differentiated from the other allied groups at the same level of inquiry, and from all groups subsidiary and superordinate across the social hierarchy. The relationships within and between these bounded entities are vulnerable to similar pressures at every level of analysis. For example, we can see boundary corruption or enmeshment within the dyad between parent and child, between family systems, between communities, and so on.

Complexity and Coherence

Complexity theory explains how systems function and change over time. In the present context, complexity theory invites us to understand relationships as nonlinear systems composed of multiple interacting subsidiary components operating under multiple convergent pressures. This is the difference between the relatively simple task of explaining how a single line of dominoes fall one into another in succession and the enormously more complex task of explaining the movement of those same pieces if they are all dropped to the floor. Complexity theory provides an overarching means of understanding how subsidiary components interact and affect one another.[2]

Complexity theory allows us to understand the otherwise illogical idea that the whole is greater than the sum of its parts. It relies on two

2. Chaos and Complexity in Psychology: The Theory of Nonlinear Dynamical Systems (Stephen J. Guastello et al. eds., 2009).

key concepts to do so: self-organization and emergence. Self-organization describes the pressures within the system that spontaneously create discernible and redundant patterns. Physicists refer to these pressures as including feedback, encapsulation, autocatalysis (that is, when an effect serves as its own cause), synchronization, criticality, connectivity, and adaptation.[3] Self-organization is evident in conflicted family systems when, for example, a child's innocuous and benign alignment with one parent snowballs into a full-blown polarization between the co-parents.

Emergence describes qualities or attributes associated with a system but not associated with any of its component parts. In its boldest example, emergence describes the appearance of life when certain amino acids self-organize. In the present context, emergence describes the behaviors associated with a system that do not exist when one examines the individuals who compose that relationship and the ways in which the system feeds back to shape the individual. "Through understanding the connections among mental processes, relationships, and brain functioning, we can build an interpersonal neurobiological foundation for the ways in which experiences—both early in life and through adulthood—continue to play a central role in shaping the emerging mind."[4]

Power and Control

Chief among the many pressures that contribute to systemic self-organization and the emergence of associated qualities are power and control. These are two among the many variables that collectively co-determine the hierarchy of relationships within biological systems. We see this playing out dramatically in Nat Geo WILD programs among the members of a wild herd of buffalo or a troop of primates as members vie for alpha status and organize relationships accordingly. We humans do no less and sometimes do so even more dramatically. Hierarchies of power and control emerge within systems contributing to the definition

---

3. David O'Sullivan, *Complexity Theory, Nonlinear Dynamic Spatial Systems*, *in* International Encyclopedia of Human Geography (Rob Kitchin & Nigel Thrift eds., 2009).

4. Daniel J. Siegel, The Developing Mind: How Relationships and the Brain Interact to Shape Who We Are (3d ed. 2020).

of subsidiary boundaries and alliances and to the relationships among superordinate systems.

Human systems differ by degree from animal systems in that power and control do not necessarily or exclusively correlate with physical appearance, size, strength, or stamina. Our relationships order themselves at least as often around access to critical resources (from food, clothing, and shelter, to money and Wi-Fi) and (legal) decision-making authority. Within the family system, this is evident in a parent's delegation of specific privileges and opportunities to a child (e.g., to cross the street, to borrow the car, to play video games). Within political systems, this is evident in the government's designation of adult responsibilities to individuals who achieve a certain age, often with little regard for that person's cognitive, social, or emotional maturity. Within the family court system, this includes the division and/or delegation of decision-making authority over children when parents separate and divorce.

Dynamics

Dynamics are patterns of behavior that characterize relationships. The dynamics in our own lives tend to be predictable and familiar. They're as likely to be reassuring as they are tiresome or painful or excruciating. They can be as mundane and benign as the "hi, how are you?" exchange between acquaintances who often ride the same elevator and as insidious and destructive as the recurrent domestic violence that occurs in many marriages. Human dynamics tend to become more rigid and pronounced when systems are stressed and more adaptive and malleable when that stress is relieved.

The dynamics of human relationships illustrate the emergent and self-organizing qualities of complex systems. When two individuals encounter one another, each brings his own constellation of needs, expectations, hopes and fears, and strengths and weaknesses into that moment. Uncountable hundreds of sensory cues combine with those (usually unconscious) thoughts and feelings, each becoming both a cause and an effect in the interaction, feeding back on themselves in unspoken and unknowable ways. The result filters through our sensory organs and brains, colored by a million other unannounced pressures to generate a "gut reaction" or "first impression," which is then carried forward into the next encounter, predisposing our thinking, dictating our behavior, and influencing our emotions.

Section II of this book catalogues the dynamics of conflicted family systems. These dynamics are generally destructive, pathological, and/or pathogenic to the extent that they interfere with healthy child development. They are driven by words, actions, and expressed emotions that serve adult needs rather than children's needs. As a result, they often work to undermine relationship hierarchies, to shift the balance of power and control within the system, and thereby to corrupt relationship boundaries.

Co-parental conflict, separation, and divorce need not harm children. Healthy parents put their children's needs first no matter the status of the adult relationship, reassuring that parent-child love is always intact, empowering healthy expression of emotions, and insulating children from the stresses of the adult conflict.

That conflict can become unhealthy in a number of ways, most powerfully when the child becomes triangulated amidst the adult tensions. Triangulation occurs when parents pull their child directly or indirectly, intentionally or otherwise, into their differences. Triangulation is discussed in detail in Chapter 7. The child's experience of triangulation is modulated by factors including the nature, chronicity, and severity of the triangulating acts, the child's emotional maturity and resilience, and how the child understands (that is, the script used to explain) what's happening within the family system.

Chapters 8 through 15 describe the family system dynamics that are played out on the stage of triangulation. Enlisted as a spy by one parent and a courier by the other, exposed to the adults' rage and acts of verbal and physical violence, discovering one parent's infidelity or the other parent's addiction, some children become chameleons, changing their emotional colors to fit into the proximal emotional environment (Chapter 8). Some become polarized amidst the adult conflict, aligning with Parent A and resisting or rejecting Parent B (Chapter 9). Many become the victims (or beneficiaries?) of shifts of power and control, compromising identity and becoming enmeshed with one parent (Chapter 10), prematurely promoted to serve as that parent's friend and ally (Chapter 11) and even as that parent's caregiver (Chapter 12). Others compromise their own development to fulfill a needy parent's needs (Chapter 13).

Chapters 14 and 15 describe dynamics likely to be more familiar to many readers. Estrangement or justified rejection occurs when a child's experience contributes to resistance/refusal of contact with Parent B. Alienation occurs when the child's experience of Parent A's unwarranted negative words, actions, and expressed emotions about Parent B are in play.

Why Does This Matter?

You can enjoy birds without caring about or learning to recognize the difference between the Kentish plover found in northern China and the white-faced plover found in southern China. Chances are that the distinction means little to most people, even though it has startling evolutionary meaning to ornithologists.[5]

Chances are that you enjoy relationships without needing to understand how adultification, parentification, and infantilization are distinct and nonexclusive forms of enmeshment found amidst some high-conflict family systems, unless you happen to be a family law professional or a family therapist. If you are, then—like the ornithologist fascinated by plovers—you're likely to find the descriptions and distinctions that fill these pages relevant and provocative and valuable. It is only by making these distinctions and refining them over time as experience and empirical data accumulate, that we can improve the quality of our communication and begin to identify necessary and appropriate legal and therapeutic remedies.

5. Xuejing Wang et al., *Demographic Histories and Genome-Wide Patterns of Divergence in Incipient Species of Shorebirds*, 10 Frontiers Genetics 919 (2019).

Chapter 3
Healthy Child and Family Development

"The traditional family model of two, middle class, heterosexual parents in which the woman is a full-time housewife and the man has full-time paid employment outside the home, which has long been assumed to be the structure most favourable to healthy child development, is now a minority."[1]

If you happen to be an aspiring family law attorney, mediator, guardian ad litem, family court judge, therapist, or forensic mental health professional of any ilk, here's critical advice: take at least one course in child and family development.

We often have the opportunity to conduct advanced professional trainings around the world. Our informal surveys in these varied settings find that regardless of guild affiliation, professional role, culture, age, or gender, fewer than half of all family law professionals acknowledge ever having taken a course in child or family development. The truth is that many participants in these trainings believe that having once been a child, having children, or having grandchildren is good enough. It is not.[2]

Raising kids (and grandkids) may facilitate empathy for the parents with whom we work, but it is just as likely to create bias. Having been married, divorced, widowed, abandoned, or abused; having raised a stepchild or a child with attention-deficit/hyperactivity disorder

1. *Re* K. Adoption, [1995], 23 O.R.3d 679, https://canlii.ca/t/fn0jr.

2. The United States Supreme Court in *Troxel v. Granville*, 530 U.S. 57 (2000), entered the field of family structure with its foray into state grandparents' visitation acts and the constitutional rights of parents to be free of government interference absent compelling reasons. Why the Court did so remains a mystery given that family law has been traditionally left to the states. *See* Sandra Day O'Connor, *The Supreme Court and the Family*, 3 U. Pa. J. Const. L. 573 (2001).

(ADHD); or having a chronically ill child, for example, can create unacknowledged super-ego lacunae—holes in an otherwise mature individual's feelings and thinking—that can cripple our impartiality and leave us at risk of doing harm. The remedies for these universal and often unrecognized blind spots are simple and necessary but never wholly sufficient: routine peer consultation, working as part of a collaborative team, everyday self-care, and ongoing education.[3]

Sadly, even the most dedicated student is unlikely to find a course in *family development*. Historically, psychology's focus has almost exclusively been on ontogeny—that is, the study of individual human development. This has generated many and varied and valuable descriptions of specific domains of development (e.g., cognitive, psychosexual, moral) that are as insightful and valid as they are myopic. Luminaries like Piaget and Kohlberg and Erickson and Levinson[4] write eloquently and accurately about stages and ages of development but pay little or no attention to the *relationship ecology* in which they occur.[5]

If we recognize that human development occurs in a web of intimate emotional relationships and that each affects the other—the individual affects the relationships within which she develops at least as much as those relationships affect her development—then the need for a systemic view becomes clear. The systemic view requires pulling back the lens in order to see individuals as component parts of larger, more-or-less cohesive, more-or-less bounded, and more-or-less well-adapted superordinate units, the

---

3. *See, e.g.*, Daniel B. Pickar, *On Being a Child Custody Evaluator: Professional and Personal Challenges, Risks, and Rewards*, 45 Fam. Ct. Rev. 103 (2007).

4. Whereas much of developmental psychology is focused on areas of growth within childhood, some studies have described universal stages of adult development very much like those ascribed to childhood:

> This sequence of eras and periods exists in all societies, throughout the human species, at the present stage of human evolution. The eras and periods are grounded in the nature of man as a biological, psychological and social organism, and in the nature of society as a complex enterprise extending over many generations.

Daniel J. Levinson, Seasons of a Man's Life 322 (1978).

5. "Relationship ecology" describes the social/emotional environment in which an individual functions and grows. *See, e.g.*, Heather A. O'Mahen et al., *Relationship Ecology and Negative Communication in Romantic Relationships: A Self-Evaluation Maintenance Perspective*, 26 Personality & Soc. Psych. Bull. 1343 (2000).

same way that we typically consider arms and legs and eyes as component parts of a cohesive individual person. It is only at this *meso* level of analysis that we can begin to understand the idea of family development.[6]

Unfortunately, the idea that systems develop over time has largely been neglected by psychology and the law.[7] A handful of notable exceptions appear in the literature,[8] but these tend to be linear, stepwise models that ignore the reciprocal, chaotic interactions between individuals and the systems that they create. They also tend to be very specific to the era and the culture in which they were conceived.

> Duvall's theory of family development persists in the literature despite many broad criticisms and efforts at revision.[9] Her approach focuses on single generations, and is restricted to healthy, middle-class, white, heterosexual, married America circa 1950.[10] In broad overview,

(continued on next page)

6. Sociologists distinguish three levels of analysis: the micro level studies individuals; the macro level studies entire cultures or societies; and meso analysis studies social units between the two. "In general, meso-level entities can be understood as smaller scale, lower level social arrangements or units with a different set of guidelines for societal organization." Matthias Richter & Nico Dragano, *Micro, Macro, but What about Meso? The Institutional Context of Health Inequalities*, 63 Int'l J. Pub. Health 163, 163 (2018).

7. J.B. Ruhl, *Complexity Theory as a Paradigm for the Dynamical Law-and-Society System: A Wake-Up Call for Legal Reductionism and the Modern Administrative State*, 45 Duke L.J. 849, 853 (1996) ("The major schools of American legal theory have been so mired in reductionist thought that they have failed to see the system behaviors").

8. *See* Joan Aldous, *Family Development and the Life Course: Two Perspectives*, 52 J. Marriage & Fam. 571 (1990); Joan Aldous, *Family Interaction Patterns*, 3 Ann. Rev. Socio. 105 (1977); *see also* Roy H. Rodgers & James M. White, *Family Development Theory, in* Sourcebook of Family Theories and Methods: A Contextual Approach 225 (Pauline Boss et al. eds., 1993).

9. *See* Stan J. Knapp & Greg J. Wurm, *Theorizing Family Change: A Review and Reconceptualization*, 11 J. Fam. Theory & Rev. 212–29 (2019), https://doi.org/10.1111/jftr.12329; J. Scott Crapo & Kay Bradford, Multidimensional Family Development Theory: An Evolution of Family Development (National Council on Family Relations, Theory Construction and Research Methodology Workshop, Working Paper No. 007-01, 2017), https://www.ncfr.org/system/files/2017-08/TCRM%202%20-%20Multidimensional%20Family%20Development.pdf.

10. *See* Tracey A. Laszloffy, *Rethinking Family Development Theory: Teaching with the Systemic Family Development Model*, 51 Fam. Rel. 206 (2002).

Duvall described eight stages of family development: (1) married couple without children; (2) childbearing families with the oldest child between birth and 30 months; (3) families with preschool children; (4) families with school-age children; (5) families with adolescent children; (6) launching families (first to last child is leaving home); (7) middle-age families ("empty nest" to retirement); and (8) aging families (retirement to death of both spouses).[11] Her approach generally lacks any definition of the patterns of thinking, feelings, and behavior that are both the cause and the effect of systemic change across time, allowing that she does acknowledge a "constant need to adapt one individual to the other and to conditions of the environment."[12] Of course from today's perspective, the theory furthermore cheats anyone who is not monogamous, heterosexual, married, healthy, and fertile from consideration.

Defining Family Systems

The most common and familiar concepts are often the hardest to define. *Family* is one of these.

At the most general level, we use the word *system* to refer to any collection or organization of human relationships. The word telegraphs the constant iterative interactions among constituent members, each impacting and being impacted by others, reshaping and being reshaped by the emergent system they co-create across time. The citizens of a country, the members of a club, the employees of a company, the residents of an apartment building, and the members of an intimate couple or a professional partnership can each be identified as constituting a system.

Family is one type of system.

11. *See* Evelyn Millis Duvall, Family Development (1957).
12. *See id.*

Family is too diverse and amorphous to be captured in a single, simple definition.[13] In the interest of inclusion and clarity, from this point forward we will write FAMILY in capital letters to refer to the concept in its broadest sense—that is, everything from the single parent–child dyad, to the childless couple, to the longhouse or kibbutz-like multigenerational collectives familiar in some cultures. The attributes and dynamics described throughout this volume often apply at this broad level of definition but are targeted at a narrower subset of intimate relationships that we distinguish in lowercase letters.

As family law professionals, we are concerned with *family* (lowercase) as defined as any emotionally entangled group of three or more human beings that include at least two adults and one minor child. Within this definition of one subtype of FAMILY, we make no assumptions about culture, language, race, or religion, ever mindful that these and related contextual factors both shape FAMILY and are shaped by FAMILY.[14] To wit:

> [T]he Western view of childhood may be very different from that of other cultures, in that the Western culture views childhood as a sacred time that should be reserved for children to

---

13. "When does a household become a family? I doubt that many individuals among the large percentage (17.21%) of single male households without children revealed by their analysis would define themselves as a family. And I wonder when a cohabiting couple thinks they have become a family. On the day they move in together? When the couple makes a long-term commitment to each other? When they have a baby together?" Robert E. Emery, *Families as Systems: Some Thoughts on Methods and Theory*, *in* Emerging Methods in Family Research 109, 111 (Susan M. McHale et al. eds., 2014) (volume 4 of the National Symposium on Family Issues book series), https://doi.org/10.1007/978-3-319-01562-0_7.

14. Michael R. Butz, Chaos and Complexity: Implications for Psychological Theory and Practice (1997); Applying Complexity Theory: Whole Systems Approaches to Criminal Justice and Social Work (Aaron Pycroft & Clemens Bartollas eds., 2014); Chaos and Complexity in Psychology: The Theory of Nonlinear Dynamical Systems (Stephen J. Guastello et al. eds., 2008); David Green & Fiona McDermott, *Social Work from inside and between Complex Systems: Perspectives on Person-in-Environment for Today's Social Work*, 40 Brit. J. Soc. Work 2414 (2010); Christopher G. Hudson, *At the Edge of Chaos: A New Paradigm for Social Work?*, 36 J. Soc. Work Educ. 215 (2000).

develop and that children should be protected by adults until they become adults and are able to make adequate decisions for themselves.[15]

We similarly have no preconceptions about the health, gender, generation, or sexual preference of the adults; about the legal status of the relationship(s) among those adults; nor the genetic, biological, or gestational relationship between each of those adults and their child or children.

Although the paradigm that is a FAMILY (in caps) persists regardless of the age of its members, for the sake of this discussion we speak of family (lowercase) as necessarily including at least one child who is a legal minor (as defined by jurisdiction). We also assume the adults are legally competent, and at least one of the adults has a legal right and responsibility to care for that child.

In this construction, we speak of the simplest and most common unit we consider *family* as composed of Parent A and Parent B who are together the biological, genetic, and gestational parents of a school-aged child whom we arbitrarily refer to as Billy or Sally.

This is the prototype or central concept of our definition of *family*.[16] The variations on this theme within this particular subset of FAMILY are many, but include, as examples, still-married, never-married, or divorced same-sex partners with adopted, stepchildren, and half-children, multiple intergenerational partners (e.g., Mom, maternal grandmother, and maternal aunt) sharing the care of Mom's several children by different partners, one of whom shares care for his child episodically, and never-married intimate partners now contesting the future care of their mutually adopted autistic daughter. Billy and Sally could be newborns or teenagers with drivers' licenses. They could be physically healthy or

15. Lisa M. Hooper et al., *Characterizing the Magnitude of the Relation between Self-Reported Childhood Parentification and Adult Psychopathology: A Meta-Analysis*, 67 J. Clinical Psych. 1028, 1031 (2011).

16. *See* Benjamin D. Garber, *Of Beasties and Butterflies: Evidence for the Stability and Domain-Specificity of Individual Differences in Categorization*, 54 J. Personality 647 (1986).

multiply impaired. They could be subject to the timesharing demands of a court-mandated parenting plan or migrating at their whim between homes, or residing entirely with one parent and refusing contact with the other.[17]

What Is a Healthy Family System?

If our goal throughout the remainder of this book is to catalogue the dynamics of the conflicted family system, we are obligated to first articulate our assumptions about what constitutes a psychologically healthy family system. Acknowledging the tremendous variation in family composition, function, and roles across race, ethnicity, language, culture, socioeconomic status, and religion (to name just a few of the relevant variables), we define the psychologically healthy family system as follows:

1. The evolutionary, social, and emotional purpose of *family* is to serve the psychological needs of its children first and foremost, acknowledging that these needs change over time, and always distinguishing the children's psychological needs from the children's wishes and from the adults' respective needs and wishes.
2. The family's shared purpose and resources create boundaries that define it as a system distinct from but frequently interacting with allied and superordinate systems that together create community.
3. Chief among every child's psychological needs is the opportunity to make and maintain a healthy relationship with both/all

17. This description begs the question of whether this prototypical family of three (Mom, Dad, and child) once separated is better described as two distinct FAMILIES (Mom and child; Dad and child). As a clinical matter—that is, in the interest of facilitating the child's coping and comprehension—we believe that the two-FAMILY presentation is best. *See, e.g.*, Benjamin D. Garber, Keeping Kids Out of the Middle: Parenting Effectively in the Midst of Adult Conflict, Separation, and Divorce (2008). However, for the sake of conceptualization and at the risk of confusion, we refer throughout this book to the separated FAMILY of two (that is, the parent-child dyad) as still constituting a single unit.

family members.[18] These relationships constitute familial subsystems (e.g., the mother-child dyad, father-child dyad, and the sibling subsystem).

4. Power, control, and access to resources are distributed unequally within the family system, creating a hierarchy among the family's constituent members that often corresponds to roles and evolves over the course of development (e.g., parent, child).
5. When adults share decision-making authority, they collaborate. That is, they engage in constructive, child-centered, and proactive communication so as to understand and cooperatively serve the child's needs. This is the co-parenting subsystem.
6. Each family member's thoughts and feelings are respected without fear or threat of consequent violence, abandonment, rejection, or loss.
7. The child's thoughts and feelings are given weight by the decision-making adult(s) as a function of the child's emotional maturity (often correlated with but never to be confused with age),[19] the child's relevant capacities, and the law. The weight thus assigned to the child's thoughts and feelings often gradually increases over time such that the balance of power, control, and access to resources shifts until ultimately the child separates from the family system. We refer to this process as launching.

---

18. Although this premise is broadly codified by the law across jurisdictions, research often advises that we must "avoid the simplistic assumption that contact with both parents after separation is always in the child's best interest." Anna M. Forssell & Asa Carter, *Patterns in Child-Father Contact after Parental Separation in a Sample of Child Witnesses to Intimate Partner Violence*, 30 J. Fam. Violence 339, 346 (2015).

19. The weight given to the child's wishes varies dramatically across jurisdictions. In Georgia, for example, children aged 14 and older are permitted to choose with whom they will reside barring evidence that the parent selected poses a risk to the child. *See* Ga. Code Ann. § 19-9-3(5) (2019); *see also* United Nations Convention on the Rights of the Child, Nov. 20, 1989, art. 12, 1577 U.N.T.S. 3 ("State Parties shall assure to the child who is capable of forming his or her own views the right to express those views freely in all matters affecting the child, the views of the child being given due weight in accordance with the age and maturity of the child.").

Development Is Contextually Driven

The development of any system must be understood in the context of its allied,[20] subordinate, and superordinate systems. Thus, understanding six-year-old Sally's development requires a perspective on how her unique strengths and weaknesses are variously nurtured or inhibited by her peer relationships and within the context of the family system that holds her. Pulling back our focus—understanding how Sally's family develops—requires a perspective not only on that system's unique strengths and weaknesses, but also on how the allied systems with which it interacts (e.g., neighbors, colleagues, fellow churchgoers), its subordinate constituent systems (e.g., Sally, her annoying little brother, Mom, and Dad), and the superordinate community that contains it nurture or inhibit its growth. As we shift the level of inquiry, the question remains constant: How do allied, subordinate, and superordinate systems affect development and how are they affected in turn?

Implicit in this idea is the iterative reciprocity among systems. Just as Sally's development is affected by her experience of her annoying brother, her peers, and her parents, the development of each of those systems is affected by Sally. At every level of inquiry, development must inevitably—and we think obviously—be shaped by and will itself shape the context in which it occurs. The process is a befuddling, nonlinear, emergent, and self-organizing quality of complex systems.

How Can Development Be Both Cause and Effect?

Our brains are built for linear thinking. It's easy to understand orderly sequences of cause and effect like so many dominoes in a single row. If you wonder why a specific domino fell, all that is necessary is to examine the domino that preceded it. A pushes B, which pushes C . . . and onward down the line.

(continued on next page)

20. For want of a better word, we use "allied" in this context to describe systems on the same level of hierarchy (i.e., peer-like) without intending to communicate alliance in the sense of shared needs, interests, or goals.

Linear cause-effect thinking is simple and clear and how the law is intended to function. It's how judges and juries are supposed to approach questions about guilt versus innocence, perpetrator versus victim, truth versus lie. It is not, however, how relationships work. This is one among many reasons why family law matters do not belong in conventional courts.[21]

Relationships defy linear logic. Relationships are systems in which B can be both a cause and an effect of either A or C or both. This alternate, Escher-like reality is as common as it is complex and enigmatic: a Gordian knot of emotion and behavior. We live it all the time, but seldom genuinely grasp it. It flies in the face of conventional math and physics and usually provokes naysayers who reasonably demand proof.

The problem understanding nonlinear systems is as much perceptual as it is cognitive. When we see domino B push over domino C, the relevant variables are readily apparent: two stamped wooden rectangles subject to momentum and gravity. Resistance due to inertia is overcome by kinetic energy. To the extent that invisible forces like wind and atmospheric pressure and temperature and altitude are relevant, they're usually negligible.

(continued on next page)

---

21. "The nature of divorce proceedings frequently encourages parents to view the dispute through a purely adversarial lens, a circumstance that negatively impacts the shared parenting role that endures long after the accusations have been made in court. As the divorce proceeding transforms the parenting relationship into one that is predicated on mutual animosity, the likelihood of reaching settlement becomes increasingly unlikely. This stems from the tradition of 'zealous advocacy' that has characterized divorce proceedings, one which emphasizes identifying the opposing party's flaws in order to gain tactical advantages." Thomas D. Vu, Student Note, *Going to Court as a Last Resort: Establishing a Duty for Attorneys in Divorce Proceedings to Discuss Alternative Dispute Resolution with Their Clients*, 47 Fam. Ct. Rev. 586, 587 (2009). As noted throughout this book, the process of resolving family conflict has even more systemic and structural burdens for the poor that requires careful reflection. *See* Elizabeth L. MacDowell, *Reimagining Access to Justice in the Poor People's Courts*, 22 Geo. J. on Poverty L. & Pol'y 473, 496 (2014) ("Several decades of gender and race bias studies show pervasive bias against litigants in private family law cases, including cases relating to domestic violence, divorce, custody, and support.").

> When we see Billy push Sally, however, the same physics can only be understood in the context of multiple, significant extradyadic invisible and historic pressures. These include each participant's experience and emotions and expectations and motivations. Did Ralph push Billy on the playground at school yesterday? Did the teacher ignore the incident and thereby condone it in Billy's eyes? If domino B could learn from his encounter with domino A the way that Billy and Sally have learned about one another over time and each has learned about Mom, its interaction with domino C might be quite different.

Stage-driven theories of development are static, like a road map printed on paper. They more or less accurately describe the route one might take, but they cannot account for weather and accidents and flat tires and impulsive last-minute decisions to visit the world's largest ball of twine *on display for viewing today only*! Stage theorists generate these static maps by studying hundreds of subjects and distilling the commonalities in their development as a function of age and/or sequence the same way that you might describe each step in a staircase. These averaged observations are then used to establish norms, discarding the variability around the norms (standard deviation) as individual differences or confounding artifacts.[22]

Sure, you can measure all the second graders in the classroom and calculate their average height. At issue is how you understand why some children are shorter and other children are taller.

Understanding variability as context rather than as confound adds both complexity and verisimilitude to the process. Life has shown us

22. "In sum, ontogenetic stage theories conceive of the developmental process as uniform and constant. Since the sequence is invariant, the causal factors must be invariant as well; *the enormous range of environmental variability is thus logically required to be causally unimportant.* The environment . . . is the 'scene or setting' of development. It is not conceptualized as a force that can constitute or redirect development stages or sequences." Dale Dannefer, *Adult Development and Social Theory: A Paradigmatic Reappraisal*, 49 Am. Socio. Rev. 100, 104 (1984) (emphasis added) (citation omitted).

that our relationship ecology matters. We know on a gut level, even if the science is much harder to grasp, that growing up is less like a line of dominoes and more like a pool ball, launched by nature across a more-or-less nurturing green felt table, colliding with others and impacting their trajectories at least as much as they impact our own.[23]

Internal Working Models

John Bowlby is the father of modern attachment theory, developmental psychology's most rigorously researched, reliable, and broadly validated conceptual model. Some would say that Bowlby is to developmental psychology what Einstein is to physics and Darwin is to evolution.

Bowlby determined that young primates implicitly distill their experience with each specific caregiver so as to anticipate the availability of future care. That is, babies spontaneously generate their own internal Yelp-like reviews of Mom's and Dad's past caregiving so as to adjust their future behavior when Mom is around differently than when Dad is around. If Mom has been sensitive and responsive or distant or overwhelming to the child in the past, the baby will expect more of the same in the future and respond in kind. The child's experience creates expectations that shape behavior that yield further experience. The resulting distilled representations are known as internal working models (IWMs).[24]

23. "In this perspective, parenthood is designed as a 'triangular function' that takes place not only within the dyadic exchange between each parent and the child, but also within the systemic interrelationship between the two parents and their child, who, together with families of origin, form the emotional context within which the child builds and develops his/her own identity." Giancarlo Tamanza et al., *Separation and Divorce in Italy: Parenthood, Children's Custody, and Family Mediation*, 51 Fam. Ct. Rev. 557, 562 (2013).

24. Cognitive psychology discusses schema (or schemata) in a similar way. Schema are internal representations of the physical environment that make human information processing easier and more efficient by reducing stimuli to familiar models and focusing on novelty or discrepancy: "Ongoing experience is the result of a matching process between the characteristics of currently available particular instances and a representation stored in memory of the gist of previous similar experiences." Allan T. Purcell, *Environmental Perception and Affect: A Schema Discrepancy Model*, 18 Env't & Behav. 3 (1986).

An IWM is a distillation of experience of a specific individual that yields predictions about that person's likely future behavior. These predictions are adaptive to the extent that they allow us to seek out individuals whom experience has taught us will likely be sensitive and responsive to our needs. Ideally, IWMs are always in flux, assimilating or accommodating new information and shaping expectations accordingly. Clinical experience teaches us, however, that some IWMs can become rigid and unresponsive, fixed as if cast in cement. This concept arises again and again throughout this book. For example, in Chapter 5, we talk about individuals' experiences of one another as distinct from any objective measure of that person. In Chapter 14 we discuss relationships as existing "in the eye of the beholder." In Chapter 9 we discuss this yet again as it bears on understanding the polarized child and resist/refuse dynamics.

To illustrate: Over time, ten-year-old Joey has watched Ms. Smith, his new fourth-grade teacher, respond calmly and warmly to his classmates. She made eye contact, smiled warmly, and was very helpful when he had trouble with math. Across these experiences, Joey has implicitly distilled an IWM of Ms. Smith as approachable, nurturing, and supportive. This gave Joey the confidence to approach her yesterday about a problem he had with a peer, expecting that she would once again be kind and attentive.

When Joey returned to class after Christmas break, however, something was different. Ms. Smith seemed gruff and distracted. She ignored some children's requests and barked at others. She barely looked up when Joey needed help with a homework assignment. These experiences quickly tainted Joey's working model, leaving him anxious and avoidant when another problem came up in the belief that she would not be helpful.[25]

---

25. Acknowledging that some would argue that a teacher is not an attachment figure (i.e., an internalized source of emotional security) but has a bond. *See, e.g.*, Karine Verschueren & Jantine L. Spilt, *Understanding the Origins of Child-Teacher Dependency: Mother-Child Attachment Security and Temperamental Inhibition as Antecedents*, Attachment & Hum. Dev. 1 (2020). The dynamics are nonetheless the same. Experience yields expectations specific to an individual, which shape behavior.

Cause and Effect Merge Once Again

For all of its predictive power and insight, attachment theory often fails to acknowledge the reciprocity of the system: not only does Billy's experience of Mom contribute to his ever-evolving IWM of Mom and thereby his expectations about her future caregiving, Mom's experience of Billy shapes her IWM of him. Each develops in the context of the relationship with the other and together function as a system subject to the pressures imposed by other systems.

In this instance, the effect is not entirely reciprocal. Because Mom's life experience is so much broader than Billy's, her expectations about the child are colored not only be their past interactions, but also by a lifetime of other experiences. Was her mother sensitive and responsive to her needs? Was Billy's older sister, Sally, responsive and accepting of her nurturance? How do the stresses in her relationship with Billy's father, with her best friend, and with her boss at work bear on her availability to Billy when he's needy? How does Billy's father's account of his experiences with Billy color her expectations?

IWMs Are Shaped from Both within and outside the Relationship

Pain and hunger and thirst and exhaustion and overstimulation can cause a baby to cry. In the ideal, Mom is sensitive and responsive to the child's cry, contributing to the child's experience of Mom as a source of stress reduction. Each time Mom responds successfully, the child experiences internal hemostasis as brain signals regulate heart rate, respiration, digestion, and sleep-wake cycles, our "hidden regulators."[26] This experience is distilled in the form of an IWM that teaches the child to find Mom's approach rewarding and to turn to Mom for future stress reduction. Rewarded by the baby's responses, Mom distills an image of the child as

26. Myron A. Hofer, *Hidden Regulators in Attachment, Separation, and Loss*, 59 Monographs Soc'y for Rsch. Child Dev. 192 (1994).

loving and miraculous and looks forward to their interaction. A healthy and adaptive dynamic is born of this idealized process, eventually imparting to the child the security necessary to tolerate separations.

Of course, most relationships are flawed approximations of this ideal. Imagine, for example, what happens when Mom develops post-partum depression, is drug-addicted, or is consumed by chronic pain. The baby's cries sometimes go unanswered and, when she does respond, she's irritable and distant. Experience leaves the child to distill a working model of Mother as unreliable, impatient, and cold, which prompts avoidant or rejecting behavior. This behavior communicates to Mom that her baby is difficult to comfort, which informs her working model of the child and how she responds to him in the future. The resulting dynamic is just as adaptive as the first, but less healthy to the extent that the child's coping resources are compromised.

Necessity Is the Mother of . . . Metaphor

Relationship dynamics and development are often easily communicated in the easy vernacular of automobiles and gas stations. In healthy relationships, we turn to one another for precious emotional fuel. Roles and experience determine who refuels whom. In this prototypical Mother-infant scenario, Mother is the gas station to which the child returns over and over again to fill his tiny little gas tank. Intimate partners (e.g., husband-wife) refuel one another, albeit usually at different times. In general, subordinate systems are refueled by allied and superordinate systems.

The metaphor is useful both to this discussion and in day-to-day practice in a number of ways. It invites us to ask you, for example, how you get refueled. If parents are their children's sources of fuel, it becomes critically important to understand how the parents themselves get refueled. An intimate partner? Extended family? A club or team or spiritual affiliation? The metaphor allows us to very concretely show the well-intended, self-sacrificing parent or

(continued on next page)

professional that you can't refuel others if your own tank is empty.[27] This is the path to burnout and vicarious trauma, subjects discussed in detail in Chapter 18.

The refueling metaphor also helps us talk about emotional maturity. The newborn can hold a thimbleful of gas and needs frequent refueling. Healthy development means growing a larger gas tank and improving mileage so as to go further and further before needing to come home to fill 'er up. Transitional objects (e.g., teddy bears and blankies) are portable red gas cans that allow the child to refuel while apart from his main gas stations.[28] Distance media (e.g., cell phones, FaceTime, and Twitter accounts) and "virtual visitation" play into these dynamics as well, although we're not yet sure whether the effect is for better or worse.[29] For most healthy children, adolescence means developing emotional waystations or "transitional affiliations" in the form of teams and clubs and gangs that serve to launch the child beyond the orbit of Mom and Dad and off to develop intimate partners with whom the cycle is repeated.[30]

---

27. This is part of the lesson learned from studies of resilience. People who have a broad and diverse support system are far more likely to manage stress than those who are socially isolated. Edith H. Grotberg, *The International Resilience Research Project*, *in* International Perspectives on Human Development 379 (Anna Laura Comunian & Uwe Peter Gielen eds., 2000).

28. *See* Benjamin D. Garber & Dana E. Prescott, *On the Value of Teddy Bears and Barbie Dolls: The Place of Children's Transitional Objects in Family Law*, 49 Sw. L. Rev. 189 (2020).

29. "On one hand, virtual visitation does potentially refill the child's emotional gas tank so as to better manage separation. On the other hand, virtual visitation does not draw on a child's representation of or association to the absent parent in that the parent is present, albeit removed from all but visual and auditory experience." Benjamin D. Garber, *For the Love of Fluffy: Respecting, Protecting, and Empowering Transitional Objects in the Context of High Conflict Divorce*, 60 J. Divorce & Remarriage 552 (2019) (citations omitted).

30. "These group associations become new sources of emotional fuel visible in the prominent colors and brands and symbols that define membership or belonging. These 'transitional affiliations' serve as launching pads that help children, at various developmental phases and over a life span, move constructively away from family-of-origin toward intimate partnerships." Garber & Prescott, *supra* note 28, at 198 (footnotes omitted).

As challenging as these concepts may be, this is only the tip of the interactional iceberg. In order to grasp the full complexity of family system dynamics, we must allow that each member's working model of each of the other family members is informed not only by direct experience with that person, but also by a host of extradyadic pressures.

It may seem obvious, for example, that Mom's own developmental history bears on the expectations that she brings to mothering. All of the hopes and dreams and fears accumulated across her life are cast on the blank slate that will be known as Billy soon after birth.[31] These conscious and unconscious historical pressures affect her expectations, color her interpretations of the baby's coos and smiles and cries, and shape her responses. Entirely ignorant of these pressures, Billy distills his experience of Mom to create his own IWM and responds accordingly.

But a systemic focus requires that we think even further outside the dyadic box. We have to allow that Mom's expectations about and reactions to Baby Billy are also influenced by contemporaneous third-party variables. Her experience with her best friend's baby, and what she learns via Google, and how she interprets the pediatrician's raised eyebrow of concern, and her intimate partner's worries and fears all shape and reshape her expectations and her behavior like many hands shaping wet clay on a potter's wheel. Relationship dynamics are dynamic, after all. Mom's working model of Baby Billy is not a fixed and static canvas colored by history and contemporaneous influences and then left to dry. It's fluid and constantly in flux, assimilating and accommodating new information from many sources, including not only Billy himself, shaping her behavior with the child on thousands of occasions across a lifetime.

The same is true of Billy as a function of development and socialization. At birth, the scope of social, emotional, and cognitive/verbal

---

31. In various studies now decades old, interviews with pregnant mothers reliably predicted as much as 75 percent of the variance among their children's attachment security at 12 months of age. *See* Peter Fonagy et al., *Maternal Representations of Attachment during Pregnancy Predict the Organization of Infant-Mother Attachment at One Year of Age*, 62 Child Dev. 891 (1991). Attachment studies require careful exposition before being generalized to child custody litigation and current gender roles within family systems. For a current review of the literature, see Daniel J. Siegel, The Developing Mind: How Relationships and the Brain Interact to Shape Who We Are (2020).

pressures on Billy's working model of Mom is limited practically, perceptually, and cognitively. As he develops and his social ecology expands, as his sensory skills begin to focus and as his verbal and paraverbal comprehension emerge, the number and variety of extradyadic sources coloring Billy's experiences of Mom grow exponentially. Grandma smiles toward Mom. Babysitters laugh with Mom. Dad yells at Mom. A baby sister arrives screaming in Mom's arms. Peers talk about their mothers. Media sources introduce a million different ideas about moms.[32] Each of these can contribute to Billy's expectations and thereby his behavior toward Mom, which, in turn, contributes to Mom's experience of Billy and her expectations of their next encounter.

Now imagine these same interwoven, chaotic, and complex dynamics as they simultaneously play out between Billy and Dad, and between Mom and Dad, each informed by history and direct experience and myriad extradyadic pressures, constantly updating a working model of the others and the system that they make together. The complexity is mind-boggling. This explains, in part, why theorists have often defaulted to propose linear, stepwise descriptions of development. For all of its appeal, however, simple and clear do not make a theory correct. Sometimes we have to grapple with complexity if we hope to genuinely understand.

Development Is a Gradual Progression from Undifferentiated to Optimal Differentiation and Back Again

No matter how you focus the lens of that orbiting telescope, from a study of the microscopic to a study of the cosmic, all healthy development follows the same general course. The life of a galaxy and the life of a planet and the life of a person all begin in an undifferentiated singularity. Development is the gradual process of differentiation toward a state

32. Alessondra Villegas, *The Influence of Technology on Family Dynamics*, Proc. N.Y. St. Comm. Ass'n, Oct. 17, 2013, at 1, https://docs.rwu.edu/cgi/viewcontent.cgi?article=1062&context=nyscaproceedings.

of bounded autonomy and the inevitable decline from that state back toward an undifferentiated singularity.

A simple visual metaphor illustrates this development-as-differentiation idea plainly: Start with a glass of water. Dip a finger into the water, and then slowly withdraw the finger. A single drop will adhere to your fingertip. That particular, bounded bubble of water has never existed before. It was an undifferentiated, unbounded part of an oceanic pool contained in your glass. It is now unique and autonomous and has an identity apart from the pool from which it arose, and to which it will return with a flick of your wrist.

In this model, development at every level of analysis is the gradual definition and then the inevitable degradation of the boundaries that define each drip as distinct from its undifferentiated oceanic origins and from all other drips.[33] The child is born into family and community undifferentiated. He has no sense of self as distinct from experience. Everything is me. This is the oceanic, undifferentiated self from whence we all emerge. Healthy development means experiencing stress and stress reduction in the context of sensitive and responsive relationships such that the child gradually begins to distinguish *me* from *not-me* and thereby to distill a sense of bounded identity distinct from all others.

We use the words *bounded* and *boundaries* to define the differentiated system and to distinguish what *belongs in* from what *belongs out*. The drip of water is bounded by surface tension. The healthy individual is physically bounded by skin and psychologically bounded by identity. The healthy family is physically bounded by walls and psychologically bounded by a sense of membership or coherence. The same is true at every fractal level of inquiry, from neighborhood to community to species to universe.

When speaking of human systems—relationships—we contend that across time and cultures, *systems* are bounded by their constituent

33. The general concept and the specific reference to the newborn's "oceanic" sense of self is associated with Freud. *See* Sigmund Freud, Civilization and Its Discontents (David McLintock trans., Penguin Classic 2002) (1930).

members' greater expectations of stress reduction from within than from without.[34] Needs trigger stress. Stress is resolved by need fulfillment. Thus, systems are bounded by their constituent members' expectations of greater need fulfillment from within the system than from outside of it.

This is essentially an analysis of variance, a statistical calculation that defines identity by determining that the differences between members of a group is less than the differences between groups. Thus, a system is said to be differentiated, bounded, or coherent to the extent that it is more self-contained than it is reliant-upon-others. By this definition, the newborn is far from psychologically differentiated within his family system in that he depends entirely on family members for psychological need fulfillment,[35] but the family is well differentiated from other families to the extent that it fulfills Mom's and Dad's and Baby Billy's needs largely from within.

This allows us to add to the definition of *family* offered earlier in this chapter: family is a collection of at least two adults and one minor child who are more reliant on need fulfillment from one another than they are reliant upon others. The family can be augmented by incorporating others who seek need fulfillment primarily within the system (e.g., adoption of a new baby) and redefined or dissolved when one or more family members seek basic need fulfillment outside of the system. The latter state occurs in the natural course of development when a child is launched toward independence, when the family system suffers powerful and/or prolonged stresses (e.g., death, disaster, disease), and when one or both adults begin to seek need fulfillment outside of the family system as can occur in the case of infidelity.

---

34. One fascinating example of how between versus within group definitions emerge and dissipate as a function of relationship ecology can be seen in Sherif's classic Robbers Cave experiments. Muzafer Sherif, *Experiments in Group Conflict*, Sci. Am., Nov. 1956, at 54; Muzafer Sherif, *Superordinate Goals in the Reduction of Intergroup Conflict*, 63 Am. J. Socio. 349 (1958).

35. This defines healthy enmeshment as discussed in Chapter 10.

Stress Is the Test

It is difficult or impossible to determine how a system gets its psychological needs fulfilled when everyone is comfortable and safe. Its only when a family is observed under stress that dynamics are cast in *bas relief.*

Ainsworth recognized this when she created the Strange Situation protocol, the standardized, reliable, and repeatedly validated measure used to assess parent-child attachment security.[36] The protocol observes if and how a toddler uses an accompanying parent to manage the stresses of interaction with an unfamiliar stranger in an unfamiliar setting.[37] Children who turn to the parent and accept comfort, calm, and resume play are implicitly communicating that they have experienced that parent as a reliable source of comfort in the past. This is referred to as a secure attachment relationship.

Children who ignore or dismiss or resist the accompanying parent upon reunion are communicating their historical experience of that parent as relatively insensitive and unresponsive to their needs. Turning to them for succor in the past has failed, so they struggle on their own in the present. These relationships are deemed insecure.

We apply the same principle to understanding systems at every level of analysis. Child custody evaluation, for example, is in part an examination of whether and how the child is able to get his needs fulfilled now that the constellation and function of the familiar family system has changed.[38]

---

36. *See* Mary D. Salter Ainsworth et al., Patterns of Attachment: A Psychological Study of the Strange Situation (1969); Mary D. Salter Ainsworth & Silvia M. Bell, *Attachment, Exploration, and Separation: Illustrated by the Behavior of One-Year-Olds in a Strange Situation, in* 4 Determinants of Infant Behavior 111 (Brian M. Foss ed., 1961).

37. "The entire separation literature suggests that the response to reunion after separation may well yield a clearer picture of the state of attachment than did the response to separation itself." Ainsworth et al., *supra* note 36, at xlii (citation omitted).

38. Importing the concepts implicit in the Strange Situation paradigm can make child custody evaluation both more informative and more efficient. *See* Benjamin D. Garber, *Exploring a Process-Oriented Forensic Family Observation Protocol,* 54 Fam. Ct. Rev. 261 (2016).

Resilience

If human relationships are defined by their internal ability to reduce stress, then we must understand resilience as one critical variable relevant to this process. Resilience is a system's ability to bounce back from stress.[39] A materials scientist concerned with the qualities of a particular alloy can calculate its resilience (μ) by observing the limits of its stress tolerance in a laboratory setting. Stress deforms materials like steel I-beams. Resilience is the material's relative ability to bounce back to its original size, shape, and strength after exposure to stress. Resilience is thus a measure of how much pressure an I-beam can manage before it breaks.

Systemic resilience can be understood in the same way at every level of inquiry, although there is no absolute metric with which to measure it. Every system from the individual human being to the family to the community and up the nested hierarchy to the level of species can be said to have its own specific resilience coefficient, a measurement that can only be taken under stress and in the context of its relational ecology.

Psychologists interested in human resilience have identified variables that help to determine how much stress individuals can withstand. Chief among these variables is social relatedness. The more socially interconnected a person is, the more likely she will be to bounce back from stress.[40]

---

39. *See* Nicholas J. Thompson et al., *Coping Strategies as Mediators in Relation to Resilience and Posttraumatic Stress Disorder*, 225 J. Affective Disorders 153 (2018). Note in this regard that "how the individual labels, assigns meaning to, and is disrupted physically and psychologically by an event will contribute to whether or not it is experienced as traumatic." Substance Abuse and Mental Health Services Administration, U.S. Department of Health and Human Services, SAMHSA's Concept of Trauma and Guidance for a Trauma-Informed Approach 8 (2014) (SMA 14-4884).

40. "Children can develop areas of resilience in their lives when they are protected by the positive actions of adults, by good nurturing, by their assets, and by policies and practices that support their healthy development and reduce risk across key systems (family, legal, judicial, educational, and community) that affect their lives." JoAnne L. Pedro-Carroll, *Fostering Resilience in the Aftermath of Divorce: The Role of Evidence-Based Programs for Children*, 43 Fam. Ct. Rev. 52, 53 (2005).

The International Resilience Project has summarized the elements of childhood resilience in a beautiful statement entitled "I have, I am, I can":[41]

The resilient child says I have:

- People around me I trust and who love me, no matter what
- People who set limits for me so I know when to stop before there is danger or trouble
- People who show me how to do things right by the way they do things

The resilient child says I am:

- A person people can like and love
- Glad to do nice things for others and show my concern
- Respectful of myself and others
- Willing to be responsible for what I do
- Sure things will be all right

The resilient child says I can:

- Talk to others about things that frighten me or bother me
- Find ways to solve problems that I face
- Control myself when I feel like doing something not right or dangerous
- Figure out when it is a good time to talk to someone or to take action
- Find someone to help me when I need it

Applying this understanding of human resilience to systems theory creates an interesting paradox: On one hand, the theory suggests that the more connected a system is within its relational ecology, the more resilient it will be. On the other hand, the more the members of a system

41. *See* Grotberg, *supra* note 27.

seek need fulfillment outside of that system, the weaker its boundaries are likely to be.[42]

As one example, the family that constantly entertains relatives, neighbors, and colleagues, hosts playdates, affiliates with a local church, participates in every school and community activity, campaigns for its favorite candidates, takes in the needy, and contributes to charities is deeply invested in allied and superordinate systems. This family may have a great deal of community support when it faces stress but may also be creating a great deal of internal stress by being so invested in others. The same extra-systemic resources that shore it up can simultaneously tear it apart.[43]

As a second example, the community and government resources that support impoverished, immigrant, and disabled families with the best of intentions risk tearing those families apart one visitor, inspector, supervisor, observer, evaluator, case manager, and paperwork form at a time. For all of their generosity and beneficence, the family's dependence on superordinate resources can weaken its boundaries and corrupt its members' roles. This can occur, for example, among immigrant families when a child is adultified by becoming enlisted as a culture broker, a phenomenon discussed in Chapter 11.

Every system must resolve this paradox in its own way or fail, redefining its roles and rules one day to the next in the balance between rigid and permeable boundaries. Not only must this balance be carefully

---

42. Research is beginning, with more research still required, to identify mediating or moderating factors or variables that might help to explain this apparent paradox. For example, "[f]or mothers only, social support was significantly linked to parent-child warmth only when mothers had low (but not high) perceived self-control." Melissa A. Lippold et al., *Parental Perceived Control and Social Support: Linkages to Change in Parenting Behaviors during Early Adolescence*, 57 Fam. Process 432 (2018).

43. "Exosystem risk factors [for high-conflict family dynamics] include extended family taking sides, also known as 'tribal warfare' or 'cheerleaders' . . . as well as professionals taking sides serving as negative advocates. Other exosystem risk factors include the involvement of child welfare, police, or other professional institutions (e.g., lawyers, children's legal representation, child advocates, etc.)." Shely Polak & Michael Saini, *The Complexity of Families Involved in High-Conflict Disputes: A Postseparation Ecological Transactional Framework*, 60 J. Divorce & Remarriage 117 (2018) (citations omitted).

attuned to culture[44] and era and social ecology, it must also shift with the developing needs of its constituent members.[45]

Identity Is How the Individual Balances Need Fulfillment from within and Connectedness Without

These two opposing forces—the drive for need fulfillment from within the system and the resilience inherent in connectedness to those who are outside the system—create a constant push/pull tension. The drip that clings to your finger when you raise it out of the glass of water experiences this as the balance between the surface tension that defines its shape and the gravity that draws it back into its source. For the individual, this is the existential question that seeks eternally to define what is me as distinct from what is not me.

The individual who errs in the direction of inflexibility and exclusivity is seen as guarded, defensive, and isolating. The medical model speaks of these people variously as anxious, narcissistic, schizoid, and/or autistic. On the other side of the coin, the individual who errs in the direction of friable and diffuse boundaries is everyone's best friend—enjoyable, adaptable, and never disagreeable—until he she becomes intrusive, confusing self and others, unable to be alone, without direction, purpose, or self-sufficiency. The medical model speaks of these people in terms of reactive attachment disorder, disinhibited social engagement disorder,[46] psychosis, and schizophrenia.

---

44. For example, "a high level of perceived family cohesion and support has also been identified as the most distinctive dimension of Hispanic families." *See* Fernando I. Rivera et al., *Family Cohesion and Its Relationship to Psychological Distress among Latino Groups*, 30 Hisp. J. Behav. Sci. 357, 358 (2008).

45. Consistent with the observation that family cohesion must be redefined as children begin to move toward autonomy, research identifies "significant decreases in family cohesion from 6th through 10th grades." Judith Baer, *Is Family Cohesion a Risk or Protective Factor during Adolescent Development?*, 64 J. Marriage & Fam. 668 (2004).

46. The fifth edition of the Diagnostic and Statistical Manual broke the former diagnosis known as reactive attachment disorder into two distinct diagnoses. Learn more about this diagnosis at Lory Zephyr et al., *Meta-Analyses of the Associations between Disinhibited Social Engagement Behaviors and Child Attachment Insecurity or Disorganization*,

Cohesion is how family systems balance need fulfillment within and connectedness without.[47] The system that errs in the direction of rigid, exclusive boundaries is seen as disengaged, aloof, and rejecting and will likely be highly vulnerable to stress. Because its boundaries are so rigid and exclusive, its cohesion is brittle. It has no extra-systemic supports.[48] This can occur when a family's beliefs, practices, religion, and/or language is markedly different than those around it, a situation that can sometimes create distinct enclaves of like-minded families within a larger community.

On the other hand, the family that errs in the direction of creating diffuse and permeable boundaries may be seen as generous, selfless, and philanthropic, but risks losing its cohesion—the emotional glue that maintains its identity as distinct within its larger social ecology—as a result. These are differences of degree, of course. For example, many close-knit religious communities maintain relatively weak family boundaries as evident in the constant sharing of resources, community meetings

---

49 Rsch. on Child & Adolescent Psychopathology 949 (2021), https://doi.org/10.1007/s10802-021-00777-1.

47. Family cohesion is traditionally defined operationally as "emotional bonding members have with one another and the degree of individual autonomy a person experiences in the family system." David H. Olson et al., *Circumplex Model of Marital and Family System: I. Cohesion and Adaptability Dimensions, Family Types, and Clinical Applications*, 18 Fam. Process 3, 3 (1979). Using this definition, a continuum of family cohesion emerges, identified as (1) enmeshed, (2) connected, (3) separated, and (4) disengaged. *See id.* at 5 (emphasis omitted); *see also* Nick J. Porta & Kristina S. Brown, *Family Cohesion*, *in* Encyclopedia of Family Studies (Constance L. Shehan ed., 2016).

48. Others define social groups along six dimensions:

1. *Permeability* is the ease of entering or leaving the group.
2. *Consensus* is the degree to which members share norms, attitudes, and beliefs.
3. *Solidarity* refers to cohesiveness and a preference for interaction within the group.
4. *Fragmentation* refers to the existence of cliques within the group.
5. *Role differentiation* involves a clear division of labor with distinctive roles.
6. *Status differentiation* refers to differences in power and status.

Paul Amato, *Approaches to Measuring Families*, *in* Emerging Methods in Family Research 179–93 (Susan M. McHale et al. eds., 2014), https://doi.org/10.1007/978-3-319-01562-0_11.

for worship, and mutual need fulfillment within the larger and relatively rigid boundaries that define the group.

The difference between these two extremes becomes most readily apparent under stress. If forced to choose between your family and your community, what would you choose?

Contemporary American culture preaches a Goldilocks approach to this dilemma. In the same way that the fairy-tale intruder chooses among the bears' three beds, our culture recommends that a moderate degree of cohesion is just right. Our family's boundaries should be neither too rigid and thereby brittle, lacking resilience and support, nor too permeable and thereby vulnerable to enmeshment and identity dissolution.

Applying these concepts to children and co-parental conflicts, we offer the following:

> [C]lear and flexible boundaries that permit each family member to function within subsystems without the interference of other members but also access resources from the larger family system when needed . . . . Thus, cohesiveness is marked by the provision of support, warmth, and intimacy across different family subsystems without compromising the autonomy or emotional well-being of any member . . . . When disruptive events in the family (e.g., maternal relationship transitions) do occur, the well-defined boundaries between family subsystems are reflected in the encapsulation of the difficulties within the specific subsystem (e.g., interparental subsystem). Thus, *the problems experienced by the subsystem do not proliferate in a way that entangles other family members* . . . . Given that these families can successfully encapsulate problems, we hypothesize that family cohesion will serve as a protective factor, buffering children from the risk conferred by maternal relationship instability.[49]

---

49. Jesse L. Coe et al., *Family Cohesion and Enmeshment Moderate Associations between Maternal Relationship Instability and Children's Externalizing Problems*, 32 J. Fam. Psych. 289 (2018) (emphasis added) (citations omitted).

Although clinical and forensic investigators have few reliable tools with which to measure relationship dynamics, research psychologists have quite a few. Unlike the forgetful carpenter who simply borrows his tools from a friend at the work site, assessment tools aren't as easily shared. A measurement that is normed on one population (e.g., university students who volunteer to participate in a professor's research) may have no validity, however, when applied to another population (e.g., high-conflict divorcing parents and their children). Ainsworth's Strange Situation paradigm, for example, is a model of reliability and validity in the context of developmental research but faces numerous reliability and validity hurdles before it can be meaningfully incorporated into family forensic practice.[50]

Nevertheless, research instruments can and often do inform the concepts—if not the measurements—relevant to family law. For example, one recent study described an observational block-building task useful for assessing cohesion within family groups.[51] Trained observers scored interactions while families worked to build a specific block structure:

> The cohesion scale assesses the extent to which the family's interaction reflects a balanced concern for all family members' emotional and psychological well-being so that there is some flexibility, permeability, and access to resources (support, warmth, intimacy) across relationships, but it occurs within appropriate, well-defined boundaries that do not compromise any one member's autonomy.[52]

(continued on next page)

50. Benjamin D. Garber, *Attachment Methodology in Custody Evaluation: Four Hurdles Standing between Developmental Theory and Forensic Application*, 6 J. Child Custody 38 (2009).

51. Coe et al., *supra* note 49.

52. *Id.*

By contrast:

> [T]he enmeshment scale assesses the extent to which boundaries are overly diffuse or permeable. High scores on enmeshment are reserved for families where all members are overly involved in one another's activities (e.g., repeatedly interrupt or talk over one another, overly rely on others for help, grab Legos out of each other's hands).[53]

When Family Systems Fail

Conflict can disrupt the system's internal hierarchy the way that a coup d'état disrupts the internal hierarchy of government. Conflict is inevitable as systems adapt to both internal and external pressures. Systems theorists know that the goal is not to avoid conflict. The goal is to be able to manage conflict so as to maintain healthy functioning. This is evident at every fractal level of inquiry, from the teenager's internal conflicts associated with puberty to divorce as it disrupts the family system to pandemics as they force the entire species to cope with new and unforeseen stresses.

The fact that conflict is inevitable within family is inherent in the idea that family exists to launch children toward autonomy. Fulfilling this goal requires change and disruption by definition. The family's internal balance of power, control, and access to resources must be overhauled. Change is necessary in order to adapt to rapidly shifting abilities and needs. Co-parents vest their growing child with greater self-control, empowering his continued healthy movement toward autonomy. Boundaries are redrawn. A new internal balance is struck. Family is redefined.

Something similar occurs when the intimate adult relationship falters or fails. Partners fall out of love, betray one another, or otherwise encounter an insurmountable impasse. The balance of power, control, and access to resources within the fractured system is compromised.

53. *Id.*

The child's experience of security is upset if not undermined entirely. The family's internal hierarchy must be rebuilt. Boundaries need to be redrawn, roles redefined, and rules adjusted accordingly.

Seventeen-year-old Billy is breaking curfew, failing school, and generally defying Mom and Dad's authority. Dad wants to punish him. Mom thinks boys will be boys. Co-parental conflict erupts. The family system is in chaos. A therapist is brought in. School officials are consulted. Grandma offers an opinion. The family's rabbi recommends a website on parenting. Mom and Dad take all this in and together create more effective behavioral contingencies at home. The family redraws its limits and boundaries in a manner better suited to Billy's abrupt movement toward autonomy while maintaining safety and control and, by doing so, retains its cohesion. As the family's new structures begin to prove effective, the structure within the family is renewed. Conflict settles. Allied supports are withdrawn.

But when allied systems—community—are not available, not welcomed, or not sufficient to help, and family disruption persists and even escalates, superordinate systems become involved. Billy's disruptive behavior might prompt a call to the police. A teacher might make a call to child protective services. A parent might file a motion seeking a divorce. In each of these and many similar circumstances, the conflicted family system becomes subjugated to the power and control exercised by a superordinate system, namely the courts.

The Judicial System

Systems exist in a hierarchy of power and control relative to one another the same way that the members of a family exist within the family's hierarchy. The parents are superordinate to the child by virtue of exercising greater power, control, and access to resources. The judicial system is superordinate to the family in exactly the same manner, exercising these prerogatives in the best interests of the child (BIC).[54]

---

54. The BIC standard is operationalized variously by jurisdiction and is often criticized as indeterminate, but the relevant factors are actually a rather intricate taxonomy or framework for exploring and explaining what occurs between family members and within

The courts' authority to intercede in a family is derived from the common-law policy of *parens patriae*.[55] This authority is typically triggered in one of two scenarios. Either a child's well-being has been compromised by adult abuse or neglect, or conflicted co-parents can't agree on significant matters concerning their children's needs. This is how judges, guardians ad litem, lawyers, and a host of other family law professionals can find themselves mired in the intricacies and intimacies of family dynamics.

Unfortunately, family is a square peg that seldom fits in the round hole that is the judicial system. The legal process demands and therefore imposes a linear, cause-effect, logical structure to resolve conflicts. This works in civil and criminal matters when binary questions of cause and effect, guilt and innocence, are at issue. It often fails when convoluted and chaotic family system dynamics are at issue. The only way to get that square peg into the round hole is to shear away the corners. In this case, that means reducing the dynamic complexity of relationships to black versus white polarities. Tragically, forcing relationship questions into this procrustean box can feel like jumping out of the frying pan and into the fire.[56] For example:

---

those family systems. *See* Steven N. Peskind, *Determining the Undeterminable: The Best Interest of the Child Standard as an Imperfect but Necessary Guidepost to Determine Child Custody*, 25 N. Ill. U. L. Rev. 449 (2004); Elizabeth S. Scott & Robert E. Emery, *Gender Politics and Child Custody: The Puzzling Persistence of the Best-Interest Standard*, 77 Law & Contemp. Probs. 69 (2014).

55. It is well-settled that "[a] parent has a fundamental right to the care and custody of his or her child." Boswell v. Boswell, 721 A.2d 662, 668 (Md. 1998); *accord In re* Adoption/Guardianship No. 10941, 642 A.2d 201, 208 (Md. 1994) ("the right of a parent to raise his or her child. . . . is so fundamental that it may not be taken away unless clearly justified"). The state, however, has an interest in protecting a child's best interest as *parens patriae*. *Boswell*, 721 A.2d at 669. "[T]he State's interest in disputes over visitation, custody, and adoption is to protect 'the best interests of the child.'" *Id.* "Thus, while a parent has a fundamental right to raise his or her own child, this Court has held that the best interests of the child may take precedence over the parent's liberty interest in the course of a custody, visitation, or adoption dispute." *Id.*; *see also* Bafford v. Bafford, No. 03-C-18-012819 (Md. Ct. Spec. App. Sept. 29, 2020), https://casetext.com/case/bafford-v-bafford.

56. *See* Dan Simon et al., *The Adversarial Mindset*, 26 Psych. Pub. Pol'y & L. 353 (2020).

> Conflict played out in the courtroom could be fueled by the adversarial nature of the legal system and by the procedures and practices of attorneys who serve as its functionaries. Within the organizational social system, the legal system can reinforce or exacerbate high conflict via the requirement of filing affidavits in support of their application and parenting plan requests.[57]

At issue throughout the remainder of this book is what happens when family systems lose their balance, sliding in one direction toward dissolution for lack of adequate boundaries or in the other direction toward isolation within extreme and rigid boundaries, variously helped or hindered by the courts. Chapter 4 begins by considering how the biases and failings of the mental health and family law systems intended to support floundering families often exacerbate the process despite their best intentions.

57. Polak & Saini, *supra* note 43, at 127.

Chapter 4
Bias and Family Forensic Practice

"We do not see things as they are, we see them as we are."[1]

Bias is the reflexive act of using blunt and myopic algorithms to more quickly process data.[2] It is the natural tendency to only see the data that confirm our expectations that polarizes parties, causing each of us to tread the same familiar path time after time. Understandable and expectable and even necessary as bias may be, science demands an objective, impartial analysis of the facts. This is emphasized in the best interests of the child (BIC) standard and in each of a long list of ethical and guild-specific guidelines, standards, and best practice protocols that demand that family law professionals consciously and continuously work to minimize bias.[3]

Unfortunately, understanding bias is never in and of itself sufficient.[4] Some types and degrees of bias are inevitable. Our goal, therefore, must be to recognize and determine what our biases are, how they color our perceptions of any particular case, and how they can become institutionalized so as to give each square peg its due.[5]

---

1. Anaïs Nin, Seduction of the Minotaur (1961).

2. *See, e.g.*, Christine V. Rogerson et al., *Teaching Social Work Students the Influence of Explicit and Implicit Bias: Promoting Ethical Reflection in Practice*, Soc. Work Educ., Apr. 3, 2021.

3. For example: "it is crucial that evaluators remain as free as possible of unwarranted bias or partiality." American Psychological Association, *Guidelines for Child Custody Evaluations in Family Law Proceedings*, 65(9) Am. Psych. 863 item 5 (2010).

4. Marissa Zappala et al., *Anything You Can Do, I Can Do Better: Bias Awareness in Forensic Evaluators*, 18 J. Forensic Psych. Rsch. & Prac. 45 (2018).

5. The rates of wrongful criminal convictions alone should be enough to give pause when relying upon the human capacity to stereotype, the dangers of implicit bias, and need for affiliation and social acceptance. *See* Glen Whitman & Roger Koppl, *Rational Bias in Forensic Science*, 9 Law Probability & Risk 69, 71 (2010) ("Forensic science

Bias, Attitudes, Stereotypes, and Prejudice

The sheer volume of sensory and affective data in even the most bland and familiar environment is utterly overwhelming. Our brains are simply incapable of processing the constant flood of ever-changing visual, olfactory, tactile, auditory, gustatorial, proprioceptive, and emotional information. Drowning in this flood, we humans would still be an invertebrate species functioning exclusively by reflex had evolution not favored brains that reduce the flood of data by taking shortcuts.

Biases are shortcuts or assumptions. They are learned and often unconscious rules that reduce the tsunami of experience into an orderly stream of information. The benefit of bias is the ability to cope and even dedicate some excess brain power to discovering fire and hot dogs and inventing the Internet. The costs include the loss of nuance and often getting things wrong as a result of uninformed misapprehension, misdirection, and overgeneralization.

If a bias is an unconscious acquired assumption generalized across a category (e.g., age, gender, race) that facilitates survival and makes room for cognitive processing, an *attitude* is a learned evaluative valence (e.g., good versus bad) associated with that category and a *stereotype* is an association between that category and a trait or behavior (e.g., big feet, kindness, intelligence, beauty). Thus, the reflexive idea that old people can't manage digital devices is a bias. The judgment that being unable to manage digital devices is bad is an attitude. The generalization that old people are therefore stupid is a stereotype.

It's easy to imagine that expertise is the antidote to bias. One might think that intense and prolonged immersion in a subject would open one's eyes to the full breadth and depth and color of a subject. Much as expertise is to be applauded and can be immensely useful in the family court process, expertise does not in and of itself reduce bias. To the contrary, the expert may be more vulnerable to bias than most by virtue of

---

evidence is often ambiguous, and the analysis is generally subjective. In spite of such ambiguity and subjective judgement, forensic science testimony is generally categorical, essentially conveying a 'match' or 'no match' decision. The tension exists within an institutional structure that frequently puts crime labs under the administration of law enforcement agencies.").

the implicit pressures associated with the role and the emotions stirred up when the expert is challenged.[6] These factors are further amplified—increasing rather than decreasing the expert's vulnerability to bias—when the expert works in the employ of an advocate who skews the expert's access to data and compromises his supposedly impartial position:

> Being an expert entails using schemas, selective attention, chunking information, automaticity and more reliance on top-down information, all of which allows experts to perform quickly and efficiently; however, these very mechanisms restrict flexibility and control, may cause the experts to miss and ignore important information, introduce tunnel vision and bias and can cause other effects that degrade performance.[7]

Bias Drives Black-and-White Thinking

The heuristic nature of biases—the overgeneralizing assumptions that facilitate sensory processing—tend to cast experience in either/or black-or-white terms. This experience is most obvious in its most primitive form, the innate human approach/avoidance reflex. Survival demands that every new stimulus be instantly designated *friend* or *foe. Friend* invites approach that can be rewarded by camaraderie, increased resources, and the strength of numbers. *Foe* triggers avoidance in the form of reflexive fight, flight, freeze, and flock behaviors.

More generally, biases induce either/or categorical thinking. Human beings implicitly understand the world by building cognitive categories of things around a central or prototypical case. People who share the same cultural experience often share the same prototypical idea of things as simple as *chair* and as complex as *parent.* Bias helps to resolve the ambiguity of each new stimulus by determining similarities to and differences from the prototype. This generates *in* versus *out* judgments.

Does this oversized beanbag belong in the category of *chair*?

---

6. Zappala et al., *supra* note 4.

7. Itiel E. Dror, *The Paradox of Human Expertise: Why Experts Get It Wrong, in* The Paradoxical Brain 177 (Narinder Kapur et al. eds., 2011).

Does this this 40-year-old drug-addicted woman fit in my category of *parent*?

Brains are like coffee mugs. They only hold so much. The more emotion present in the cup, the less room is left for logical, analytical reasoning. As thinking capacity diminishes, reflexes kick in to compensate. Thus, biases run rampant when emotions are high. Of course, there may be no professional setting more thoroughly steeped in emotion than family law and, therefore, there may be no professional process more vulnerable to biases.

Unfortunately, the problem of unchecked bias is much larger than the well-being of the next child whose future will be determined by the court. It's bad enough when professional bias shortcuts an impartial evaluation, distorts a professional's interpretation of the data, or prompts a decision maker to lean one way and not the other. It's worse, still, when those biases gradually seep into the fabric of the institution through case law, agency regulations, procedural mandates, ethical codes, best practice standards, and legislation that affect the well-being of entire populations. This happens when one professional's unchecked bias in one case snowballs to become an essential epistemic inequity: an institutionalized bias that predisposes the system to designate one group as *friend* and another group as *foe*.[8] Epistemic inequities run rampant through our justice

8. *See* Justin D. Levinson & Danielle Young, *Different Shades of Bias: Skin Tone, Implicit Racial Bias, and Judgments of Ambiguous Evidence*, 112 Va. L. Rev. 307, 315 (2009) ("Several commentators have considered the way implicit biases are either facilitated by the law itself or how legal decision-makers may unintentionally propagate these biases."); Michele Benedetto Neitz, *Socioeconomic Bias in the Judiciary*, 61 Clev. St. L. Rev. 137, 165 (2013) ("Studies showing the pervasive nature of implicit bias highlight the need to devote more attention to identifying socioeconomic bias in its implicit form. Indeed, a review of Fourth Amendment and child custody cases reveals that this bias is indeed present in American courts."); Gregory S. Parks, *Judicial Recusal: Cognitive Biases and Racial Stereotyping*, 18 N.Y.U. J. Legis. & Pub. Pol'y 681, 696 (2015) ("Judges are human. They suffer from the same frailties, flaws, and foibles that the rest of us do. That includes being subject to a whole host of cognitive biases. Given the extent to which the valuation of whiteness and devaluation of blackness permeates American society, it is no surprise that all racial groups tend to automatically or subconsciously preference whiteness over blackness.").

See Andrea L. Miller et al., *Forging Diversity-Science-Informed Guidelines for Research on Race and Racism in Psychological Science*, 75 J. Soc. Issues 1240 (2019) (arguing that

system particularly in the form of self-perpetuating and polarizing feedback loops that favor the selective dissemination of information, power, and control to some groups more than others.[9]

Bias is a broad category that captures dozens of distinct perceptual, sensory, cognitive, and emotional shortcuts. Three among these are particularly relevant to family law and our discussion of family system dynamics. These are as follows:

1. **Confirmation bias** describes the human predisposition to perceive what one expects to perceive. Walking into a room, opening the refrigerator, or commencing a family systems evaluation with an a priori expectation can blind a person to contrary facts. This happens routinely when an evaluator approaches a family or a hearing officer approaches a case thinking top-down, taking a deductive approach, seeking to confirm or refute a preconceived hypothesis. Part of the solution to confirmation bias is bottom-up thinking, taking an inductive approach to the process.[10]

---

research on racism is strengthened when scholars (1) are mindful of historical patterns of oppression and inequality, (2) adopt a racially diverse team science approach, (3) utilize diverse samples, (4) consider the influence of multiple identity groups on human experience, and (5) promote the translation of knowledge from the laboratory to the field).

Medical science had been criticized for control group studies, which may ignore women or minorities or many other forms of diversity and oppression. *See* Vivek H. Murthy et al., *Participation in Cancer Clinical Trials: Race-, Sex-, and Age-Based Disparities*, 291 JAMA 2720, 2720 (2004) ("Applying trial results to patients who would not have been eligible to participate has been associated with harm. It has been promulgated that 'appropriate' representation of specific patient subpopulations is necessary to further understanding of race/ethnicity-based differences in presentation, prognosis, and response to therapy."); Antronette K. Yancey et al., *Effective Recruitment and Retention of Minority Research Participants*, 27 Ann. Rev. Pub. Health 1, 2 (2006) ("One must recognize that overarching contributors to health disparities are inherent in minority engagement challenges. There are relatively few investigators from underrepresented racial/ethnic minority groups in the academy, reflecting the skewed [socioeconomic status] SES distribution and sociopolitical marginalization of these populations compared with white European Americans. Increased involvement in scientific leadership of investigators from populations with substantive health disparities is critical.").

9. Dana E. Prescott, *Bending the Light of Social Science in Family Court: Epistemic Injustice and Epistemic Exceptionalism Matter*, 33 J. Am. Acad. Matrimonial Law. 99 (2020).

10. Benjamin D. Garber, *Sherlock Holmes and the Case of Resist/Refuse Dynamics: Confirmatory Bias and Abductive Inference in Child Custody Evaluations*, 58 Fam. Ct. Rev. 386 (2019).

As one author suggested more than 60 years ago, "it is difficult to avoid the subconscious tendency to reject for good reason data which weaken a hypothesis while uncritically accepting those data which strengthen it."[11]

Confirmation bias illustrates how easily objective reality can be distorted through the lens of expectation. One would think that two objective experts examining a single phenomenon should make identical observations. There is, after all, an objective truth. This should apply equally to experts asked to measure a physical distance or weight and to experts asked to assess a family. Nevertheless, judges commonly hear diametrically opposing views about a single event from eminently qualified forensic experts committed to objective measurement and sworn to tell the truth.

Of course, part of this is attributable to the complexity of the phenomenon being measured. We do not yet have the tools with which to assess the quality or impact of human interactions as precisely as we can measure the height of a wall or the distance to the moon. Those tools that we do have—psychometric assessment instruments—are vulnerable to problems associated with sampling and representativeness, cultural and demographic norms, confounding variables, generalizability, reliability, validity, administration, and unknown or unacceptable error rates. Indeed, if carpenters relied on measurements as flawed as those that we use in family law, none of our homes would still be standing.

2. **Allegiance bias** is one manifestation of confirmational bias often associated with lawyers' arguments and experts' opinions. Allegiance bias describes the human predisposition to take positions that win social acceptance, are congruent with one's affiliations, and suit the people who are paying you.[12] In the courtroom, scholars and practitioners have for generations recognized that the adversarial nature of legal proceedings creates "partisan bias in experts through unconscious affiliation with the side that hires them (i.e., adversarial allegiance) and by attorneys who

---

11. Seymour S. Kety, *Biochemical Theories of Schizophrenia (Part I)*, 129 Science 1528, 1529 (1959).

12. One might attribute the chameleon child's position, caught between warring parents, to allegiance bias. *See* Benjamin D. Garber, *The Chameleon Child: Children as Actors in the High Conflict Divorce Drama*, 11 J. Child Custody 1 (2014).

select and pressure experts to make extreme claims."[13] An ever-growing body of research from clinical and social psychology, and from behavioral economics suggests that experts are susceptible to a host of these implicit allegiance biases that may distort or influence complex scientific matters.[14]

3. **Selection bias** is a sort of allegiance bias for the masses. Selection bias occurs when researchers draw conclusions from partisan or nonrepresentative samples. For example, a pollster who surveys individuals attending the National Democratic Convention can only draw generalizations about the opinions of attendees at the convention. To use these data to try to predict the outcome of a national election is to be guilty of selection bias. The sample measured is by no means representative of the voting population.

Selection bias is unfortunately common and far too seldom recognized in some of the research concerned with alienation (Chapter 15). Studies that elicit participants by posting ads on websites and listservs catering to aggrieved parents who have lost custody are as likely to generate facts about family dynamics as Alaskans who look out their windows can predict the weather in Miami.

This simple reality seldom stops lawyers from selectively employing experts and evaluators and service providers with known track records,

---

13. John "Kai" Kellerman et al., Expert Opinion: Hot Tubbing as an Alternative to Adversarial Expert Testimony 1 (2018), http://ap-ls.wildapricot.org/resources/EmailTemplates/2018_04%20April%20AP-LS%20Newsletter/ExpertOpinionApril.pdf.

14. *See* Daniel C. Murrie & Marcus T. Boccaccini, *Adversarial Allegiance among Expert Witnesses*, 11 Ann. Rev. L. & Soc. Sci. 55, 58 (2015) ("Questions about adversarial allegiance are long-standing and widespread. Expert witnesses—particularly those from medicine and the behavioral sciences—have long been tolerated with skepticism and sometimes characterized as hired guns who can reach any conclusion to support the party that retained them."); Tess Neal & Thomas Grisso, *The Cognitive Underpinnings of Bias in Forensic Mental Health Evaluations*, 20 Psych. Pub. Pol'y & L. 200, 206 (2014) ("We think there are good reasons to be concerned. Scientific and clinical expertise in the courtroom is dependent on the expectancy that the expert seeks accuracy and avoids anything that may lead to bias in the collection or interpretation of data. Challenging that expectancy is a growing body of research suggesting that forensic examiners differ in the data they collect and the opinions they reach, depending on the social contexts in which they are involved in forensic cases.").

published works, and/or practice protocols that support the lawyer's case and thereby the litigant's wishes and then rely on those experts to opine about the case. The same self-affirming selective biases have been documented among forensic experts who are inclined to work with litigants and lawyers who share their preexisting beliefs.[15]

Confirmational, allegiance, selection, and similar biases work together to force that square peg into the round hole. They maintain and even exacerbate a black-and-white view of what we know to be a very gray experience. These individual and institutional biases act like a wedge driving conflicted parties further and further apart, exaggerating differences such that nuance and context and even the child's best interests are subjugated to the court's win/lose mentality.

Definitions, Prototypes, and Biases

Earlier we referred to shared cultural prototypes that prompt people with shared experiences to make shared judgments about what is in and what is outside of a category. Stop reading for a moment and close your eyes. Picture a chair and then read on.

Chances are that you pictured an upright, straight-backed wooden structure likely to be found at a kitchen or dining room table. Whether you imagined arms or padding or ornate woodwork doesn't matter. It's unlikely that you imagined a beanbag chair (except for those oppositional and defiant readers stuck on our earlier discussion) or a king's throne or a folding beach chair made of hollow aluminum rods. It's even less likely that you imagined a flat rock or a tree stump, both of which are good for sitting, but neither of which commonly approach the prototype of the category.

But what happens when a community does not share a prototype or a definition of a concept? What would occur, for example, if the word *chair* brought to mind flat rocks for some, thrones for others, and the person

15. *See* Daniel C. Murrie et al., *Are Forensic Experts Biased by the Side That Retained Them?*, 24 Psych. Sci. 1889 (2013); Tess M.S. Neal, *Are Forensic Experts Already Biased before Adversarial Legal Parties Hire Them?*, PLoS one, Apr. 28, 2016 (e0154434).

in charge of a meeting for still others? Although this kind of implicit jockeying about for cognitive primacy is common when new products and concepts arise, the lack of consensus inhibits further inquiry, generates ambiguous and misleading findings ("chairs are naturally occurring and enormously heavy"), and can do harm ("the committee member was fired when she attempted to sit on the chair"). In the absence of consensus, bias runs wild, ruling in and ruling out instances on the basis of idiosyncratic rules.

This has been true of systemic dynamics in family law at least since the BIC standard first required us to try to understand each child's unique needs. Concepts like enmeshment (Chapter 10), parentification (Chapter 12), and estrangement (Chapter 14) were little more than theoretical abstractions in the days of chattel when fathers owned their children like so many cows, or in the tender years era, when children were believed to need their mothers above all else.

In lieu of definitions and consensual prototypical ideas, family law practice has taken on the feel of America's Wild West. Today, rather than carrying a six-shooter and making one's own justice, family law professionals go about their business with their own idiosyncratic sense of what a family is and how it should function, the causes of family dysfunction, the place of individual psychopathology, and the remedies for those imagined causes. Confirmation biases in favor of these often many and varied, seldom empirically determined, and often conflicting concepts threaten to upset the justice system as a whole, undermining due process, and subjecting the BIC standard to each court's unique interpretation. Justice is not served when two courts hearing precisely the same case are likely to reach very different conclusions no matter whether they function on opposite sides of the country or on opposite sides of the street.

This then is the goal of this book: to begin to establish a common conceptual foundation that will facilitate communication and improve the reliability and validity of our evaluations, the courts' judgments, and the efficacy of the remedies thus ordered. In so doing, we hope to diminish bias in all of its forms and epistemic injustice throughout the judicial system, particularly as it trickles down to influence the family system and the best interests of each child.

Bias and Resist/Refuse Dynamics

The idiosyncratic state of family law is highlighted nowhere more starkly and its associated biases are nowhere more aggressive than when a family presents with resist/refuse dynamics (RRD) (Chapter 9).

RRD is the phrase used in the contemporary literature to describe those family systems in which a child has become strongly allied with Parent A and resists or refuses contact with Parent B. This child's black/white, either/or binary position within her conflicted family system precisely echoes the binary nature of her parents' conflict, the zealous advocates' polarized and antagonistic positions, and the court's win/lose institutionalized biases. Like the chicken and the egg and the rooster, it's a waste of time to argue which came first. All that we know is that the insidious interplay of biases within and between these nested systems is self-perpetuating even when the reality of the child's position is seldom black and white.

The practical pressures of the legal process and professional and institutionalized biases[16] together push many professionals and courts to attribute RRD to binary either/or causes. The logic typically holds that if the rejected parent is not abusive, then the aligned parent must be alienating.[17] This kind of forced-choice reasoning is appealing to the

---

16. The momentum of history contributes to epistemic injustice to the extent that the law's historical endorsement of either/or custody outcomes persists into the present. For example, survey data find "continued endorsement of gender differences despite the current gender-neutral best interests of the child standard." Julie E. Artis, *Judging the Best Interests of the Child: Judges' Accounts of the Tender Years Doctrine*, 38 Law & Soc'y Rev. 769, 797 (2004).

17. As an example of this type of absolutist language unrelated to the complexity of probability and statistics, in social science research, see "[I]n cases when abuse or neglect have not occurred, it is highly probable—to 99% clinical certainty—that alienation is the cause of the rejection." Linda J. Gottlieb, Reunification Therapy for Severe Parental Alienation or for an Unreasonably Disrupted Parent-Child Relationship (2019), http://endparentalalienation.weebly.com/uploads/3/1/0/9/31091731/12-22-2019_tpff_treatment_protocol_x_4_6_18_ent_protocol_for_severe_alieantion_rejection.pdf. For an analysis of the ethical and scientific challenges for courts from this kind of language, see Judith Cashmore & Patrick Parkinson, *The Use and Abuse of Social Science Research Evidence in Children's Cases*, 20 Psychol., Pub. Pol'y & L. 239, 243 (2014) ("Cherry picking involves the selective interpretation or application of research,

extent that it fits precisely into the court's guilt-versus-innocence, blame-attributing process. It serves the parents' needs to feel vindicated in the eyes of the court and the zealous advocate's need to win the motion or the trial or the greater part of the child's care. It reduces the brain-splitting complexity of many chaotic relationships into all-or-nothing simplicity. But for all of its attractiveness, such binary explanations breed bias and antagonism and do harm.

The alternative is far less attractive because it is far less well fitted to the binary structure of the legal system, even if it more closely reflects reality. This means understanding that RRD is invariably the result of multiple, interwoven practical exigencies and systemic dynamics. Like so much else about human relationships, the subject is complex and chaotic and in constant motion. Some of the possible contributing forces are benign (e.g., not wanting to miss a desirable event in one home) while others are quite malignant (e.g., explicitly being told that separation is a betrayal). Establishing consensual prototypes and definitions of each of these various factors and then carefully weighing out how each contributes to a particular system's dynamics is messy and time-consuming and less likely to crown one parent the good guy and damn the other as bad, but this is the reality that we live in. In so doing, we work to minimize bias, accepting each square peg for all of its edges and angles, unbiased by round holes.

Parents Have Biases, Too

We close this chapter by bringing our consideration of bias out of the stuffy halls of justice and into the stained and worn kitchens and TV rooms of the families whom we serve. Bias is a human tendency, not a predilection unique to professionals. Thus, armed with an understanding of bias in several of its forms we are left to consider bias in the conflicted family system.

No animal is more stressed than a parent protecting its young.

---

with research favoring a particular position being cited, but without reference to studies that do not support that position.").

The parents who enter our offices and courtrooms are functioning under extreme stress, no matter how politely or aggressively or tearfully they present to you. As emotion increases, the room left in their coffee cup brains decreases, limiting their ability to think clearly and fueling their most primitive biases.

Parents litigating custody carry with them the stresses of exposure and humiliation, the fears of loss and separation, the insult of abandonment and rejection, and the reality of a bottomless pit of debt. Like the lost souls described in Plato's Allegory of the Cave, adults who were once partners quickly take on diametrically opposed positions, inducing antagonism based in part on rigid and biased perspectives.

In this fertile ground, bias sprouts full grown overnight. The need to protect a child and to validate one's position in a life-altering and very public drama quickly distorts thinking and polarizes perceptions. Bias prompts parents to attorney-shop, trying on and switching off professionals like so many pairs of shoes in search of the one that most closely fits one's point of view. This is selection bias at its best.

Driven by confirmation bias and their attorneys' requests, these parents cherry-pick photos and text messages and anecdotes that support their case and are blind to or simply ignore others that might temper or refute it. They endorse narratives that are congruent with their wishes and overlook the bits that don't. "The nature of the adversarial process encourages hostile, polarized, black-and-white thinking with little challenge, presents perceived truths as facts and fuels and channels rage in a scripted manner."[18] This creates a self-affirming spiral wherein each confirmatory bit is reason to endorse more confirmatory bits and ignore everything else. In this way, bias becomes the wedge that drives opposing parties further and further apart. "The torn loyalties, grief, rage, humiliation, and anxiety commonly generated by these matters, compounded by zealous advocates and exacerbated by the adversarial court system can compromise rational thinking for all involved. The response is often a regression to more primitive, emotion-driven, and biased positions."[19]

---

18. Joan B. Kelly & Janet R. Johnston, *The Alienated Child: A Reformulation of Parental Alienation Syndrome*, 39 Fam. Ct. Rev. 249, 258 (2001).

19. Garber, *supra* note 10, at 389.

But leave the professionals out for a moment. Listen to how the biases inherent in family conflict corrupt roles and distort the dynamics. In one very real example, Mom heard her five-year-old report gleefully that "Daddy taught me about sex." Blinded by the anger and shame and grief of divorce and a looming custody battle, this mother panicked. She called the police and her lawyer, obtained a protective order, and alleged abuse. Many hours, three hearings, a child protective interview, and thousands of dollars later, the child told her therapist about how Daddy "taught me about 'sects: bugs and beatles and buterflies and things."

Or listen to how bias born of emotion affected the mother who heard her daughter say, "Daddy put his pee-pee in my pee-pee." Clear thinking was overcome by emotion. Confirmation bias took over. She called the police and child protective services. Weeks later a forensic evaluator asked the child to explain. Giggling, she was glad to: "I went pee-pee in the potty and forgot to flush. Then daddy went pee-pee in the potty, too!"[20]

20. David A. Martindale, Allegations of Alienation or Child Sexual Abuse in Custody Evaluations, Presentation at Palo Alto University, Co-Sponsored by CONCEPT Professional Training and Palo Alto University (June 17, 2019). Dr. Martindale credited Steven Ceci.

Chapter 5

The Motives That Yield Destructive Family Dynamics

"Human needs arrange themselves in hierarchies of prepotency. That is, the appearance of one need usually rests on the prior satisfaction of another, more prepotent need. Thus man is a perpetually wanting animal."[1]

"All happy families resemble one another, but each unhappy family is unhappy in its own way."[2]

Looking under the Hood

This book, like Audubon's field guide, emphasizes the recognition and differentiation of types, taxonomies, and classifications. Audubon relied on stunning color images to identify distinct species of birds. We rely, instead, on behavioral descriptions to identify the dynamics of the conflicted family system with sincere apologies for the absence of artwork.

The history of psychology is deeply divided over whether behavioral description is a necessary or sufficient means of distinguishing social and emotional phenomena. Think of this as the division between Freudian psychoanalysis with its emphasis on deep-seated, unconscious, and

1. Abraham H. Maslow, *A Dynamic Theory of Human Motivation*, *in* UNDERSTANDING HUMAN MOTIVATION 26 (Chalmers L. Stacey et al. eds., 1958), https://doi.org/10.1037/11305-004.

2. Leo Tolstoy, from the opening of *Anna Karenina*. LEO TOLSTOY, ANNA KARENINA (David Magarshack trans., Signet Classics/New American Library 1961) (1877).

often infantile needs,[3] and Skinner's behavioral therapy with its emphasis exclusively on observable and measurable causes and effects.[4]

Even more simply, think of this as the distinction between genotype and phenotype.

Family law professionals' early attempts at description (and even diagnosis) by presumed or inferred genotype failed miserably with negative consequences that linger to this day. This is flagrantly obvious in Gardner's now-debunked "parental alienation syndrome" with its implications about "malicious mothers"[5] and a blind eye to actual child abuse (Chapter 15).[6]

The field has tried to heal the schism created by Gardner's self-published theories by gradually shifting its focus from inferences to observations—that is, from genotype to phenotype. The result is now a near-exclusive emphasis on visible, measurable acts. This is most clearly evident in our contemporary reference to resist/refuse dynamics (Chapter 9). Of course, pendulum swings of this sort fill history in every field of endeavor. In the best of worlds, this shifting between extremes presages the gradual establishment of a more moderate, stable, and well-informed consensus position.

Writing this book while we wait more-or-less patiently for the emergence of such a consensus in family law, we are left to reach our own informed balance between genotype and phenotype. This chapter speaks to the former. We presume here to suggest some of the interior needs and motives—the genotypes—that can create, sustain, and amplify the conflicted family system dynamics discussed throughout Section II of this book. In so doing, we are figuratively taking a look under the hood. We

---

3. *E.g.*, Sigmund Freud, *Instincts and Their Vicissitudes*, *in* Foundations of Psychological Thought: A History of Psychology 353 (Barbara F. Gentile & Benjamin O. Miller eds., 2008) (1915).

4. *E.g.*, B.F. Skinner, *About Behaviorism*, *in* Foundations of Psychological Thought, *supra* note 3, at 261.

5. Ira Daniel Turkat, *Divorce Related Malicious Mother Syndrome*, 10 J. Fam. Violence 253 (1995), https://doi.org/10.1007/BF02110992.

6. Ruth A. Blizard & Morgan Shaw, *Lost-in-the-Mall: False Memory or False Defense?*, 16 J. Child Custody 20 (2019), https://doi.org/10.1080/15379418.2019.1590285.

are presuming and inferring individual thoughts and feelings and needs that are seldom measurable, seldom diagnosable, and certainly don't meet *Daubert* and comparable evidentiary standards. We do this in the strong belief that these observations are generative—that is, that understanding motivation can help to create hypotheses that might then be tested, guide evaluation, inform decision making, and become the foundation of new and better remedies.

Need fulfillment is the goal. Psychology's understanding of the motives that drive complex human behavior remains rather primitive and simplistic. Our beliefs can be summarized in four bullet points as follows:

- Across the entire span of individual development, history, and culture, human behavior is goal directed. That is, our actions are seldom random. We do what we do in order to try to achieve specific outcomes.
- Behaviors that fail to achieve goals extinguish; that is, if it doesn't work, we stop doing it.
- Behaviors that succeed in obtaining goals are reinforced; that is, if it works, we do it more often and with greater effort.
- The reinforcements that motivate us can be prioritized. Maslow presented these in the form of a hierarchy of needs, acknowledging that the freedom to pursue a higher-order goal requires first that all lower-order goals are adequately fulfilled. From most imperative to least, our needs are prioritized as follows:[7]
    (a) Survival needs (food, water, shelter, rest)
    (b) Safety needs (felt-security, safety)
    (c) Affiliation (belongingness, love, social acceptance)
    (d) Self-esteem (feelings of pride, accomplishment, recognition)
    (e) Self-actualization (self-satisfaction, self-fulfillment)

Child protective services (CPS), first responders, and the criminal and dependency courts exist to respond when a child's survival and safety needs are compromised (items a and b on Maslow's list). Psychotherapy

7. Maslow, *supra* note 1.

in all of its many forms exists to respond when a child's self-esteem is compromised (item d). Problems with self-actualization (item e) must, by definition, be managed within the self.

The family courts exist to respond when a child's affiliation needs (item c) are compromised.

Affiliation means both the subjective felt-experience of belonging and the objective, codified (e.g., in the form of a birth certificate, adoption papers, or parenting plan), and often visible evidence of belonging. Unfortunately, the subjective and the objective are often confused as when parents or the courts contaminate a child's sense of belonging with legal distinctions about the child's parents' decision-making authority and residential responsibility in a court order or parenting plan.

This conflict between the child's feelings and the structures imposed by superordinate systems frequently erupts in family law. It is once again evidence of why relationship conflicts don't belong in the conventional win-lose court system, and it is entrée into understanding the motivations that drive the dynamics of the conflicted family system.

Relationships Happen at the Nexus of Needs

As with all things nonlinear, discussing the motivations behind conflicted family dynamics is bound to be confusing. Describing child development is simple by contrast. One stage yields to another over time as a joint function of nature and nurture. One domino leads to the next in a predictable, linear succession.

Relationships are chaotic events that occur when two or more systems intersect as each moves through space and time influenced by and responsive to an unknown number of coincidental and colliding social and emotional experiences. Think about literature's prototypically star-crossed lovers, Romeo and Juliet. The youths' lives intersect in Shakespeare's play as each lives and grows toward his or her respective family's opposing purposes, their relationship relentlessly torn and (spoiler alert!) then finally destroyed by the pressured conflict between the Capulets and the Montagues.

In a similar (if somewhat less dramatic and more optimistic) manner, a child responds to her experience of Mother (an intersection described by attachment theory) who simultaneously responds to her experience of her child even while Father is responding to his experience of his child *and* to his experience of Mother/wife (an intersection we refer to as the co-parenting dyad) who is also responding to her experience of Father/husband (co-parenting), even while each family member is developing across time and the whole system is managing its relationship with allied systems (e.g., neighbors, extended family, community), subordinate systems (e.g., each parent-child dyad, the co-parenting dyad, the sibling subgroup), and superordinate systems (e.g., schools, first-responders, employers, community agencies, courts). None of these relationships ever exist in a vacuum. Each is constantly subject to multiple simultaneous social and emotional pressures within and between systems. With this in mind, our argument against diagnoses in favor of dynamics may begin to make more sense.

To evaluate each individual member of a conflicted family system and then make recommendations about custody is like studying each of the 22 balls on the snooker table individually in order to predict which of two players will win. It's the interaction that matters, how each component part affects and is affected by the others. There is a synergy to systems—that emergent, nonlinear, self-organizing, whole-greater-than-the-sum quality that allowed amino acids to first produce life—that is neglected by a focus on one ball at a time.

A child custody evaluator takes on the seemingly impossible job of capturing a snapshot of how each member of the system affects and is affected by all of the others across space and development, subject to the simultaneous pressures of the other members of the system as well as the pressures exerted and absorbed by the systems that surround and contain it. If this description isn't daunting enough, the task is further complicated by the fact that the family system being evaluated is simultaneously aware of and responsive to the (legal, judicial, child protection, psychological, accounting, and so on) systems that are evaluating it. Although the custody evaluator's ethics, guidelines, and standards call for an emphasis on relationship *fit* (e.g., the quality of the fit between parent and child),[8] even this relationship-oriented concept falls flat when one really considers the complexity of the matter.

The Child's Need for Affiliation

We speak of the child's need for affiliation in terms of her drive to win acceptance, affection, and attention from others. These are the behavioral indices of belonging. We presume *a la* Maslow and consistent with attachment theory that the need for affiliation drives much of children's behavior. This is most readily apparent in how children use their parents and family as a secure base or emotional anchor or safety net that instills the confidence necessary to grow toward autonomy.

> Harlow's experiments with rhesus monkeys illustrate this hierarchy of needs graphically: Infant monkeys separated from their mothers were given simultaneous access to two surrogates. One was a mother-shaped wire surrogate that provided milk from a bottle. The other was a mother-shaped cloth surrogate that provided tactile comfort. Given the freedom to choose, the babies spent the vast majority of their time clinging to the latter, apparently reassured by the tactile contact, retreating to the former only long enough to feed when necessary.[9]

8. "The evaluation focuses upon parenting attributes, the child's psychological needs, and the resulting fit." American Psychological Association, *Guidelines for Child Custody Evaluations in Family Law Proceedings*, 65 Am. Psych. 863, 864 (2010), https://www.apa.org/pubs/journals/features/child-custody.pdf.

9. Harry F. Harlow, *The Nature of Love*, *in* The Evolution of Psychology: Fifty Years of the American Psychologist 41 (Joseph M. Notterman ed., 1997) (1958).

Refueling

As a practical matter, particularly in discussion with parents about their children's needs, we talk about the human need for emotional nurturance and affiliation in terms of vehicles and refueling. If emotional nurturance (affiliation, affection, praise, security) is gas, then emotional maturity means increasing fuel efficiency across development—that is, becoming better able to go further on a single fill-up.

Younger, less emotionally mature, and more stressed children get extremely limited miles-per-gallon. They need to be refueled more often. Emotional security grows when the child learns that the next gas station is never far away. Fall down and skin your knee? Mom is there to pick you up, dust you off, and send you on your way.

The good news is that we humans are terrifically adaptable. We work hard to discover what works and then we stick with it. Many children's emotional and behavioral problems begin *not* as a function of genetic predisposition or diagnosable psychopathology, but because they are implicitly reinforced by the system meant to contain them. Thus, the child who discovers that Dad is too busy or depressed or addicted to pay attention until he gets in trouble, is implicitly rewarded by Dad's attention for getting in trouble. It hardly matters that the resulting attention is harsh and even hurtful. Affiliation is affiliation. The ounce or two of that precious fuel drives the behavior and shapes the system.

This is one of the traps of the medical model as applied to family systems: viewing an individual's thinking, feeling, and behavior in a vacuum presupposes the presence of pathology within that individual. Consider the case of Dustin, the disruptive sixth grader. Dustin refused to do his homework and was disrespectful in class. In response, the teacher sent Dustin to the vice principal's office. The vice principal called an emergency meeting to include Dustin, his teacher, and his divorced parents. The adults spent 20 minutes scolding the child while all that Dustin could think was how cool it was that Mom and Dad were back together and finally agreed about something. What happened the next day? The child was even more disruptive. Why? Because behavior that is individually maladaptive (Dustin was punished) proved to be systemically highly adaptive (Dustin's parents came together).

Understanding the importance of emotional fuel and the drive for affiliation helps us to understand a closely related, larger point: neglect is far more damaging even than abuse. The abused child at least is recognized. The neglected child has failed entirely to get refueled. He is forgotten and invisible.[10] Neglect leaves the child's emotional gas tank empty. Children who grow up with neglect often feel invisible and unlovable, and undeserving of or incapable of love and belonging.

This lesson gives us insight, as well, into the many dynamics of the conflicted family system. The chameleon child, for example, has learned to win affiliation in each of two disparate emotional environments by adjusting her identity to fit in to each (Chapter 8). Triangulated into her parents' war, caught up in a loyalty bind that says loving one parent means the loss of the other, she compromises self (self-esteem is a luxury on Maslow's hierarchy while affiliation is still unfulfilled) and truth (about as important as Wi-Fi to a starving man) in order to win acceptance, attention, and affection from both.

The polarized child resolves the same dilemma quite differently, relying entirely on one source of emotional fuel and rejecting the other (Chapter 9). This relieves the child's constant pressure to adapt to the proximal emotional environment at least in the short run. The logic of this outcome is as old as the aphorism that "a bird in the hand is better than two in the bush." It is as ironic as it is tragic that the polarized child often seems to align with the parent whose affection, attention, and acceptance are the weakest, most tentative, or most contingent, perhaps in the belief that the other parent's love will withstand the rejection.

10. Lane Strathearn et al., *Long-Term Cognitive, Psychological, and Health Outcomes Associated with Child Abuse and Neglect*, 146(4) Pediatrics e20200438 (2020), https://doi.org/10.1542/peds.2020-0438; *see also* Joseph R. Cohen & Hena Thakur, *Developmental Consequences of Emotional Abuse and Neglect in Vulnerable Adolescents: A Multi-Informant, Multi-Wave Study*, 111 Child Abuse & Neglect 104811 (2021).

"Trauma Bonding" and "Stockholm Syndrome"

The human capacity to rationalize is impressive. When reason and science fail, some would have us endorse black-box "counter-intuitive" concepts like so much phrenology or alchemy mysteriously managed by self-acclaimed priests.[11] This isn't science, no matter how impressive the words and the experts who speak them. Science doesn't require possession of a decoder ring, knowledge of a secret handshake, or the practice of magical incantations. Science requires transparency, reproduceable results, established error rates, and the use of reliable and valid measures.

Here's how it works: Parent A is convinced that Parent B is abusive of their children. If the child resists contact with Parent B, then Parent A takes this as certain evidence that she was correct. However, if the opposite is true—if the child doesn't resist contact with Parent B—then the same conclusion applies. The child's relationship with Parent B must be subject to *trauma bonding*.[12] In either case, Parent A's confirmation bias is confirmed, never mind that there are many and varied reasons why children resist and refuse contact with a parent, most of which have nothing to do with abuse and never mind that *trauma bonding*—like its equally ignoble first cousin *Stockholm syndrome*[13]—is not a valid scientific concept.

(continued on next page)

11. "This court finds this expert's failure to give straightforward answers to the attorney for the children's questions renders her testimony incredible and—and counterintuitive or not—inconsistent with any rational view of the family circumstances in this case." J.F. v. D.F., 61 Misc. 3d 1226(A) n.55, 112 N.Y.S.3d 438 (table) (N.Y. Sup. Ct. 2018). The court added, "Excessive litigation based on a flimsy theory can be as alienating as any other strategy. The presence of the same three experts here—at a substantial cost by the father—suggests to the court that the parental alienation theory is a new tool in the 'para-psychology-in-the-courtroom complex,' as part of a strategy to upend negotiated parenting agreements by the more aggressive and more moneyed spouse." *Id.* at 11.

12. Donald G. Dutton & Susan Lee Painter, *Emotional Attachments in Abusive Relationships: A Test of Traumatic Bonding Theory*, 8 Violence & Victims 105 (1993); *see also* Matthew H. Logan, *Stockholm Syndrome: Held Hostage by the One You Love*, 5 Violence & Gender 67 (2018).

13. Like "trauma bonding," the Stockholm syndrome has little empirical basis in the literature. *See* Michael Adorjan et al., *Stockholm Syndrome as Vernacular Resource*, 53 Socio. Q. 454 (2012); Celia Jameson, *The "Short Step" from Love to Hypnosis: A Reconsideration of*

Like the person who denies that he is in denial and thereby cannot escape the accusation, there is no way out of this sophistry because it's not science. It is not refutable, measurable, transparent, reliable, and validated. It is no more than confirmation bias dressed up in thousand-dollar-per-hour magical thinking.

Adults Need to Be Refueled, Too

The drive for affiliation and the metaphor of refueling are relevant to understanding parents' motives, as well.

When conflict erupts in an intimate adult relationship (regardless of the gender, generation, and legal status of the relationship and regardless of whether the couple cohabitates), each partner loses his or her primary source of belonging and emotional fuel. We believe (although the subject has received scant empirical study) that how the adults cope with this loss and its idiosyncratic subjective meaning is predictive of how the separation will unfold and how the family's dynamics will evolve. In particular, this bears on whether and how their children will be triangulated into the process.

When Parent B is Parent A's exclusive source of emotional fuel, the end of the adult relationship leaves Parent A alone and adrift. As Maslow would predict, self-esteem (never mind self-actualization) is undermined as the need for affiliation supersedes all but safety and survival. This parent faces the (often unrecognized) choice either to withdraw into anger and depression or to reach out to others for emotional fuel.

A healthy, resilient, and emotionally mature adult turns to other adults for support: colleagues or neighbors or extended family. He joins clubs or support groups or enrolls in therapy. He finds new ways to belong and affiliate and win others' acceptance, attention, and affection so as to keep his emotional gas tank full and thereby remain able to fuel his children.

---

the Stockholm Syndrome, 14 J. for Cultural Rsch. 337 (2010); Minu S. Nair, *Stockholm Syndrome—A Self-Delusive Survival Strategy*, 3 Int'l J. Advanced Rsch. 385 (2015).

Tragically, some adults in this situation turn to their children for affiliation and validation. This is the stage upon which enmeshment is born (Chapter 10). Some adults desperate for affection, acceptance, and attention turn inappropriately to a son or daughter for need fulfillment. Of course, the misplaced need is reciprocated because, by definition, children crave their parent's emotional fuel. If becoming Mommy's best friend (adultification; Chapter 11) or taking care of Daddy (parentification; Chapter 12) or remaining needy even while peers become more independent (infantilization; Chapter 13) wins that precious ounce of nurturance, then the behavior is reinforced. The roles are redefined. The dynamic emerges.

Keeping in mind that these dynamics are not mutually exclusive, this is also the stage upon which alienation thrives. Caught up in an unhealthy but rewarding cross-generational alliance, parent and child bond together by damning the absent parent. Sometimes this is overt and explicit, serving the aligned parent's need for validation. Other times it is born of a subtle form of bootstrapping: Dad's confirmation bias prompts him to interpret something innocuous and benign as evidence that his son also sees Mom's failings, so he agrees, "yeah, she can be nasty." He rationalizes saying this because his son "is old enough to know the truth" or "you wouldn't want me to lie to him" or something similarly self-serving and blind to the child's needs. Of course, the child responds in kind, escalating a downward spiral built around each participant's need for affiliation and the ancient idea that the enemy of my friend is my enemy. For example:

> [A] child may say something fairly neutral, but the parent will twist it into a concern about the child. To the child, it is perceived as though the aligned parent is being supportive. As soon as a child begins to define himself as a victim, the other parent begins to be defined as abusive. Once that occurs, the child has been moved into the middle of the conflict taking the lead role in rejecting the other parent, with the aligned parent taking what appears to be a passive, and supporting role.[14]

14. M.L.S. v. N.E.D., [2017], 2017 S.K.Q.B. 183 para. 179, http://canlii.ca/t/h4pqj.

Of course, there's a third option available to the adult cast adrift by the breakdown of an intimate relationship. The first is affiliation with other healthy adults. The second is an unhealthy affiliation with the child to the detriment of all. The third is affiliation with no one, leaving the gaping wound open, staunching the pain momentarily with addiction, avoidance, and denial; drugs or alcohol; exercise or dieting or work or video games or shopping or sex.[15] The addiction doesn't matter for the purpose of this discussion, even though it will matter greatly if and when remedies and recovery are considered. What matters here is the child's experience of family conflict leading to triangulation and emotional neglect.

The Parent's Need to Win

The loss of an intimate relationship can spark embarrassment and shame for the adults involved. Separation and divorce can feel to some like a public admission of failure and a disclosure of weakness. This experience is amplified because marriage is a very public proclamation by the couple to love, honor, and cherish until death do they part. The more that the relationship is invested in allied systems—neighbors, church, extended family, community—the greater shame may be associated with its ending *and* the greater social supports may be available to the process.

Shame often carries with it an intense need for vindication.

Vindication means publicly winning, which means, in turn, getting the house, getting the furniture, getting child support, getting the retirement account, and getting the kid. Any of these can be important and worth fighting over, but when the adult's need to "win" eclipses the child's needs, destructive dynamics ensue.

A parent whose drive is to win is unlikely to have any perspective on why or how enlisting a child as a co-conspirator works against the child's needs. Why not enlist the child to spy on Mom? Why not enroll the child to serve as a courier, carrying messages back and forth between homes?

---

15. "Substance-abusing parents constitute a unique high-risk group among parents whose parental rights were terminated." Vered Ben-David, *Substance-Abusing Parents and Their Children in Termination of Parental Rights Cases in Israel*, 66 Child. & Youth Services Rev. 94 (2016).

Why not ask leading questions or selectively videotape the child's rants or script and coach and bribe and threaten the child or call CPS about every new scrape, cut, and bruise?

Why not expose the child to exaggerations and lies about the other parent that more or less subtly undermine the child's relationship with that parent (alienation; Chapter 15). After all, isn't watching the child reject the other parent the ultimate validation and vindication?

Some adults never had the emotional maturity to put their children's needs first. Others regressed in the face of separation and divorce stress, losing that most mature skill as they back down the staircase of development. In either case, when adults allow their needs to supersede those of their children, children get hurt. They become triangulated like the rope in the adult tug-of-war. They suffer from anxiety and are forced to discover their own means of managing these stresses.

The Grieving Parent

Like the parent who needs to win, the grieving parent is struggling to cope with the enormous stresses of systemic change. But where one feels embarrassed and wishes to save face, the other feels destitute and empty over the loss of what may have been the safest—if not the only—emotionally refueling relationship in his life. Grief is a natural and expectable response to loss, but the associated experiences of diminished energy, loss of pleasure in usual things (anhedonia), disrupted sleep and appetite, irritability, withdrawal, and avoidance—not to mention suicidal ideation, plans, and acts—can cripple that parent's ability to fully engage in the divorce process, setting the stage for parentification of a child (Chapter 12) and/or estrangement (Chapter 14).

This may be another case of the isolated parent who turns to his child for support, or a parent whose intrinsic resilience and existing social supports fall short of his need. In either case, the child's direct and/or vicarious experiences of that parent's grief and sadness is likely to spawn anxiety, fear, and avoidance that trigger approach or avoidance. Approach means being pulled into the grieving parent's needs, becoming aligned if not enmeshed and even parentified. Avoidance means rejection. Pushing away from the grieving parent for objective reasons. He's emotionally absent. He's always crying. He's grumpy. He's no fun. This is estrangement and one of many elements that can result in resist/refuse dynamics.

But watch how these things can spiral out of control: Blind to how his grief is obvious and anxiety-inducing to his child, Dad becomes more lonely and depressed because his son refuses to spend weekends in his care. Mom takes her son's refusal as evidence of abuse (that's her confirmation bias flaring up) and more-or-less subtly reinforces the child's position. Dad believes that the child's resistance is Mom's doing (his confirmation bias) and hires a lawyer to allege alienation. CPS become involved. Father and son grow apart even as Mother and son grow closer together. By the time a custody evaluator enters the fray, the dynamics at play are entirely convoluted, complex, chaotic, and self-perpetuating.

Evolution and Self-Blame

Objectivity—the ability to understand facts without bias or emotion—is an abstract luxury that accompanies the similarly abstract and unattainable state that Maslow identified as self-actualization. Backing down his hierarchy, objectivity diminishes as more primitive needs flourish. Thus, there is nothing objective when survival is at stake other than survival itself.

Emotion Compromises Reason

It is not only objectivity that is lost in the shadow of stress. All of our cognitive and sensory capacities are compromised by emotion. Working with parents directly, we illustrate this with a coffee mug. Thinking and feeling mix like oil and water. The more feelings fill the mug, the less room there is for thinking. We discussed this idea previously in Chapter 4.

This basic lesson serves many purposes. In this context, it helps to understand the motives and mistakes of the parent intent on winning, the grieving parent, and others whose better judgment and mature functioning are compromised by the loss of an intimate relationship. Much as this explanation can help us to understand the

(continued on next page)

many dynamics characteristic of the conflicted family system, it also offers us a clue to how these dynamics can be avoided or minimized.

Beginning with the coffee mug explanation, we must help parents to understand how emotion compromises reason to the detriment of their children. This means establishing healthy adult supports early on that function as refueling stations for needy adults. Therapists and group affiliations and coaches and hobbies and sports and teams and clubs that help to keep adult gas tanks full and thereby maximize the possibility of clear thinking and child-centered decisions.

The child triangulated amidst her parents' conflict and struggling day-to-day for acceptance, attention, and affection, has a very limited capacity for objective perceptions. Emotion and primitive needs color her experience and distort her thinking. This may be most obvious in children's near-universal tendency to blame themselves for their parents' faults and flaws.

We presume that evolution has selected for this trait. The logic goes like this: a child who objectively perceives his parent's misdeeds will reject that parent in anger and resentment and fear, and thus becomes vulnerable to predation and thereby less likely to pass down those well-reasoned genes to his children. By contrast, a child who is inclined to blame himself for his parents' misdeeds carries around his guilt and self-blame but remains close to Mom or Dad, safe from predators, and grows up to pass on self-blame to his children. In this way, parent-blaming children go extinct and self-blaming children flourish.

Although science hasn't (yet) identified the genes for the attribution of blame, the clinical evidence is more than compelling. Children's need to preserve the idea that their parents are good and safe even at the cost of self-loathing is tragically obvious in the five-year-old who believes that it's her fault that Mom and Dad broke up, in the teenager whose façade of bravado crumbles in tears of guilt because Mom wouldn't have left if he hadn't gotten in trouble, and even in the adult who has lived her life carrying around the certainty that her childhood abuse was the result of choices that she made at age six.

The child's predisposition toward self-blame has at least two corollaries. Guilt can motivate well-intended but inappropriate and often inflammatory efforts at repair, illustrated, for example, in Disney's "The Parent Trap" (1961). Even more powerfully, the child's guilt can enable a parent's selfish efforts to avoid introspection and sidestep responsibility for the family change. It suits both the selfish parent and the self-blaming child to allow the child to become the scapegoat.

Structure Minimizes Anxiety

The dissolution of an intimate adult relationship usually means the breakdown of the roles and rules within the family system, at least briefly. When structures of this sort fail, people become anxious.

As anxiety fills the coffee mug, the space available for clear thinking diminishes. Bias and emotion color perceptions more and more. Conflicts are more likely, more lengthy, and more destructive. In the absence of clear structure, both children and adults misbehave. Boundaries are crossed, and unhealthy alliances are built. This is fertile ground for enmeshment in its various forms, for alienation, for stress-induced acts of violence, and their sequelae, including property damage, injury, criminal involvement, and estrangement.

Structure comes in four distinct forms:

1. Limits on behavior and associated consequences
2. Roles that define relationships
3. Boundaries that define space
4. Routines and rituals that define time

When these structures are firmly established, predictable, and consistent, anxiety diminishes. Mature thinking improves. Conflict becomes less likely, less intransigent, and less destructive. Creating and maintaining these structures within the family is the responsibility of the co-parents who rely, in turn, on allied systems (e.g., faith organizations, extended family, therapists) to establish and maintain them. When this process fails, superordinate systems often step in, resulting, in one instance, in the court generating a parenting plan.

Chapter 6

The Professional's Humility, Limitations, and Role within the System

"One of the painful things about our time is that those who feel certainty are stupid, and those with any imagination and understanding are filled with doubt and indecision."[1]

"How people react to holding power is not just a function of some abstract relation of dominance, but of the identity, beliefs, values and theories of the people involved and the political and social content of their relationship."[2]

The last step necessary to set this stage is a call to humbition.

As professionals dedicated to serving the needs of children and as individuals with the hubris to assert opinions, recommendations, and decisions that may forevermore shape the lives of others, we take on a moral responsibility that far outstrips our various ethical codes and legal mandates.

---

1. Attributed to Bertrand Russell. *See also* Nejc Plohl & Bojan Musil, *Do I Know as Much as I Think I Do? The Dunning-Kruger Effect, Overclaiming, and the Illusion of Knowledge*, Psihološka Obzorja/Horizons of Psych., Apr. 23, 2018, at 20.

2. John C. Turner, *Explaining the Nature of Power: A Three-Process Theory*, 35 Eur. J. Soc. Psych. 1, 18 (2005). For another point of view related to specialized courts, see Anthony C. Thompson, *Courting Disorder: Some Thoughts on Community Courts*, 10 Wash. U. J.L. & Pol'y 63, 63 (2002) ("In the process, community courts have begun to utilize the coercive power of the judiciary in ways that raise questions about their propriety and necessity. Interestingly, these concerns have not surfaced in the literature examining community courts.").

We write here in cold and abstract terms about Parent A and Parent B and their anonymous children. We presume to classify and hope to clarify the choreographies of their relationships. We do these things despite the fact that we are ourselves flawed and failing and biased human beings, little different from those whom we judge, separated from their plight only by the thin veil of role assignment and job title, ever mindful of the frank reality captured so well in the ancient aphorism: There but for the grace of God go I.

Humbition is a neologism in need of Webster's endorsement, the Oxford English Dictionary's reification, and an engraved plaque set at eye level in every evaluator's office, mediator's conference room, and judge's chamber. To wit:

> Working in an emerging area of practice requires a delicate balance of courage and caution—courage to pursue new paths, caution to ensure the well-being of those we serve. This balance is expressed through the virtue of "humbition:" a fusion of humility and ambition. Applied to the field of healing disrupted parent-child relationships, humbition allows social scientists and practitioners to balance an ambitious application, extrapolation, and expansion of available knowledge, experience, materials, and procedures with an acceptance of realistic limits to our ability to help parents and children . . . .[3]

We have modeled this book on the work of Audubon, a brilliant naturalist, artist, and teacher. But where Audubon was insulated from the subject of his studies by the certainty that man and bird are distinct species, that he would never himself be faced with the challenges of migration or plumage or predatory raptors in any but the most metaphoric sense, we have no such security. Indeed, experience suggests that a large number of family law professionals have themselves been subjected to the vicissitudes of the family law process, an unexplored reality that certainly

3. Richard A. Warshak & Mark R. Otis, *Helping Alienated Children with Family Bridges: Practice, Research, and the Pursuit of "Humbition,"* 48 Fam. Ct. Rev. 91, 91 (2010) (citation omitted).

compounds the already weighty burden of bias (Chapter 4). We explore some of the ramifications of this reality in Chapter 18.

Roles within Adversarial Systems

The fractal nature of nested systems suggests that the same corrupted roles, misplaced alliances, and polarizing forces that we attribute to the conflicted family can exist at every other level of inquiry, including among family law professionals. Blind to these dynamics, we risk adding layers of expensive acrimony to the family's essential conflict and thereby failing our most critical obligation—that is, to do no harm.

Our roles as evaluator, lawyer, mediator, guardian ad litem, expert, and judge (to name just a few) are earned in classrooms, codified by institutions, documented on sheepskin, telegraphed by an alphabet soup of post-nominal appendages, and conveyed upon us by legislative bodies, administrative agencies, professional organizations, and sometimes even by popular vote. Any attendant authority is earned or granted and sometimes audaciously presumed.[4] No matter our respective pedigrees, when we work within the judicial system, the judge is the parent, and we are the children subject to her exercise of power and control. The family court (itself subject to the dictates of its superordinate parents, the appellate courts on one side and the legislature on the other) ultimately dictates the rules and roles of the system, effectively superimposing a structure on the family courts in much the same way that the family courts impose structure in the form of parenting plans on the conflicted family system. The distribution of power, control, and access to resources and the alliances within this superordinate system trickle down to influence how families manage their crises and eventually how parenting rights and responsibilities are allocated and exercised in the home.[5]

---

4. This authority to delegate is the subject of intense debate. *See* Milfred D. Dale et al., *Parenting Coordination Law in the U.S. and Canada: A Review of the Sources and Scope of the PC's Authority*, 58 Fam. Ct. Rev. 673 (2020); Dale R. Koch & Amy Pincolini-Ford, *Parenting Coordination in Domestic Violence Cases*, Juv. & Fam. Just. Today, Summer 2006, at 16.

5. Tom R. Tyler & Justin Sevier, *How Do the Courts Create Popular Legitimacy?: The Role of Establishing the Truth, Punishing Justly, and/or Acting through Just Procedures*, 77 Alb. L. Rev. 1095, 1098 (2013/2014).

When Families Enlist Professional Helpers

Before conflicted families enter the judicial system, they often engage a scattered collection of volunteer and hired helpers. This is the diverse collection of mental health providers, victim advocates, faith-based counselors, coaches, experts, soothsayers, and new-wave practitioners whose practices may be circumscribed by jurisdictional mandate, guild-specific ethical codes, and affiliation-specific guidelines (or not at all), but are generally not regulated by the courts.[6] We like to think that these therapists,[7] mediators, alternative dispute resolution (ADR) providers, and specialty and diversion services[8] help a significant percentage of troubled families to resolve their differences amicably and thereby minimize the number who require the family courts' intercession, but no one knows if this is true.[9]

Together, these providers create a fractured system unto themselves caught in an odd hierarchical purgatory somewhere superordinate to the family but subordinate to or perhaps allied with the courts. Because these players tend to be hired on an ad hoc basis, engaged either when emotions flare or functioning fails, and tend to become aligned with individuals or subsystems (e.g., father and stepmother) while ignorant of and totally unknown to other members of the family, chaos reigns.

6. *See* Tiffani DiPrizito, *Play by the Rules: Why States Should Adopt Uniform Court Rules for Forensic Psychologists in Child Custody Evaluations*, 54 Fam. Ct. Rev. 512 (2016).

7. For mental health professionals working with any of these families who may have contact with courts, there is wisdom in better understanding that you may become "forensic" even if unwillingly. *See* Dana E. Prescott, *Flexner's Thesis Was Prescient: Ethical Practices for Social Workers "in the Trenches" Requires Forensic Knowledge*, 16 J. Soc. Work Values & Ethics 40 (2019).

8. Turner, *supra* note 2, at 18. For another point of view related to specialized courts, see Thompson, *supra* note 2, at 63 ("In the process, community courts have begun to utilize the coercive power of the judiciary in ways that raise questions about their propriety and necessity. Interestingly, these concerns have not surfaced in the literature examining community courts.").

9. Various types of criminal court diversion programs have published mixed data concerning outcomes with the conclusion that results are uncertain. *See* Karen P. Hayhurst et al., *The Effectiveness of Diversion Programmes for Offenders Using Class A Drugs: A Systematic Review and Meta-Analysis*, 26 Drugs: Educ. Prevention & Pol'y 113 (2017). We are not aware of any comparable data relevant to family law diversion-type programs, but such a study would be very expensive, ethically challenging, and complex to conduct.

The Siloed Therapist

This describes the therapist, counselor, or coach Mom or Dad hires to help manage the family turmoil and who proceed with no perspective on the larger family system. They sympathize with their client's pain and validate their client's perspective because that is, after all, what therapists are trained to do. Thus validated and refueled by a professional with a framed diploma on the wall, a nice suit, and a handful of impressive letters after his name, the parents return home with their opposing positions reinforced and escalate the battle. The result drives the wedge between the partners deeper, compounding tensions and biases and the pain for all involved.

This is the dilemma of the siloed therapist, the professional who presumes to support the needs of an individual without any perspective on the larger systems in which that individual functions. Working from the comfort of a nicely furnished black box, the professional's only point of reference is an experience of reality communicated exclusively by his client. This means that the siloed therapist is incapable of considering anything but individual psychopathology.

Imagine, by analogy, that you've signed on as therapist for one of the three blindmen who encountered an elephant for the first time from the ancient parable.[10] Your client talks clearly and consistently about the creature's long, sinuous nature; its snakelike flexibility; and its curious, probing behavior. Knowing nothing more, you write a letter to the court advocating for your client's point of view.

---

10. "The parable of the blind men and an elephant originated in the ancient Indian subcontinent, from where it has been widely diffused. It is a story of a group of blind men who have never come across an elephant before and who learn and conceptualize what the elephant is like by touching it. Each blind man feels a different part of the elephant's body, but only one part, such as the side or the tusk. They then describe the elephant based on their limited experience and their descriptions of the elephant are different from each other. In some versions, they come to suspect that the other person is dishonest and they come to blows. The moral of the parable is that humans have a tendency to claim absolute truth based on their limited, subjective experience as they ignore other people's limited, subjective experiences which may be equally true." Wikipedia, *Blind Men and an Elephant*, https://en.wikipedia.org/wiki/Blind_men_and_an_elephant (last edited July 13, 2021).

Meanwhile, each of your client's blind friends has commenced his own therapy. One convinced his therapist to advise the court that the beast surely was short and squat and immovable. The other man's therapist testified that the very same beast was huge and rounded and solid.

The court assumes that all three accounts can't be true. Two of the three stories must be lies. Reinforced by experts and evidence and impressive testimony by impressive professionals, no one understands that all three accounts are true. Your client encountered the elephant's trunk. Another encountered its leg. The third encountered its belly. In the absence of any perspective outside of individual psychotherapy, the whole of the beast can never be fully understood.

The problem of the siloed therapist may be most destructive when the client is a child. In this too-familiar story, a well-meaning but systemically blind professional responds to one parent's plea on behalf of her child. Engaging the child with only that parent's perspective in mind feeds confirmation bias and risks exacerbating the child's polarization within the adult conflict (Chapter 9), commonly contributing to and exacerbating the child's resist/refuse behaviors.

By contrast, "a more integrated, collaborative perspective is likely to produce more optimal outcomes for parents and children than current siloed attempts to improve child and family well-being encourage the increased use of systematic data in making decisions about how to allocate scarce resources for family support."[11]

Recognizing this problem, the Association of Family and Conciliation Courts recommends in relevant part:

> The CIT [court-involved therapist] must, whenever possible, obtain each parent's perspective in the treatment process and maintain professional objectivity when interpreting statements and behaviors of children. The CIT should use particular

11. Carolyn Pape Cowan & Philip A. Cowan, *Enhancing Parenting Effectiveness, Fathers' Involvement, Couple Relationship Quality, and Children's Development: Breaking Down Silos in Family Policy Making and Service Delivery*, 11 J. Fam. Theory & Rev. 92 (2019).

caution in interpreting statements, play or drawings that appear to express positions on adult issues to avoid inaccurate or incomplete assessment of a child's developmental needs, expressed thoughts and feelings.[12]

The Judicial System

When the family fails to settle its differences, when allied systems (e.g., community and extended family) are unavailable or unsuccessful in their best efforts to help, and when the members of this scattered, interstitial therapeutic support system do more harm than good, superordinate systems become involved. Moving up through the hierarchy of power, control, and access to resources adds layers of people the same way that a snowball rolling downhill accumulates mass and speed and destructive potential. Entering the judicial system means that the family system, already encrusted with layers of extended family and professional helpers, must now add lawyers and experts and judges (not to mention paralegals and clerks and bailiffs and so on), compounding the risk that the roles and boundaries and the hierarchies within and between these systems will become intractably entangled and blurred.

As a result, it's not uncommon to see lawyer and client reenacting the marital conflict, prompting the lawyer's withdrawal, the parent's search for new counsel, adding frustrating delays to an already frustratingly slow process.[13] Anticipating these dynamics, "[l]awyers should think about what emotions could be expected from clients generally and from their particular clients and should be prepared to respond to these feelings."[14]

Mom hires an expert who immediately eschews contact with her and directs all communication to her lawyer in the interest of impartiality

---

12. Association of Family and Conciliation Courts, Guidelines for Court-Involved Therapy 1.2(d) (2017).

13. *See* Marjorie A. Silver, *Love, Hate, and Other Emotional Interference in the Lawyer/Client Relationship*, 6 Clinical L. Rev. 259 (1999).

14. Gail E. Silverstein, *All's Well That Ends Well: The Importance of Full and Effective Closure in Lawyer-Client Relationships*, 19 Clinical L. Rev. 555, 568 (2013).

and the protection of privilege.[15] This process is sound, but the resulting relationship dynamic triggers Mom's anxiety about secrets, rejection, and abandonment, recreating within this odd subsystem (lawyer-client-expert) the same destructive schism that erupted in the marriage.

Or perhaps more familiar among the dynamics of the legal system is the divorce-like conflict that erupts between Mom's lawyer and Dad's lawyer, polarizing already antagonistic colleagues, triangulating the guardian ad litem, and infusing the fact-finding process with explosive, unresolved trickle-down emotion. More than an abstract problem of relationship dynamics, the cogs of this Rube Goldberg-like machine can quickly jam and sputter to a stop.

Role Corruption within the Family Court System

Few people think about how extraordinary it is to have a court decide when a child is picked up at school, how long a weekend lasts, whether and where a parent may relocate with a child, or who will serve as that child's teacher, therapist, or physician. As much as these details may appear to be tedious and trivial wastes of family resources and professionals' time, they can become the kindling that result in a hundred-thousand-dollar, three-week long litigious conflagration.

This exercise of power, control, and the allocation of resources—that is, the imposition of the court's authority on the minutiae of a family's day-to-day life—is empowered by the British common law idea of *parens patraie*, the court's responsibility to intercede in the otherwise sacrosanct autonomy of the family in order to protect citizens who prove unable to protect themselves.[16]

---

15. "A reviewer who meets with a litigant begins to formulate opinions concerning the merits of the litigant's position in the dispute before the court. The information offered by a litigant to a retained reviewer is, by its very nature, insufficient and skewed, and it cannot be appropriately analyzed. Consequently, the weight to be assigned to the information simply cannot be ascertained in an unbiased manner." David A. Martindale, *Forensic Consultation in Litigated Custody Disputes*, 35 J. Psychiatry & L. 281, 294 (2007).

16. *See, e.g.*, Daniel E. Witte, Notes & Comments, People v. Bennett*: Analytic Approaches to Recognizing a Fundamental Parental Right under the Ninth Amendment*, 1996 BYU L. Rev. 186, 227–34 (1996).

The court's exercise of its *parens patraie* authority often prompts lawyers to hire experts to advise the court. The admission of an expert's testimony is subject to *Frye*, *Daubert*, and similar standards depending upon jurisdiction, standards that are often interpreted loosely by family courts with the caveat that it will hear an expert's testimony and thence "assign it the weight that it deserves."

Lay versus Expert Roles

As a threshold matter, it is important to define what it means to be an *expert* in any adversarial system. The Federal Rules of Evidence[17] define what is *not* expert evidence by first defining lay evidence:

> If a witness is not testifying as an expert, testimony in the form of an opinion is limited to one that is: (a) rationally based on the witness's perception; (b) helpful to clearly understanding the witness's testimony or to determining a fact in issue; and (c) not based on scientific, technical, or other specialized knowledge within the scope of Rule 702.[18]

An opinion by a lay or fact witness may be permissible if based on her perceptions, but those perceptions must be "adequately grounded on personal knowledge or observation just as would be the case with simple statements of fact."[19]

By contrast, expert opinion is based upon facts "perceived by or made known to the expert at or before the hearing,"[20] and derived from specialized knowledge "not within the realm of the ordinary layperson."[21] Simply put, "if an opinion requires specialized knowledge and is not

---

17. For an excellent review of the rules of evidence as applied to family matters, see Steven N. Peskind, The Family Law Trial Evidence Handbook (2013).

18. Fed. R. Evid. 701; *see* Divine v. Robbins, 683 S.E.2d 286, 294 (S.C. 2009) ("Ms. Emery's opinion regarding Mother's behavior was based on her personal interaction with Mother as Daughter's guardian [ad litem] and was probative in determining which parent was best suited to obtain custody of Daughter.").

19. Mitchell v. Kieliszek, 900 A.2d 719, 723 (Me. 2006) (internal quotations omitted).

20. Fed. R. Evid. 703.

21. *Mitchell*, 900 A.2d at 723 (quoting Chrysler Credit Corp. v. Bert Cote's L/A Auto Sales, Inc., 707 A.2d 1311, 1317 (Me. 1998)).

based on personal perception, it is an expert opinion, even if it is offered on the 'fact issue' of credibility rather than the 'expert issue' of the standard of care."[22]

These rules define roles and limits and boundaries within the judicial system in the same way that healthy co-parents work together to define roles and limits and boundaries within the family system. Within these two distinct but overlapping systems, structure dictates how members are allowed to behave. The court and legislature define what lawyers and their experts are allowed to do very much the same way that parents define what children are allowed to do. This means, for example, sustaining counsel's objection when Mom's therapist (a fact witness testifying that Mom did, indeed, attend therapy) tries to offer an opinion about custody or when the child's school counselor (a fact witness testifying that Dad attended teacher meetings) opines about alienation.[23] However, in the absence of an objection or when the court overrules such an objection, these well-intended but ill-advised and often unethical actions[24] blur boundaries, corrupt roles, mislead the court,[25] and work to the detriment of the child.

---

22. *Id.* at 724.

23. For example: "These statements are not only speculative, but amount to a lay diagnosis or prognosis regarding a complex medical issue. Ms. Rose is not qualified to do that, as she was not qualified as a psychiatrist, psychologist, or licensed clinical social worker." *In re* Yve S., 819 A.2d 1030, 1067–68 (Md. 2003).

24. For example: "[P]sychologists provide opinions of the psychological characteristics of individuals only after they have conducted an examination of the individuals adequate to support their statements or conclusions." American Psychological Association, Ethical Principles of Psychologists and Code of Conduct 9.01(b) (2010).

25. In one study, jurors viewed clinical therapist and forensic testimony as equally scientific but more heavily weighed the therapist testimony in their decision making. *See* Daniel A. Krauss & Bruce D. Sales, *The Effects of Clinical and Scientific Expert Testimony on Juror Decision Making in Capital Sentencing*, 7 Psych. Pub. Pol'y & L. 267 (2001). This outcome has been replicated in research and, in the authors' anecdotal experiences, even with judges in bench trials, despite the fact that clinical opinion is far more riddled with bias and unreliability than forensic opinion.

Judges, Experts, and Blurred Boundaries

Experts, unlike lay witnesses, are allowed to offer an opinion on the ultimate issue on the basis of research, clinical interviews, and data collected from therapists, teachers, and other first-hand sources who are not present in the courtroom and who therefore cannot be cross-examined.[26] When an expert brings unique knowledge of a field of study to bear on the particulars of a case and the court weighs the expert's opinion as a function of his credentials and impartial, insightful, and comprehensive grasp of the fact pattern at hand, justice is served. This is a healthy legal system at its best.

What becomes troublesome is the possibility that a court will weigh an expert's opinion at least in part on that professional's prestige and presentation, rather than on his specialized knowledge grounded on reliable, generalizable, and reproduceable methodology and research.[27] Televised interviews, book publications, high-profile celebrity endorsements, and expensive suits and haircuts are not in and of themselves the substance of science, credibility, or admissibility. For that matter, the number of cases a professional has testified in has no necessary bearing on her ability to contribute to a case.[28] This dilemma is captured most readily in the half-joking but commonly expressed belief that the value given an expert's opinion is directly related to how far that expert traveled to testify.[29]

---

26. Judith Cashmore & Patrick Parkinson, *The Use and Abuse of Social Science Research Evidence in Children's Cases*, 20 Psych. Pub. Pol'y & L. 239 (2014).

27. Victor E. Schwartz & Cary Silverman, *The Draining of* Daubert *and the Recidivism of Junk Science in Federal and State Courts*, 35 Hofstra L. Rev. 217 (2006).

28. George J. Alexander, *Big Mother: The State's Use of Mental Health Experts in Dependency Cases*, 24 Pac. L.J. 1465 (1993); Daniel W. Shuman & Stuart A. Greenberg, *The Expert Witness, the Adversary System, and the Voice of Reason: Reconciling Impartiality and Advocacy*, 34 Pro. Psych.: Rsch. & Prac. 219 (2003).

29. Gary Edmond et al., *Contextual Bias and Cross-Contamination in the Forensic Sciences: The Corrosive Implications for Investigations, Plea Bargains, Trials, and Appeals*, 14 Law Probability & Risk 1 (2015); Saul Kassin et al., *The Forensic Confirmation Bias: Problems, Perspectives, and Proposed Solutions*, 2 J. Applied Rsch. Memory & Cognition 42 (2013).

The forensic expert's privilege to speak to the ultimate issue in a case requires competence and integrity that ethically and rationally informs decision making about a person or a system.[30] An expert who allows his personal experience, biases, beliefs, and remuneration to affect his testimony is doing harm.[31] So too is the expert who compromises her professional boundaries in the interest of ego, authority, or prestige.

Chapters 11 and 12 describe the dilemma of the enmeshed child who is adultified or parentified within the family system. Enlisted by an immature, isolated, overwhelmed, or incompetent parent to serve either as ally or caregiver, these children give up their childhoods, compromise their identities, and are conscripted into the adult war. The adults who enable and nurture these unhealthy dynamics have abdicated their parenting responsibilities. Further:

> [J]udges tend not to be knowledgeable about the research that forms the knowledge base for forensic psychological opinions. . . . [I]t is difficult for judges to distinguish between acceptable and unacceptable practices for qualified members of a legitimate discipline. Others have expressed concern regarding the ability of judges to discern sound from flawed methodology. Forensic psychological experts functioning as communicators to

---

30. American Psychological Association, *Specialty Guidelines for Forensic Experts*, 68 Am. Psych. 7 (2012); American Psychological Association, *Revision of Ethical Standard 3.04 of the "Ethical Principles of Psychologists and Code of Conduct" (2002, as Amended 2010)*, 71 Am. Psych. 900 (2016); Harry T. Edwards, *The National Academy of Sciences Report on Forensic Sciences: What It Means for the Bench and Bar*, 51 Jurimetrics 1 (2010); National Research Council, Strengthening Forensic Science in the United States: A Path Forward (2009).

31. Tarika Daftary-Kapur et al., *Gender-Intrusive Questioning: A Survey of Expert Witnesses*, 32 Behav. Sci. & L. 180 (2014); John F. Edens et al., *"Hired Guns," "Charlatans," and Their "Voodoo Psychobabble": Case Law References to Various Forms of Perceived Bias among Mental Health Expert Witnesses*, 9 Psych. Services 259 (2012); Tess Neal & Thomas Grisso, *The Cognitive Underpinnings of Bias in Forensic Mental Health Evaluations*, 20 Psych. Pub. Pol'y & L. 200, 206 (2014); Marissa Zappala et al., *Anything You Can Do, I Can Do Better: Bias Awareness in Forensic Evaluators*, 18 J. Forensic Psych. Rsch. & Prac. 45 (2018).

> the court can assist triers of fact in being more informed consumers of custody evaluation reports.[32]

A similar sort of abdication of authority occurs in the courts when a judge, overwhelmed by the facts of the case, intimidated by the science, or otherwise unwilling to exercise his authority instead implicitly vests his decision-making authority in an expert. We see this occur most robustly when the courts delegate quasi-judicial authority to parenting coordinators or "reunification" therapists.[33] Although the dynamic is more subtle, it can be seen just as clearly when experts opine about ultimate issues.[34]

The parallel between what sometimes happens within the justice system and what sometimes happens within the family system is eerie. At both levels of inquiry, the authority feels relieved to be able to rely on someone who seems to understand what's happening even while guilt and anxiety over the abdication of authority runs rampant. Meanwhile, the adultified or parentified individual is simultaneously giddy with the authority figure's gift of respect and recognition and power, and overwhelmed by the responsibility. Others involved in the dynamics are enraged and confused, feeling disenfranchised and resentful. At both levels of inquiry, the resulting dynamic is disorienting and fuels universal anxiety as rules and roles are arbitrarily rejected and redefined, all to the detriment of the child.

---

32. Martindale, *supra* note 15, at 292 (citations omitted).

33. For example, the New Hampshire Supreme Court wrote:

> Wife asserts that "[p]lacing Ms. Tucker in the role of fact finder and decision maker as to how and when [she] may progress towards seeing her children constitutes an avoidance of official judicial responsibility and an impermissible delegation of it to a private citizen." . . . It is the trial court's responsibility . . . to determine parental rights and responsibilities in cases of divorce and legal separation, and we now hold that the court may not delegate that responsibility to a third party.

In re Kamil, 242 A.3d 801, 812–13 (N.H. 2020) (citations omitted).

34. Jon K. Amundson & Glenda M. Lux, *The Issue of Ethics and Authority for Licensed Mental Health Professionals Involved in Parenting Coordination*, 54 Fam. Ct. Rev. 446 (2016).

Science, Not Séance

Successful relationships require the simultaneous and sometimes contradictory processes of validating both emotion and fact. Our feelings are real and meaningful but must not be confused with science. This is as true of the parent-child dyad as it is of young lovers as it is of a lawyer's representation of a cuckolded father as it is of the weight a judge gives to an expert's testimony. Both emotions and facts exist. The first is born of subjective experience and clouds perception. The second is born of objective reality and opens us up to the full breadth of perception. In order to function as successful adults in society and to do our jobs as family law professionals, we must not only know the difference between facts and emotions, but proactively and transparently distinguish them.

This distinction arises again and again when cross-examining family law experts. Many seem to consciously take advantage of the family court's greater latitude to allow their personal agendas to color their testimony.[35] They hide their biases, flawed theories, and empirical failings behind a shiny veneer of expertise bejeweled with self-published treatises, websites, and degrees.[36] They put on a good show, brag about the scores of courts that have heard their spiel, and overwhelm jurists and juries alike with supposed terms of art and magical skills worthy of Harry Potter's evil nemesis, Voldemort, their hubris as obvious and as seldom

35. Scholars have often noted that the qualifications and reliability of expert opinions in family court should adhere to the same rules of scientific methodology and evidence as other matters in court:

> Using a *Daubert* analysis should likewise result in the exclusion of the expert's testimony on "best interests." A decision on the ultimate issue requires legal analysis and consideration of many factors, some of which may not be known to the expert. Because the best interest standard is admittedly indeterminate, it is not possible to critically assess the expert's predictions on which outcome would serve the child's best interests. In other words, the expert's opinion would not have scientific validity and should not be allowed under *Daubert*.

Sarah H. Ramsey & Robert F. Kelly, *Social Science Knowledge in Family Law Cases: Judicial Gate-Keeping in the Daubert Era*, 59 U. Miami L. Rev. 1, 22–23 (2004).

36. We encourage consumers of science and scientific testimony to read John P.A. Ioannidis, *Why Most Published Research Findings Are False*, 2 PLoS Med. 696 (2005) (article e124), https://doi.org/10.1371/journal.pmed.0020124.

challenged as "The Emperor's New Clothes."[37] Left unchecked, the risk is that these hired guns will not only corrupt a particular case and do harm to a particular child, but that their shallow theories and facile methods will become entrenched, creating or concretizing systemic biases.

Stay in Your Lane

Systems fail when need and emotion corrupt roles and rules. This occurs within the family court system when professionals trip over their egos, motivated by hubris, greed, and a need to win, treating families like so many notches on one's gun belt. The antidote includes constant and intentional self-care (Chapter 18). We close this chapter with a focus on the least often acknowledged and perhaps most important aspect of the family law professional's self-care, the simple idea of knowing and accepting one's limits.

None of us wears a cape on our backs or an *S* emblazoned on our chests. Iron Man and Wonder Woman are projections of lingering childhood dreams of omnipotence and one way that healthy adults cope with the reality of our helplessness. We all have very real limits of ability and knowledge and competence. We must work to discover and embrace these limitations with humility or deny them at our peril.

Any person's report of any particular event or knowledge of any particular subject is necessarily limited. No one can know all things from all perspectives. Acknowledging one's limitations—being comfortable saying "I don't know" and being open to new information that might change an opinion—is a sign of emotional health and maturity. Doing these things as a professional is a sign of humility and compliance with an ethic essential to our various professional roles.

Adapting numerous professional guilds' various ethical codes and best practice standards to our more general purpose, we believe that family law professionals should universally be responsible to:

---

37. Hans Christian Andersen, Fairy Tales Told for Children (1837).

1. Recognize, openly acknowledge, and work to minimize the inevitable biases, attitudes, and prejudices that compromise objectivity.
2. Recognize and respect the unique roles, relationships, needs, and wishes of the people whom we serve.
3. Act intentionally to understand the impact of culture, religion, language, gender, sexual orientation, and other historical and contextual factors that bear on the identity and the relationships among the people whom we serve.
4. Exercise the power, control, and access to resources inherent in a particular professional role equitably, within the limits of that role, and with humility.
5. Engage in and otherwise encourage a documented, transparent, empirically informed, and reproduceable process.
6. Base our opinions on diverse methods and reliable and valid techniques whenever possible and sufficient to substantiate our findings.[38]
7. Proactively disclose error rates, contrary data, alternate theories, and opinions.
8. Provide testimony "in ways that promote understanding and avoid deception."[39] This means, in part, taking care "not to distort or withhold relevant evidence or opinion in reports or testimony."
9. Recognize that relationship questions require an understanding of interpersonal dynamics within and between systems, including the ways in which the intrusions of the legal system itself shapes and is reshaped by the relationships being examined.

---

38. American Psychological Association, *supra* note 24, EPPCC Standards 2.04, 9.01.

39. *Id.* SGFP 5.01.

SECTION II
Taxonomy: The Dynamics of the Conflicted Family System

"A true conservationist is a man who knows
that the world is not given by his fathers,
but borrowed from his children."

—Wendell Berry

Chapter 7
Triangulation

"The psychologist described Andrew's plight as an involvement 'in a sad and intense triangulation between the parents . . . [a] tug of war over the soul of th[e] child.' The report observed that the parents, 'although physically divorced, remain enmeshed with each other and the children are caught in this conflictual triangle.'"[1]

Definition:	Triangulation occurs when a third person or system is exposed to or drawn into the relationship that exists between two other people or systems. In the context of divorce, a child is triangulated into the adult conflict when she is exposed to or enlisted to play a part in that conflict. Triangulation is the common precondition for all of the dynamics described throughout this book including enmeshment, estrangement, and alienation.
Reasonable precautions:	Communities should proactively educate parents about the harm that children experience when they become triangulated amidst adult conflict. This includes simple, clear direction about closing doors in the interest of privacy and taking reasonable steps to assure that children do not have access to adult communication media.

1. Margolin v. Margolin, 796 S.W.2d 38, 41 (Mo. Ct. App. 1990) (alterations in original).

What to look for:	Triangulated children know too much about their parents' conflict and one or both parents' individual lives. They may feel as if they caused the conflict and/or are responsible to resolve it. Energy that should be invested in learning and growing and friends is redirected to adult and family matters (e.g., "I hope we can pay the rent this month.").
Caution:	Beware that children can become triangulated into their parents' conflict due to other actors' (e.g., extended family, older siblings, stepparents) intentional or incidental choices.
How to respond to the adults:	Begin with group educational and support opportunities. The goal is insulating children from adult matters so as to reassure and to minimize anxiety. Direct parents to read and/or watch educational videos. Follow-up discussions, quizzes, and written reports can help assure compliance. When triangulating behaviors persist, psychological evaluations and/or court sanctions can become appropriate.
How to respond to the child:	The triangulated child needs reassurance that she will be okay even as the adults work out their differences. She may need "a port in the storm" (i.e., a healthy, safe, and impartial adult relationship in which to gain perspective on the family transition, family roles, and rules).[2] A carefully structured and systemically informed child therapy is one way to provide this support.
Implications for custody-related decisions:	Intentional and persistent acts to triangulate the child leave the child at increased risk of enmeshment and/or alienation. Many best interests formulations and associated "friendly parent" rules would weigh custody outcomes in favor of the parent who succeeds in insulating the child from adult matters.

2. Noting that "[p]ets, like therapists and grandparents and coaches and neighbors and siblings, can thereby serve as a child's emotional 'port in the storm'; that is, a secure base or relationship anchor to relieve some of the anxiety associated with parental conflict, separation, and divorce." Benjamin D. Garber & Dana E. Prescott, *On the Value of Teddy Bears and Barbie Dolls: The Place of Children's Transitional Objects in Family Law*, 49 Sw. L. Rev. 189, 210 (2020).

The concept of triangulation as applied to family systems has its recent roots in the work of Bowen[3] and Minuchin.[4] As a transitive verb, the word describes the dynamic in force when two or more members of a system incorporate a third person into their relationship as a means to achieve a desired outcome. Triangulation can be intentional or incidental, mutually beneficial, or selfishly destructive.

Triangulation is often conflated in the family systems literature with other distinct dynamics, most notably including enmeshment.[5] Upon closer examination this confusion is understandable because triangulation commonly co-exists with and serves as the foundation upon which these other dynamics develop. Caught between the shifting tectonic plates of a highly conflicted family system, the triangulated child suffers constant and increasing pressure to resolve the conflict—to adapt her behavior to her explosive relationship ecology—simply to fulfill her need for nurturance and affiliation.

Healthy Triangulation?

Context is everything. We use the phrase "relationship ecology" to describe the interpersonal context in which dynamics evolve. Whether and to what degree any particular dynamic is healthy or destructive can only be understood in its native interpersonal environment. For the

---

3. *See* Murray Bowen, Family Therapy in Clinical Practice (1978); Murray Bowen, *The Use of Family Theory in Clinical Practice*, 7 Comprehensive Psychiatry 345 (1966).

4. *See* Salvadore Minuchin, Families and Family Therapy (1974); Patricia Minuchin, *Families and Individual Development: Provocations from the Field of Family Therapy*, 56 Child Dev. 289 (1985).

5. "The concept of triangulation is one that has been conceptualized, operationalized, and labeled in many different ways, and the processes subsumed under these labels are myriad. For some investigators, the heart of the triangulation construct is the child's inappropriate participation in the executive functions of the family . . . . [O]thers define triangulation as inappropriate involvement of the child in the interparental relationship . . . [or as occurs] when one parent is successful in creating a special bond with the child that excludes the other parent." Patricia K. Kerig & Julie A. Swanson, *Ties That Bind: Triangulation, Boundary Dissolution, and the Effects of Interparental Conflict on Child Development*, *in* Strengthening Couple Relationships for Optimal Child Development: Lessons from Research and Intervention 59 (Mark S. Shulz et al. eds., 2010).

purpose of discussion throughout this book, we speak of a dynamic as healthy to the extent that it facilitates the family's purpose—that is, safely helping the child develop toward autonomy (Chapter 3). We speak of dynamics as unhealthy or destructive to the extent that they work counter to this goal.

In the broadest view, triangulation can be a healthy and adaptive means of intervening to resolve dyadic conflicts. When Sally can't adequately express her needs to her new teacher, she asks her mother to attend their next conference. When co-workers can't resolve their differences, a human resource worker sits in with them. When intimate partners reach an impasse in their relationship, they might turn to a mediator or a couples' counselor. We speak of these and many other familiar examples as healthy and adaptive because the triangulated (third) party is impartial to the dyadic conflict, aware of and accepting of the role, and has the emotional maturity to manage the associated stresses.[6]

Consider, for example, two cases in which children are routinely and knowingly triangulated into extrafamilial conflicts:

1. **Children as peer mediators**. Preteens and adolescents are sometimes enlisted to serve as peer mediators in their schools. This model endeavors to teach healthy conflict resolution methods and to empower a student body by training and supervising carefully selected children to help peers settle their differences. These students are helped to take a structured, defined, and intentionally triangulated role in their peers' conflicts so as to help all involved develop new conflict resolution skills.

The literature concerned with peer mediation focuses largely on training, supervision, and effectiveness within the classroom or school

---

6. For example, immigrant children who are triangulated into their parents' acculturation needs are discussed later in this chapter:

> In contrast to teachers and counselors who receive training on culture brokering and are able to maintain an emotional distance from those they help, children of immigrant families who act as culture brokers are thrown into a situation that they may not be prepared to deal with and are not able to keep an emotional distance from.

Curtis J. Jones, *Immigrant Adolescents as Culture Brokers: Families from the Soviet Union*, 145 J. Soc. Psych. 405 (2003).

setting.[7] The efficacy of the process has often been demonstrated[8] and may be generalizable to the larger community.[9] However, very little attention has been paid to the social and emotional impact of the process on the triangulated student/peer mediator's functioning and development.[10]

The only exception to this observation that we know of is found in a 2014 dissertation concerned with the effects of peer mediation training on third- through fifth-grade peer mediators. That young author observed that "students demonstrated higher levels of social competence as a result of receiving peer mediation training, but lower levels of self-esteem and resiliency."[11] The suggestion, then, is that even carefully scripted, structured, and supervised triangulation may take a significant toll on the child's psychological development.

2. **Children as "culture brokers."** Some immigrant children are triangulated into adult matters to facilitate their parents' functioning and acculturation. These children are described in the professional literature as "culture brokers" or "language brokers." Research finds that as many as 90 percent of immigrant children are enlisted to varying degrees in this role.[12] For example:

---

7. *See* Inmaculada Usó et al., *Impact of Peer Mediation Programmes to Prevent Bullying Behaviors in Secondary Schools*, 39 Infancia y Aprendizaje: J. for Study Educ. & Dev. 499 (2016).

8. Robert D. Harris, *Unlocking the Learning Potential in Peer Mediation: An Evaluation of Peer Mediator Modeling and Disputant Learning*, 23 Conflict Resol. Q. 141 (2004).

9. Vitus Ozoke, *From Peers to Community: Transferring Peer Mediation Skills from School to Community*, *in* The Mediation Handbook: Research, Theory, and Practice 243 (Alexia Georgakopoulos ed., 2017).

10. Retrospective research seeking to associate childhood training as a peer mediator with particular long-term outcomes would likely face criticism about selection bias. In short, it would be extremely difficult to know whether the children chosen for training were selected because they had already proven to have certain predisposing character traits (e.g., insight, perspective taking, impulse control, compassion). For an example of such research strategies and their limitations and challenges when applying to courts and policy, see Bruce Smyth, *A 5-Year Retrospective of Post-Separation Shared Care Research in Australia*, 15 J. Fam. Stud. 36 (2009).

11. Deanna J. Cardoza, *Peer Mediation and Its Effects on Elementary Student Perceptions of Self-Esteem and Social Competence*, 74 Dissertation Abstracts Int'l Sec. A: Human. & Soc. Sci. 12-A(E) (2014) (Ed.D. dissertation, California State University, Fresno).

12. Vanja Lazarevic, *Effects of Cultural Brokering on Individual Wellbeing and Family Dynamics among Immigrant Youth*, 55 J. Adolescence 77 (2017).

> Immigrant children and adolescents often acquire the new language faster and accept the new norms and values more easily than their parents, so that the parents turn to them for assistance in understanding the new language, practices, and more. Consequently, children often become language and culture brokers for their parents.[13]

Whereas triangulation in the context of divorce places children in the midst of a conflict *within* the family system, triangulation in the context of immigration places children in the midst of the conflict *between* the family system and allied (e.g., neighbors, community, church) and superordinate (e.g., police, healthcare, judicial) systems. Child culture brokers serve as buffers between systems on the front lines of the persistent battle that erupts between cultures and languages and rituals by translating, advocating, interpreting, and managing money for their parents and extended family.

The child triangulated between systems—like the child triangulated within her family system—benefits from consequent pride, nurturance, and affiliation at the cost of an additional burden of anxiety. The child triangulated as a culture broker, for example, is exposed to many of the harsh realities of the adult world prematurely, most notably the ugly underside of poverty, social exclusion, adult needs, epistemic injustice, and prejudice. This child, very much like the child peer mediator and the child triangulated amidst her parents' conflict, is forced to divert a portion of her finite and precious emotional energies from the necessary tasks of development to manage others' needs instead.

Research in this field teaches us that immigrant children are more likely to become triangulated as their parents' culture brokers when their elders remain deeply enmeshed in their native cultures[14] and less likely to

---

13. Olga Oznobishin & Jenny Kurman, *Understanding Language Brokering and Self-Perceptions among Young Immigrants from the Former Soviet Union in Israel*, *in* LANGUAGE BROKERING IN IMMIGRANT FAMILIES: THEORIES AND CONTEXTS 98 (Robert S. Weisskirch ed., 2017).

14. Edison J. Trickett & Curtis J. Jones, *Adolescent Culture Brokering and Family Functioning: A Study of Families from Vietnam*, 13 CULTURAL DIVERSITY & ETHNIC MINORITY PSYCH. 143 (2007).

do so when their parents are more educated and have better English fluency, higher social status within the native culture, higher economic status in the adopted culture, and longer residency in the adopted culture.[15]

We know that as immigrant families rely more and more on children as culture brokers, those teenagers report *both* greater family conflict and greater family adaptability. This means that from the triangulated youths' points of view, their families are more stressful on the inside but more flexible on the outside.[16]

The same research finds that immigrant families' reliance on child culture brokers is unrelated to those children's reports of family cohesion.[17] Keeping in mind that this reflects the triangulated child's point of view (and not the parents' reports), this outcome is nonetheless startling. We would expect that the intrafamilial pressures that cause a child to take on an adultlike role outside the family system would compromise family boundaries, diminish cohesion, and even prompt that child to separate from the family prematurely.[18]

Recognizing these realities, many educational, child protection, healthcare, and legal professionals discourage immigrant families from relying on their children as culture brokers.[19] Like the scant research examining the development of children vested as peer mediators, the

15. Curtis J. Jones & Edison J. Trickett, *The Adolescent Culture Broker Role: A Study of Adolescents and Mothers from the Former Soviet Union*, 145 J. Soc. Psych. 405 (2005).

16. If this were an individual rather than a family system, she would be described as internalizing or "bottling up" stress. These individuals can become powder kegs destined to explode in anger and/or implode in depression.

17. *See* Trickett & Jones, *supra* note 14.

18. This discussion raises fascinating questions yet to be studied about the current generation of children serving as "technology brokers" for their parents and grandparents, facilitating access to software, cloud-based technologies, and video platforms such as Zoom. *See* Teresa Correa et al., *The Complexities of the Role of Children in the Process of Technology Transmission Among Disadvantaged Families: A Mixed-Methods Approach*, 13 Int'l J. Commc'n 21 (2019).

19. "There is well-founded professional resistance to the use of children in the [language broker] role in sensitive or challenging meetings, but for some purposes many immigrant parents and grandparents prefer a language broker from within their own family to an external professional interpreter." Tony Cline et al., *Child Language Brokering in Schools: A Discussion of Selected Findings from a Survey of Teachers and Ex-Students*, 31 Educ. & Child Psych. 33 (2014).

research supporting this position is mixed.[20] Regardless, the unfortunate fact is that there are seldom enough skilled case workers, advocates, and professional translators available to relieve the pressures that inevitably triangulate these children.

Pathological Triangulation

Triangulation into others' needs and conflicts carries with it the burdens of that knowledge and the pain of exposure to the associated emotions. This is why even the most highly trained and successful professional mediators are at high risk of burnout and compassion fatigue (Chapter 18). When the triangulated party is immature, unprepared for and perhaps even unaware of her role and unable to manage the associated stresses, the experience becomes destructive.

In the same way that we each rely on internal defense mechanisms to manage the otherwise overwhelming flood of sensory and emotional experiences in our world, we also rely on societal defense mechanisms for the same purpose. These are the laws and professional roles and superordinate systems that society simultaneously relies upon and rages against exactly the same way that children rely upon and rage against the rules set forth by their parents. These include things as varied as the laws that dictate the age of majority, rating systems that alert us to media content, government agencies that manage the dissemination of information, professional licensing standards, and health regulations.

Much as we rail against restrictions on the press, government secrets, failures of transparency, and autocracy in any form, we also depend upon these superordinate powers to protect us emotionally. The child inevitably rails against parental control, but needs it to manage her reality. Triangulation removes these protective filters, demanding that a subordinate system compromise its own needs to serve those of a superordinate system.

---

20. For example, teens serving as their parents' translators may improve their academic performance. *See* Raymond Buriel et al., *The Relationship of Language Brokering to Academic Performance, Biculturalism, and Self-Efficacy among Latino Adolescents*, 20 Hisp. J. Behav. Sci. 283 (1998).

Imagine what would happen if surgeons involved their patients in every incision and stitch, if the military informed the public about every possible threat, or if health officials advertised every suspected pathogen. Imagine how society would function if we could look over the president's shoulder at every briefing, meeting, and conference. At every level of inquiry, those with greater power, control, and access to resources are responsible to shield those with less. Being exposed to the flaws and foibles of those superordinate processes or worse, being conscripted to address them directly, might make you feel important and valued but will simultaneously undermine your security. This is the experience of the child triangulated amidst her parents' conflict.[21]

We return repeatedly throughout this text to the metaphor of the coffee cup: a familiar vessel able to contain a finite amount of liquid. The metaphor is an important way to illustrate our own very human limited capacity to manage emotion and sensory input.

That coffee cup comes up again in the context of discussing triangulation within the conflicted family system. Our job as parents is, in part, to create an environment in which our children can devote as much of their finite energies as possible to *childing*, the intransitive verb akin to *parenting* that describes the immature human being's process of learning and growing and making friends, learning ABC and 1-2-3.

When children are triangulated into their parents' needs, they are forced to invest some of their finite energies in managing adult emotions and behaviors. The coffee cup begins to fill with adult matters. This depletes resources that should be invested in other childing activities and can thereby compromise development more generally. The fact that some types of triangulation can cause the child

(continued on next page)

21. "In positive co-parenting relationships former partners avoid undermining one another and the triangulation of children, and engage in cooperation related to parenting tasks." Lynda M. Ashbourne et al., *Orienting Services to Separated/Divorced Fathers*, 51 Fam. Ct. Rev. 666, 670 (2013) (citation omitted).

to feel special or valued or needed (thereby serving the child's need for affiliation) is critically important to those who seek to understand family systems but is never an adequate justification for the outcome. Expressed most simply: as adults we share a responsibility to insulate our children from adult stresses so that they can devote their resources to development.

When Children Are Triangulated within the Family System

High-conflict adult relationships, marital separation, and divorce are ideal environments in which to observe the destructive effects of intrafamilial triangulation, or what some studies refer to generically as "interparental boundary problems."[22] Having once publicly promised to love, honor, and cherish an adult partner, having come to rely upon that partner as a primary source of emotional fuel, having developed an internal working model of that person as a source of emotional security, all that is lost. Angry and sad and scared and embarrassed and needy, each of the adults individually is suddenly cast adrift in search of new ways of fulfilling needs formerly fulfilled by one another. Healthy adults turn to healthy adult relationships: friends, extended family, faith-based supports, a therapist, mentor, colleague, or a new intimate partner. Allied and superordinate systems catch them in the safety net of community, church, or support group, and refuel needs for affiliation so that these parents, bruised and battered by their adult loss, can nonetheless continue to serve their children's needs.

Whether and how a parent's reliance on extrafamilial resources acts to settle or exacerbate the adult conflict is unimportant to this discussion,[23]

22. *See* Gregory M. Fosco et al., *Interparental Boundary Problems, Parent-Adolescent Hostility, and Adolescent-Parent Hostility: A Family Process Model for Adolescent Aggression Problems*, 3 Couple & Fam. Psych.: Rsch. & Prac. 141 (2014).

23. As when, for example, a siloed individual therapist validates his client's point of view without any knowledge of the larger family system. *See* Chapter 6.

as long as the children are neither exposed to nor involved in the process. Think of this as an aircraft crew's responsibility in case of a problem in flight. The goal is to reach the assigned destination safely without upsetting the passengers and certainly without asking them to help to fly the plane.

Unhealthy adults allow their emotions to contaminate the child's experience and compromise her security. These adults allow their own needs to eclipse their children's needs. Some turn to addictions, deny their neediness and neglect self-care, sink into depression or anxiety, or rage and/or project their needs onto their kids. Sometimes this happens out of ignorance because a parent simply doesn't know that children need to be protected from adult conflicts. Sometimes it happens because a parent doesn't have the benefit of other systems' supports. And sometimes it happens simply because the parent never had the ego strength, emotional maturity, and sensitivity to separate his own needs from those of a child. What we know is that "chronic, unresolved interparental discord can strain the co-parental relationship and lead to children being drawn into parental conflict in an effort to resolve it or diffuse the resulting tension."[24]

This is triangulation in its most pathological and pathogenic form. These are the tectonic pressures that can distort, suspend, and even reverse a child's otherwise healthy development toward autonomy and the fertile ground upon which the seeds of even more destructive systemic dynamics can take root.

Triangulation in the midst of co-parental conflict can be understood from either or both of two theoretical perspectives:

> *A spillover perspective* . . . argues that mood or affect is transferred from one relationship to another. From this perspective, parents in distressed interparental relationships are more likely to be angry and hostile with their adolescents, which places adolescents at risk for adjustment problems. *A social interaction*

24. Although the why and how of "the diffusion of negativity from interparental to parent-child subsystems are less clear." Gregory M. Fosco & John H. Grych, *Adolescent Triangulation into Parental Conflicts: Longitudinal Implications for Appraisals and Adolescent-Parent Relations*, 72 J. Marriage & Fam. 254 (2010).

> *learning perspective* . . . emphasizes the role of contingencies in family interactions that reinforce hostile or aversive adolescent behavior. Within the family, adolescents' hostile or angry behavior toward parents may be reinforced if such behavior serves to disrupt parental disagreements.[25]

Triangulation by spillover occurs when adults fail to adequately insulate their children from corrosive and confusing feelings, words, and behavior. Doors are left ajar, text messages are left exposed, e-mail accounts are shared, and phone calls are overheard. Experienced family law professionals encounter these "oops! I guess I gave him my cell phone with all my text messages to his father on it" incessantly. Adult character pathology, addiction, and/or the regression associated with stress can erode previously healthy intergenerational boundaries, creating destructive emotional spillover.

In its most explicit and egregious form, spillover sets the stage for adultification—that is, premature enlistment of the child as an adult's peer or partner (Chapter 11). This can occur when a child who is incidentally exposed to co-parental conflict is drawn into the fray the way that an innocent bystander gets drawn into two strangers' fight. In one familiar example, an overwrought father notices his ten-year-old son standing in the doorway during a marital spat and calls out, "Hey Billy, you heard what she said. Does that make any sense to you?"

The social interaction learning perspective explaining triangulation is just as familiar and just as destructive. Recall that the motives that drive human behavior are finite and primitive. Behaviors that are rewarded are repeated and become more frequent. One of the most powerful rewards is the praise of valued others. Thus, when Sally's confession to her father that she argued with her mother elicits the adult's self-serving smile or a vindictive chuckle or even his explicit praise, what might first have been an expectable part of adolescent rebellion becomes a weapon in the adult war.

25. Fosco et al., *supra* note 22, at 142.

Children as Agents of Triangulation?

When a child's behavior accidentally interrupts her parents' conflict, that behavior is reinforced. Listening intently to his parents' argument from atop a staircase, Billy slips and falls down the entire flight. His injuries are minor, but his upset startles the adults into action. Ice packs and bandages and a trip to the emergency room. Billy discovers that he can control his parents' conflict by distracting them. Triangulation can thus be an emergent, self-organizing attribute of the chaotic system.

"One potentially maladaptive way children may attempt to cope with marital discord is to actively intervene in interparental conflicts."[26] We know that teenagers are more likely than younger children to insert themselves into adult conflicts.[27] The relief that these youths experience associated with even a short-lived cessation of adult tensions can implicitly reinforce both the child's well-intended efforts to mediate or distract and terribly dysfunctional behaviors ranging from school failure to running away to suicide attempts.

Does Adult Intent Matter?

When one or both parents' emotional spillover triangulates the child into the co-parental conflict, someone inevitably alleges that the act was intentional. Is the mother who talks about Dad in front of her daughter aware that this is hurtful to the child and purposely acting to disparage the man and win the child's alliance? Or is this more simply evidence that she is impulsive and immature and needy, failing to think through the consequences of her actions and to put the child's needs first before her own? This quandary will reappear chapter after chapter throughout this book as we discuss the various dynamics of the conflicted family. It rears its ugly head nowhere as plainly and as often as it does in the literature concerned with alienation (Chapter 15). "Although it may be difficult to

---

26. Patricia K. Kerig, *Triangles in the Family Circle: Effects of Family Structure on Marriage, Parenting, and Child Adjustment*, 9 J. Fam. Psych. 28 (1995).

27. The research in this area is rather vast, but see, for example, Patrick T. Davies & Evan M. Forman, *Children's Patterns of Preserving Emotional Security in the Interparental Subsystem*, 73 Child Dev. 1880 (2002).

contain their negative feelings toward their former spouse, parents have to work actively at putting their children's needs first by supporting the child's relationship with the other parent."[28]

Obviously, the question of intent must be considered on a case-by-case basis. However, research examining the effectiveness of group parent education programs can inform this inquiry in some limited ways.[29] One co-parenting education course, for example, documented significant decreases of triangulating behaviors among never-married, co-parent participants.[30] Another program found in a sample of divorcing adults who completed their program that

> 88% of participants reported that they would definitely avoid bad-mouthing their ex-spouse; 90% reported that they would definitely avoid sending messages via children; 78% reported that they would definitely avoid questioning their children about the private life of the other parent; 90% reported that they would definitely be supportive of their child having a good relationship with both parents; and 91% reported that they would definitely keep children out of arguments.[31]

Taking these outcomes at face value, one might infer that many triangulating behaviors are often the result of ignorance and that the frequency and severity of these destructive behaviors can be avoided or curtailed through education. This conclusion opens the door to consider

---

28. John H. Grych, *Interparental Conflict as a Risk Factor for Child Maladjustment: Implications for the Development of Prevention Programs*, 43 FAM. CT. REV. 97, 101 (2005).

29. Much as the authors have suggested throughout this book, research in this area confronts the same challenges when trying to suggest efficacy to the courts: selection bias, small sample sizes, cultural, socioeconomic, and racial homogeneity, and outcomes that rely largely or entirely on participant self-report. This does not mean that these programs are without important value to parents as many parents do benefit from learning to reflect before responding and the potential risks to their children from subtle and explicit forms of conflict. *See* Cindy Eira Nunes, *Co-Parenting Programs: A Systematic Review and Meta-Analysis*, 70 FAM. RELATIONS 759 (2021).

30. Heidi E. Stolz et al., *Parenting Together: Evaluation of a Parenting Program for Never-Married Parents*, 58 J. DIVORCE & REMARRIAGE 358 (2017).

31. JoAnne Pedro-Carroll, *Assisting Children through Transition: Helping Parents Protect Their Children from the Toxic Effects of Ongoing Conflict in the Aftermath of Divorce*, 39 FAM. CT. REV. 377, 386 (2001).

the potential benefits of instituting universal prophylactic adult education in the basics of child and family development, parenting, and co-parenting.

> The first author (Garber) has long espoused a self-sustaining universal prophylactic parent education program serving precisely these goals. In short:
>
> 1. The U.S. federal government will rescind the automatic dependent child tax deduction.
> 2. A national online program of Continuing Parenting Education (CPE) courses will be instituted. Curricula will include a broad menu of topics in child and family development, parenting, and co-parenting, as well as specialty topics (e.g., special education services, chronic childhood illness, screen time, gifted and talented children).
> 3. Parents who complete a predetermined number of annual CPE credit hours will receive a certificate that will entitle them to earn back the dependent child tax deduction.
> 4. Those parents who fail to complete required CPEs in any given year will not be eligible for the tax deduction.
> 5. The additional tax dollars collected from non-completers will pay for the maintenance and routine updating of the program.
> 6. Those tax dollars will also pay for a long-term study to determine whether children and families who complete annual CPEs are more successful in school, in the workplace, and in relationships.

Is Education Enough?

These promising parent education studies fulfill our hopes and confirmation biases. We want to discover remediable ignorance rather than selfish and intentional acts of malice and abuse. Unfortunately, it may be a mistake to take these studies at face value. Their otherwise impressive statistical findings are contaminated by selection bias and the absence of control group comparisons, by the study respondents' wishes to please and impress those who taught them and administered the surveys, and by the absence of external validity measures.

External validity asks whether research participants actually do what they say they will do. It's not at all uncommon to find that people will say one thing but do another. To illustrate, teenagers asked to describe how they would behave in hypothetical situations seldom actually behave in those ways in real life. Knowing is one thing. Doing can be entirely another.

Detouring and Scapegoating

"Parents may unite to blame their child for their conflict or focus on the child's behavior in an effort to avoid addressing problems in their marriage—a process known as scapegoating."[32] Minuchin referred to this as a "detour."[33] He recognized that many family systems avoid and distract from their conflicts by deflecting attention, for example, to the child's acute academic, medical, or psychological needs. As a result, the adult war is suspended while the child gets surgery or bailed out of jail or is rushed into detox. By giving the adults a shared purpose around which they can join, however briefly, everything else is temporarily forgotten. This may be adaptive in the short run, but it leaves the adult conflict to fester and incentivizes the adults to perpetuate rather than resolve the child's difficulties in the medium and long run: "Detouring couples in particular are hypothesized to contribute to the emotional problems and psychosomatic symptoms in children, who may take on the role of the identified patient in order to maintain homeostasis in the family system."[34]

Chicken or the egg? Does the child act out to try to defuse the parents' conflict or does the parents' conflict cause the child to act out?

Not only is the answer usually unknowable, it is also irrelevant. If relationships were subject to the orderly laws of linear logic, the argument might be worthwhile. Because we know that relationships are complex and chaotic, more like something that Escher would draw than a

32. Grych, *supra* note 28, at 100.
33. *See* Minuchin, *supra* note 4.
34. Kerig, *supra* note 26.

row of dominoes falling in succession, all that we can understand are the dynamics at play. Which came first simply doesn't matter.

> We can see your raised eyebrows and hear your guttural noises of disapproval. Asserting that the primacy of actions is unimportant—never mind unknowable—goes against everything we've learned since our respective blue-haired kindergarten teachers insisted that every upset first be addressed by asking "who started it?"
>
> *Who started it?* may be knowable and is certainly relevant in most areas of the law, in conventional physics, and elsewhere throughout the sciences. For most of us, the question carries a fulfilling sense of righteous vindication and validation. It reassures that there is justice and that good decisions are rewarded and bad decisions are punished. It reminds us that the superordinate systems that we trust to contain us are paying attention.
>
> But *who started it?* becomes a bottomless pit in the context of chaotic family relationships. Your kindergarten teacher might have been better off to focus on a specific behavior in a specific context (e.g., who hit whom first), but the larger relationship dynamic is not amenable to sequential, linear, or logical dissection. Too many simultaneous and interwoven pressures converge from both within and outside of the interaction to ever answer the question. Thus, approaching the child's triangulation as a chicken or egg (or rooster) formulation is misleading and a waste of resources. The better and necessary question is how to change the dynamics that sustain it. "Dynamics," plural. There is seldom or never only one problematic relationship at work.

The Developmental Impact of Triangulation

Some researchers concerned with the impact of one form of triangulation contend that the impact of triangulation is in the eye of the beholder. That is, "if a child sees the advantages of caregiving roles, responsibilities, and relationships, and maintains that view believing in the cultural appropriateness or deriving a sense of self-importance, then those views about the experiences can inform a positive self-evaluation." Any associated positive outcome must, however, be weighed against the reality that "[c]hildren who are charged with taking care of their family members are often robbed of performing their own developmental tasks, as well as activities with their peers."[35]

Remember the coffee cup metaphor? When kids are pulled into others' conflicts, some portion of their finite resources are redirected away from the critical tasks of childhood. When this process is intentional, when the child is able to remain impartial and emotionally disconnected from the conflict, benefits might accrue. Children who serve as peer mediators come away with improved conflict management and self-advocacy skills. Children who serve as their family's language and culture brokers develop superior language and social skills and master the subjects (e.g., healthcare, education, paying bills) that they mediate. But no matter the context or the content that the child is triangulated into, the emotional and developmental costs incurred can be painful and lasting.

Unfortunately, the research concerned with triangulation is muddied by disparate definitions and operationalizations of the term.[36] Relevant data tend to rely on uncorroborated self-report measures. Aware of these failings, we are carefully distinguishing intrafamilial triangulation from the various subsidiary dynamics discussed in the pages that follow.

Despite differences of definition and operationalization and measurement, we find a credible common thread among researchers who conclude that intrafamilial triangulation comes with distinct and lasting developmental costs. For example, "triangulation was associated with increased self-blame and diminished parent-adolescent relations."[37] We know that children drawn into their parents' arguments are more likely

---

35. Judyta Borchet et al., *We Are in This Together: Retrospective Parentification, Sibling Relationships, and Self-Esteem*, 29 J. Child & Fam. Stud. 2982, 2983 (2020).

36. For example: "high-conflict parents often involve and enmesh children in the conflict. This type of behavior is not only damaging to a child's emotional well-being but facilitates loyalty binds in children and strained parent-child relationships." Shely Polak & Michael Saini, *The Complexity of Families Involved in High-Conflict Disputes: A Postseparation Ecological Transactional Framework*, 60 J. Divorce & Remarriage 117, 125 (2018).

37. Fosco & Grych, *supra* note 24.

to experience depression, engage in antisocial acts, and be at odds with their parents.[38]

Clinically (and without the rigors of empirical support) we believe that children triangulated amidst their parents' conflicts often take away at least one misconception that can misdirect their development forever after. This is the belief that anger ends love. Being drawn into the rage and fear and despair that can erupt between warring co-parents and the very loud, very painful end of their marriage not only communicates that love is conditional. This experience powerfully communicates that anger can undo love and therefore must be feared and avoided at all costs. These children grow up unable to tolerate their own and others' necessary and natural experience of anger at tremendous developmental and relationship costs. One facet of this dilemma—the child's chameleon-like adaptation—is discussed in Chapter 8.

Institutionalized Efforts to Prevent Triangulation

The legal system is acutely aware that co-parents sometimes expose and otherwise triangulate their children amidst their adult conflicts. This awareness has sparked a great variety of responses evident across jurisdictions in three predominant forms.

A number of state legislatures have enacted what are commonly called "friendly parent" statutes. These are standards that guide the courts to award primary custody to the parent who is determined to be most likely to support the child's relationship with the other parent.[39] Cooperation and courtesy are certainly good factors to live by in life generally and in custody cases particularly. Although these statutes should, in

---

38. *See* Kay Bradford et al., *When There Is Conflict: Interparental Conflict, Parent-Child Conflict, and Youth Problem Behaviors*, 29 J. Fam. Issues 780 (2008).

39. As of 2011, 32 states had some version of the "friendly parent" factor or statute. Interview with M. Bud (Oct. 14, 2020). This concept has its legitimate critics just as presumptions of joint physical custody raise concerns with power imbalances and perception over facts in custody trials. *See* Elisabeth Godbout et al., *Positions Taken by Judges and Custody Experts on Issues Relating to the Best Interests of Children in Custody Disputes in Quebec*, 29 Int'l J.L. Pol'y & Fam. 272 (2015); Richard A. Warshak, *Securing Children's Best Interests While Resisting the Lure of Simple Solutions*, 56 J. Div. & Remarriage 57 (2015).

theory, work against triangulation at least as long as the family remains under the microscope imposed by the family courts, they can also work against Parent A's efforts to protect his child when Parent B is abusive or neglectful.[40] With this in mind, some states have modified their friendly parent language. For example, the Colorado statute relies in relevant part upon

> [t]he ability of the parties to encourage the sharing of love, affection, and contact between the child and the other party; except that, if the court determines that a party is acting to protect the child from witnessing domestic violence or from being a victim of child abuse or neglect or domestic violence, the party's protective actions shall not be considered with respect to this factor.[41]

Many jurisdictions across the English-speaking world now require divorcing parents to participate in some form of co-parenting education. Although these programs are notoriously too little and too late, their curricula typically include education about the damaging effects of triangulation and its subsidiary dynamics.[42]

Finally, many jurisdictions have either recommended or mandated that parenting plans include specific language prohibiting parents and their allies from exposing or engaging children in their conflicts. For example, the default parenting plan template created by the state of New Hampshire includes the following language: "Each parent shall promote a healthy, beneficial relationship between the child(ren) and the other parent and shall not demean or speak out negatively in any

---

40. This concept has its critics. One parent's friendly can be another parent's gaslighting. As always, nuance matters. "Children are thought to do better when allowed or encouraged to maintain a close relationship with both parents. Therefore, custody should be awarded to the parent most likely to foster the child's relationship with the other parent. On close examination, however, the friendly parent concept presents a dangerous paradox. It works against the interests of children. The normal functioning of the courts is undermined." Margaret K. Dore, *The "Friendly Parent" Concept: A Flawed Factor for Child Custody*, 6 Loy. J. Pub. Int. L. 41, 56 (2004).

41. Colo. Rev. Stat. § 14-10-124(1.5)(a)(VI).

42. David G. Schramm & Emily H. Becher, *Common Practices for Divorce Education*, 69 Fam. Rel. 543 (2020); Stolz et al., *supra* note 30.

manner that would damage the relationship between either parent and the child(ren)."[43] Even more explicitly, a child-centered family law organization in Toronto, Canada, recommends this language: "We will keep our children out of our conflict. We will not ask them to pick sides, carry messages, or hear our possible complaints about the other parent."[44]

On balance, we read these data as supporting our focus on the value and integrity of hierarchically nested systems, from the individual to the dyad, to family and FAMILY and community.[45] The very limited literature on triangulation within the family system and between the family system and the allied (e.g., peer group mediators) or superordinate (e.g., culture brokers) systems demonstrates time and again that the dynamic may serve the survival needs of the system at a potentially grave emotional cost to the child. Like a wild animal caught in an inhumane trap, some systems are willing to sacrifice a part in order to save the larger whole.

---

43. State of New Hampshire Judicial Branch, Parenting Plan, https://www.courts.state.nh.us/forms/nhjb-2064-f.pdf (current as of Aug. 7, 2018).

44. Association of Family and Conciliation Courts, Ontario Chapter, Parenting Plan Template, https://afccontario.ca/wp-content/uploads/2020/01/AFCC-O-Parenting-Plan-Template-Jan-17-2020.docx (current as of Jan. 2020).

45. Urie Bronfenbrenner, *Toward an Experimental Ecology of Human Development*, 32 Am. Psych. 513 (1977).

Chapter 8
The Chameleon Child

"Q: If you had a wish for yourself and your family, what would your wish be?
Frances (age 12): [That] there was two of me, then I could be with mum and I could be with dad at the same time and I could see my friends."[1]

"[Alienating parents] withdraw love and affection when the child talks positively about the [targeted parent] . . . leading the child to fully and openly reject the [targeted parent], or to compartmentalize their feelings and show one 'face' to the [alienating parent] and another to the [targeted parent]."[2]

Definition:	Like the lizard of the same name, the chameleon child copes with the pressures of having been triangulated amidst her parents' conflict by changing her emotional colors to earn acceptance, affection, and attention in each of two (or more) disparate and warring emotional environments.[3]

1. Carol Smart, *From Children's Shoes to Children's Voices*, 40 Fam. Ct. Rev. 307, 316 (2002).
2. Jennifer J. Harman et al., *Parental Alienating Behaviors: An Unacknowledged Form of Family Violence*, 144 Psych. Bull. 1275, 1279 (2018).
3. Benjamin D. Garber, *The Chameleon Child: Children as Actors in the High Conflict Divorce Drama*, 11 J. Child Custody 1 (2014).

Reasonable precautions:	The chameleon child has seen conflict end love and therefore fears that conflict will cost her one or both parents' love. These children must be reassured in word and in deed that their parents' love is for them unconditional even if their love for one another was not. This often requires cognitive behavioral interventions intended to help these children better recognize and find healthy ways to express their strong emotions.
What to look for:	Children who say and do what they believe the immediate audience wants to hear and see. Their presentations prove to be contradictory when their listeners compare notes but, in the absence of healthy communications, these differences fuel adult confirmation bias and exacerbate conflict.
Caution:	When Parent A reports that Sally said one thing and Parent B reports that Sally said the opposite, both may be true. This isn't lying. It's coping.
How to respond to the adults:	The chameleon child is adapting to her experience of disparate and warring caregiving environments. Thus, the best response is to maximize consistency and communication between parents. Even when the conflicts persist, co-parenting interventions intended to improve caregiving structures within and between homes may help.
How to respond to the child:	Healthy development demands the acceptance and learned ability to express the full range of emotional experience. Chameleon children need to experience (not simply to understand) love as unconditional. They often need healthy models and direct instruction concerned with identifying and expressing strong feelings.
Implications for forensic process:	Professionals must be hypervigilant for the effects of relationship context, proximity, and recency on children's words, actions, and expressed emotions, taking care not to allow children's chameleon-like words and actions to fuel parents' confirmation biases.

Adaptation Means Survival

Adaptation is the evolutionary force that Darwin realized had created the great variety of finch species catalogued years earlier by his mentor, Audubon. It is exactly the same force at work within the family system—albeit prompting behavior change within generations rather than genetic changes across generations—thereby generating the variety of family dynamics catalogued in this volume.

Adaptation means adjusting behavior to fit into the proximal environment in order to obtain critical resources. More than just food, clothing, and shelter, we know that primates are very highly motivated to adapt in order to obtain emotional nurturance (Chapter 5).[4]

Every child works to balance two simultaneous and competing needs: the need for affiliation experienced via parental attention, affection, and acceptance, and the need to separate and grow toward autonomy. The strength of these competing needs varies over time and circumstance, creating at best a seesaw-like tension that alternates between dueling messages: "hold me tight" and "let me go."[5]

When early parent-child relationships are secure—that is, when the child's experience of caregiving is calm, consistent, and dependable and caregivers are sensitive and responsive to the child's needs—children feel confident in the knowledge that they can push off from that secure base to explore and return to be comforted and refueled. Gradually moving further and further away from Mom and Dad, the child practices autonomy incrementally, learning first to carry love and affection around in the form of a teddy bear or blanky (i.e., transitional objects), then finding affection and acceptance among peers (i.e., transitional affiliations), and finally internalizing these critical resources so as to be able to live apart and develop lasting and mature adult bonds.[6]

---

4. Harry F. Harlow et al., *Total Social Isolation in Monkeys*, 54 Proc. Nat'l Acad. Sci. U.S. 90 (1965), https://www.ncbi.nlm.nih.gov/pmc/articles/PMC285801/pdf/pnas00159-0105.pdf.

5. Benjamin D. Garber, Holding Tight/Letting Go: Raising Healthy Kids in Anxious Times (2016), https://www.unhookedmedia.com/stock/holding-tight-letting-go.

6. Transitional objects and transitional affiliations are discussed in the context of high-conflict divorce in Benjamin D. Garber & Dana E. Prescott, *On the Value of Teddy Bears*

When those same early parent-child relationships are insecure—that is, when experience teaches a child that emotional nurturance is contingent and that caregivers can't be relied upon to read and respond to his needs—that seesaw tension between hold-me-tight and let-me-go is thrown out of balance. Behaviors must be adapted and needs compromised in the interest of survival. The child has to find some way to maintain his precious emotional fuel. Some withdraw into the very primitive helplessness of depression. Some lash out in rage and defiance. Some dissociate in order to protect themselves from trauma. And some have the good fortune to find need fulfillment elsewhere, from a grandparent or nanny or teacher or even a therapist. "One of the most valuable insights of the systemic perspective is that children's and parents' problem behaviors often serve a function in the family system—they arise in response to patterns of relationship within the family and represent understandable, if misguided, attempts at adaptation."[7]

Fortunately, most of us struggle through these relationship challenges relatively unscarred. Innate human resilience, the child's capacity for adaptation, the malleability of the attachment subsystem, and most parents' ability to ultimately put their children's needs first before their own carry us through. The people who consume 90 percent of family law professionals' time actually represent less than 10 percent among divorcing parents. These are the minority of family systems in which healthy adaptation fails to compensate the child for his parents' selfish, destructive choices.

We don't yet know which variables predict how any given child will manage these intense relationship pressures. Age (likely as a quantifiable

---

and Barbie Dolls: The Place of Children's Transitional Objects in Family Law, 49 Sw. L. Rev. 189 (2020), and in Benjamin D. Garber, *For the Love of Fluffy: Respecting, Protecting, and Empowering Transitional Objects in the Context of High Conflict Divorce*, 60(7) J. Divorce & Remarriage 552 (2019).

7. Patricia K. Kerig & Julie A. Swanson, *Ties That Bind: Triangulation, Boundary Dissolution, and the Effects of Interparental Conflict on Child Development*, *in* Strengthening Couple Relationships for Optimal Child Development: Lessons from Research and Intervention 59 (Mark S. Shulz et al. eds., 2010).

proxy for emotional maturity) matters.[8] Older children simply have more power, control, and access to resources than younger children. We also know that the child's social ecology is relevant: isolation works against adaptation. Conversely, the breadth of a child's social relatedness across multiple allied systems is associated with resilience and healthier outcomes. A child who has siblings, who feels connected to his neighborhood, church, and school, who belongs to clubs and plays on teams, or who spends time with extended family is more likely to adapt to the stresses of family conflict than a child who does not.

When the triangulated child's safety net fails, his persistent need for emotional fuel forces more extreme outcomes. This chapter describes the chameleon child, the son or daughter who resolves the painful tensions of the parents' war and the loyalty bind that makes loving one a betrayal of the other by constantly changing her emotional colors to suit the proximal relationship. Becoming chameleon-like is a brilliant adaptation in the short run. Like the lizard of the same name, the effect is to avoid predation. Agreeing with Mom when you're with Mom and agreeing with Dad when you're with Dad wins each parent's time and attention, even if it fuels the adult conflict and costs the child the opportunity to develop his own unique identity. To illustrate:

> They learned to please by becoming nonpersons by making no demands. These children usually presented as good, conforming and patient. They were seldom identified as having any problems or causing any trouble. Their hallmark was their constriction of affect. Some lacked spontaneity, seemed vacant, joyless, and withdrawn to the point of looking mildly but chronically depressed. They were not only unexpressive of their feelings, they appeared walled off from access to their emotional life.[9]

---

8. "[C]hildren in high-conflict divorces who were younger than nine years old felt torn in their loyalty to each parent, but . . . nine- to twelve-year-olds tended to ally with one parent or the other, perhaps as a way of resolving the loyalty conflict." John H. Grych, *Interparental Conflict as a Risk Factor for Child Maladjustment: Implications for the Development of Prevention Programs*, 43 Fam. Ct. Rev. 97, 100 (2005).

9. Janet R. Johnston et al., *Latency Children in Post-Separation and Divorce Disputes*, 24 J. Am. Acad. Child Psychiatry 571 (1985).

Dynamics, Not Diagnoses

We use the shorthand "chameleon child" and "triangulated child" and "polarized child" and a handful of other facile labels in an effort to communicate clearly and concisely. It's important to keep in mind that each of these references intends to capture a snapshot taken from our orbiting, infinitely powerful telescope focused not on the individual, but on the family system. Mistaking any of these labels for diagnoses akin to those catalogued in the Diagnostic and Statistical Manual (DSM) is like mistaking a single frame for the entire movie. The child's chameleon-like adaptation may work for him today given his experience of today's many confluent and interwoven social and emotional pressures, but that can change tomorrow. Adaptation is by definition fluid and responsive. As much as this fact confounds our natural wish to pin things down and label them once and for all, as clinicians and family law professionals we rely on the system's malleability in order to produce change.

The Chameleon Effect

Adapting words and feelings to the proximal emotional environment is not at all unique to children whose parents are engaged in high-conflict litigation. It's an entirely natural process observed universally. Mammalian (and likely other) brains are hardwired to spontaneously adapt through imitation.[10] This spontaneous, unconscious phenomenon has been recognized for decades: "The *chameleon effect* refers to nonconscious mimicry of the postures, mannerisms, facial expressions, and other behaviors of one's interaction partners, such that one's behavior passively and unintentionally changes to match that of others in one's current social environment."[11]

---

10. Anthropologists suggest that nonconscious mimicry creates affiliation, and that affiliation can be expressed through nonconscious mimicry, with all the attendant social and evolutionary benefits. *See* Jessica L. Lakin et al., *The Chameleon Effect as Social Glue: Evidence for the Evolutionary Significance of Nonconscious Mimicry*, 27 J. Nonverbal Behav. 145 (2003).

11. Tanya L. Chartrand & John A. Bargh, *The Chameleon Effect: The Perception-Behavior Link and Social Interaction*, 76 J. Personality & Soc. Psych. 893 (1999).

Across species, adopting the behaviors and attitudes of a dominant partner or the proximal group is a very common and successful means of winning social acceptance, signaling affiliation, and maximizing survival in the here and now. Adopting the mannerisms, attitudes, and speech patterns of the social group can reduce conflict and facilitate transitions. Mimicry may be nowhere more obviously at work than in adolescence when wearing the right clothes, adopting the right postures, using the right language, and immersing in the right media (among many other variables) defines "cool" and means acceptance.[12]

But mimicry can be maladaptive in the long term. Wearing a social mask can get in the way of discovering who you really are. When chameleon-like mimicry compromises a child's opportunity to discover and define an identity, the developmental costs of the short-term coping mechanism can be dramatic.[13] For example, children coping with the death of a parent "may become chameleons, looking for clues and models of behavior in their new environments to make and sustain connections. In the process, they may struggle to develop a coherent sense of self."[14]

The Chameleon Effect and High-Conflict Divorce

Emotionally mature adults navigate their conflicts without compromising their children's security. They act to insulate and reassure their kids largely by putting their own needs second to those of the child. In this healthy environment, the adults manage their relationship without

12. Mimicry is associated with the functioning of mirror neurons, brain structures that facilitate the comprehension of action. Mirror neuron deficiencies are theoretically associated with autistic spectrum disorders. Marco Iacoboni & Mirella Dapretto, *The Mirror Neuron System and the Consequences of Its Dysfunction*, 7 Nature Revs. Neuroscience 942 (2006).

13. Of all of the peer-reviewed research and young adult novels written on this subject, we suggest that the most apt is Dr. Seuss's "The Star-Bellied Sneetches" wherein mimicry goes awry, "until neither the Plain nor the Star-Bellies knew whether this one was that one . . . or that one was this one . . . or which one was what one . . . or what one was who." Dr. Seuss, The Sneetches and Other Stories (1961).

14. Allison Werner-Lin et al., *There's No Place Like Home: Preparing Children for Geographical and Relational Attachment Disruptions Following Parental Death to Cancer*, 38 Clinical Soc. Work J. 132, 134 (2010).

triangulating the child, thereby never requiring the child to divert her finite emotional energies away from the healthy tasks of development.

By contrast, parents who triangulate their children amidst their adult conflict are selfishly putting their own needs first. This child is forced to find some way to cope, diverting those same finite energies to manage the family's dynamics. Drawn into the fray, forced to become the rope in the parents' tug-of-war, and observing that anger ends love, many of these children grow up believing that their own anger will elicit rejection and abandonment and rage and must therefore be avoided at all costs. These children learn that love means doing and saying what the proximal adult wants to hear and see. Thus, these children "compartmentalize their feelings and show one 'face' to [one parent] and another to the [other parent]."[15] As one child stated:

> You sort of change, depending what house you're at. I don't know about other people, but I find that I'm a different person at . . . a different house. 'Cause the different environment and . . . my parents react differently to different things. It is difficult to explain. So I adapt to my environment, I suppose.[16]

Consequences of the Child's Chameleon-Like Adaptation

The immediate goal of the child's chameleon-like adaptive strategy is affiliation, acceptance, affection and emotional nurturance, and need fulfillment. These outcomes are rewarding, thus strongly motivating the child to do more of the same. But this success often comes at a very substantial cost.

Recall the constant tension between hold-me-tight and let-me-go that defines the healthy family's gradual movement toward launching the

---

15. Harman et al., *supra* note 3. "Children in high conflict situations are faced with the overwhelming demand of having to adapt between their warring caregivers, needing to change their emotional presentation and responses depending on their caregiving environment." Shely Polak & Mike Saini, *Children Resisting Contact with a Parent Postseparation: Assessing This Phenomenon Using an Ecological Systems Framework*, 56 J. Divorce & Remarriage 220 (2015).

16. Quoting a 16-year-old girl from research interviews concerned with her experience of divorce. Smart, *supra* note 2, at 312.

child off into autonomy. When that seesaw balance is thrown off-center by adult conflict and the scarcity or contingency of emotional fuel, the chameleon child overinvests in hold-me-tight in the belief that let-me-go means conflict and conflict, in this child's experience, means rejection, abandonment, and the end of love.

Healthy development requires conflict. Children test limits. Healthy parents respond firmly, calmly, clearly, and consistently. Conflict is safe within the confidence of noncontingent love. This is how the radius of the child's life centered around the parents gradually expands until he finally breaks free of their gravity to go off on his own.[17]

But when conflict threatens loss, the costs of the child's natural let-me-go limit-testing can become intolerable. Thus, the chameleon child becomes a model of compliance in each home, eagerly anticipating and validating each parent's perspective but never getting the opportunity to discover his own. As an adult, this child is likely to be incredibly empathic and attuned to others but needy and empty and profoundly unhappy. Further:

> Children who exhibit complete changes of behavior and interests from one parent's home to the other's are in trouble. They become over-adaptive. They are extremely vulnerable to peer pressure because their primary fears are rejection and abandonment. If they happen to be in the company of thugs, they act as thugs act. If they associate with a cult, they become true believers. If their peers use drugs or alcohol or join gangs, so will they. They do not develop a sense of self or an internal set of values.[18]

How and how much a chameleon child's identity is compromised is mitigated by a number of variables, most notably her emotional maturity. Emotional maturity—the child's emerging ability to understand and regulate her own affective states—is grossly approximated by reference to

---

17. Sabrina Keopke & Jaap J.A. Denissen, *Dynamics of Identity Development and Separation-Individuation in Parent-Child Relationships during Adolescence and Emerging Adulthood—A Conceptual Integration*, 32 Developmental Rev. 67 (2012).

18. Anne Kass, *Chameleon Kids*, http://www.alllaw.com/articles/family/child_custody/article9.asp (accessed Nov. 23, 2010) (article removed).

age. Thus, the longer a child has lived in a healthy family system before becoming triangulated amidst her parents' conflict, the more social and emotional resources she is likely to have to cope when she becomes triangulated and the less vulnerable she is to compromising her identity.[19] At the extreme of older adolescence, for example, some children can escape the family's destructive dynamics by overinvesting in otherwise expectable peer relationships. At the other extreme of age, however, the young child has little or no experience apart from his parents' war and few emotional resources outside of the home. The long-term developmental impact of chameleon-like adaptation on this child can be deeply pathological.

Confirmation Bias and the Chameleon Child

This is the perfect storm of distorted needs and dynamics. The child says what he believes the parent wants to hear in order to avoid rejection and get his most basic emotional needs fulfilled. The overwhelmed, financially drained, grieving, angry, and scared parent needs to feel validated and vindicated in his own and in the public's eyes. This parent's coffee mug is full of emotion, leaving room for just a drop or two of clear thinking and healthy perspective. Not only is he naturally inclined to see the world in black and white terms, but the legal system reinforces this view. His lawyer demands that he produce evidence that can be used to win his case.

Riddle me this: What's more powerful than a thread of cryptic text messages, an album of loving photographs, and a 50-page sheaf of e-mail communications? The answer: A child who says, "I hate her!"[20]

---

19. *See* Paul R. Amato, *Life-Span Adjustment of Children to Their Parents' Divorce*, 4 Future Child. 143 (1994); *see also* Christy Kleinsorge & Lynne M. Covitz, *Impact of Divorce on Children: Developmental Considerations*, 33 Pediatrics Rev. 147 (2012). By analogy, think of child development like the construction of a skyscraper. A building with a solid foundation is far more likely to weather a storm than a building with a flaw in its cornerstone.

20. "The myside bias predicts that adversaries will routinely construe the factual situation as supportive of their own position." Keith E. Stanovich, *Myside Bias, Rational Thinking, and Intelligence*, 22 Current Directions Psych. Sci. 259 (2013).

The parent's confirmation bias and the child's chameleon-like adaptation together create a powerful self-affirming feedback loop. Need fuels need round and round until the system has generated its own reality that is artificially validated by those vested in believing it and often goes unchecked by others who stand outside the system and outside the emotion trying to grasp some objective larger truth.[21]

In this self-serving mindset, Mom hears Billy's agreement that Daddy is a jerk as validation of her own beliefs and as selfish vindication of her decision to divorce him. She has no perspective on the child's desperate need to maintain her love and caring, a need that can drive him to say and do what she herself desperately needs to hear. For his part, Billy sees Mom's nurturing, supportive, us-against-them response to his statement as reinforcing, so he says more.

Blinded by their own needs to the child's desperate efforts to cope with the pressures inherent in his triangulated position, Mom and Dad implicitly ask leading questions and tacitly communicate their emotional positions eliciting further chameleon-like validations. A self-affirming feedback loop is created within each parent-child dyad whereby the child's "honesty" and "bravery" are rewarded by a parent who finds the child's words and actions rewarding, thereby inviting the child's further admissions and disclosures and revelations.

When the parent takes the data to lawyers and siloed therapists and overworked child protective service professionals, the spiral of bias escalates.[22] Eventually, the molehill that was the child's innocent effort to win an overwhelmed parent's love becomes a mountain that separates litigating parents. The court is once again faced with two, diametrically opposed, and mutually exclusive stories and proceeds in its linear logic to conclude that only one can be true and we must therefore divine who is

21. See our discussion of the *etic* versus the *emic* in Chapter 18.

22. "Siloed" systems are insular and biased. Applying family systems concepts at this superordinate level of inquiry, one might describe a siloed therapist as enmeshed with the patient. For example: "the Center for Creative Arts and Play Therapy declined [to accept as patients] the [C]hildren as they did not wish to be enmeshed with Mother's continuing campaign of false allegations of sexual and physical abuse against Father." N.D.J. v. D.E.J., 237 A.3d 463, 2020 WL 2537216, at *2 (Pa. Super. Ct. May 19, 2020).

telling the truth and who is lying, who is the better parent, and on that basis, how parental rights should be allocated.[23]

Interviewing and the Chameleon Child

The child who demonstrates chameleon-like behaviors poses two specific challenges for the forensic family evaluator. These concern recency and proximity effects and rapport. Because no one can know in advance how any particular child is coping with her family dynamics, it's impingent on every evaluator to take every reasonable step to minimize these confounds.

1. **Recency and proximity effects.** The chameleon child is socially hypervigilant. She has learned to read her relationship ecology more easily and clearly than you are reading these words. In her experience, context is identity. This means that every professional tasked to interview a child must take into account where that child woke up on the morning of the interview, who drove the child to the interview, how the child understands the interview process, how the child understands the limitations of privacy or confidentiality, whether the child believes that the accompanying parent is nearby and listening in, and what the child anticipates about the drive home. These parameters have been described as the bookends of the interview.[24] Together, they constitute the recency and proximity variables that risk contaminating any child's presentation in interview, but none more so than the chameleon child:

> Like a chameleon, the child who has recently spent several consecutive days in mom's care is reasonably expected to have adapted to that environment, arriving for interview with all of the tensions and pressures, beliefs and emotions that allow her

---

23. "[R]esponding differently to the social environments as provided by each parent, out of the child's need to adapt, and thus inadvertently escalating conflict when parents misinterpret the child's contextualized words and behavior." Jean Mercer, *Are Intensive Parental Alienation Treatments Effective and Safe for Children and Adolescents?*, 16 J. Child Custody 67, 78 (2019).

24. David A. Martindale, Allegations of Alienation or Child Sexual Abuse in Custody Evaluations, Presentation at Palo Alto University, Co-Sponsored by CONCEPT Professional Training and Palo Alto University (June 17, 2019).

> to survive in that home. Because her presentation may be quite different following a period of time spent in dad's care . . . the interviewer must carefully document and try to balance these effects.[25]

This means much more than simply recording who drove a child to interview on a particular morning. It means designing each assessment protocol so as to minimize and mitigate recency and proximity effects. At the least, we know that one interview is never enough.[26] Optimally, child interviews and observations are balanced in a manner that allows one to draw inferences about how a child's presentation varies as a function of recency and proximity with each caregiver.[27]

2. **Rapport?** Chameleon kids are a pleasure to engage. They tend to be models of compliance and precocious social skills. Experience has taught them to read the room and to respond in kind. This skill has helped them navigate their powerful family dynamics, so why would they do anything differently with you?

In fact, your pleasure interviewing a child may be a clue.[28] We should expect most children to have some degree of anxiety and avoidance in

---

25. Benjamin D. Garber, The Voice of the Child in High Conflict Divorce: Understanding and Minimizing Contextual, Systemic, and Process Confounds (2012).

26. "[O]ne observation session alone is not sufficient in helping to make valid inferences about the general style of interactional behavior in families. . . . On the other hand, it is perhaps unrealistic and overly costly to routinely carry out the numerous observational sessions . . . . [T]here is good rationale for conducting a minimum of two 45- to 60-minute observation sessions with each parent." Daniel J. Hynan, *Parent-Child Observations in Custody Evaluations*, 41 Fam. Ct. Rev. 214, 219 (2003). "When structuring interviews, evaluators shall consider a range of hypotheses and base their interview strategies on published research addressing the effects upon children's responses of various forms of questioning. Evaluators shall have knowledge of and shall consider the factors that have been found to strongly affect children's capacities as witnesses." Association of Family and Conciliation Courts, Model Standards of Practice for Child Custody Evaluation 9.1 (2006).

27. Consider the forensic family evaluation protocol recommended by Benjamin D. Garber, *Exploring a Process-Oriented Forensic Family Observation Protocol*, 54 Fam. Ct. Rev. 261 (2016).

28. Of course, precocious social skills can be a clue to other non-mutually exclusive dynamics and conditions, as well.

forensic interview. The child who manages this process glibly with precocious social skills is subtly communicating something about her experience with adults. For example, the six-year-old who first greets you with a hearty handshake, excellent eye contact, and compliments is not that way because you're such an excellent interviewer. Don't trip over your ego here. Check your own anxiety and your selfish need for validation at the door. This is the trap that the parents fell into. Your job is to help the child feel comfortable while you look in from outside the relationship, looking down from that infinitely powerful telescope, trying to understand who she is and what she needs and how she is trying to get it.

Relying on a structured interview process can help to reduce your anxiety, minimize the risk of leading questions, and allow you an opportunity to consider apples-to-apples comparisons between children you've interviewed using the same protocol.[29] Recording the interview may also help, allowing you (and subsequently the court) to look back on both the child's answers and her interpersonal presentation from outside of the immediate pressures of the interaction.[30]

Are Chameleon-Like Behaviors Evidence of Alienation?

Not necessarily.

Some have suggested that a child's context-dependent presentation is evidence of other destructive family system dynamics. For example: "Another indicator of alienation is a child who shows affection to the target parent when the other parent is absent but acts indifferently or defiantly to the target when in the presence of the other parent. Such an 'inconsistent chameleon' quality is a diagnostic hallmark of [alienation]."[31] We disagree. This is binary thinking. Although chameleon-like responses can

29. "Unfortunately, researchers have repeatedly shown that these research-based and expert-endorsed recommendations are widely proclaimed but seldom followed." Michael E. Lamb et al., *A Structured Forensic Interview Protocol Improves the Quality and Informativeness of Investigative Interviews with Children: A Review of Research Using the NICHD Investigative Interview Protocol*, 31 Child Abuse & Neglect 1201, 1203 (2007).

30. Orly Bertel, *Let's Go to the Videotape: Why the Forensic Interviews of Children in Child Protective Cases Should Be Video Recorded*, 50 Fam. Ct. Rev. 344 (2012).

31. Chaim Steinberger, *Father? What Father? Parental Alienation and Its Effect on Children*, 38 N.Y. St. B.A. Fam. L. Rev. 10, 21 (2006).

be associated with the child's exposure to Parent A's unwarranted expression of negative words, actions, and/or emotions about Parent B (i.e., alienation as discussed in Chapter 15), these behaviors can also occur in the context of a host of other dynamics. For example, a parentified child (Chapter 12), invested in caring for a parent's well-being, may be prone to chameleon-like responses even in the absence of alienation. Thus, to assert that the chameleon child has necessarily been exposed to alienation or to consider it a manifestation of the dynamic is akin to saying that seeing stripes is evidence that a zebra is in the room. It may be true, but it's just as likely to be a tiger or a skunk.

The Chameleon Child and Custody Determinations

Dr. Brilliant recognizes that nine-year-old Jimmy's reality is very flexible. He claimed to be scared of whichever parent was absent on each of four different occasions across the course of a family system evaluation. He simultaneously proved to be caring and engaged, compliant, and fun with whichever parent was present. Dr. Brilliant wondered if there were two Jimmys, one allied with Mom and the other allied with Dad.

Gently confronted about the inconsistency, the child tried to sidestep the issue. He could offer no insight into his own labile, context-dependent emotional reactions.

Do these observations in and of themselves bear on if and how Dr. Brilliant should advise the court about the future allocation of the parents' rights and responsibilities? No; however, the data should prompt the evaluator to consider two hypotheses: (1) the parents have triangulated Jimmy, exposing and possibly even enlisting him to participate in their conflict, and (2) despite Jimmy's social skills, he may be quite emotionally immature.[32] If supported by additional data, the former would call

32. "He or she may be particularly verbally or socially precocious (and may have been groomed so as to develop these attributes), but is likely to be far less emotionally mature. The resulting developmental decalage is fertile ground in which to develop anxiety, depression, anger, and in which to plant the seeds of later character pathology." Benjamin D. Garber, *Parental Alienation and the Dynamics of the Enmeshed Parent-Child Dyad: Adultification, Parentification, and Infantilization*, 49 Fam. Ct. Rev. 326 (2011) (citations omitted).

for adult education and court-ordered strictures intended to insulate the child from adult matters. The latter observation may be reason to suggest that Jimmy commence or continue in a systemically informed individual psychotherapy[33] with the goals of shoring up interpersonal boundaries, helping him to identify and feel confident expressing his own thoughts and feelings, giving him a "port in the storm" relationship outside the fray, and monitoring the child's risk of becoming polarized between and/or further enmeshed within the family dynamics.

33. For example, compliant with the Association of Family and Conciliation Courts, Guidelines for Court-Involved Therapy 1.2(d) (2017).

Chapter 9
The Polarized Child

"The relentless conflict between the parents has established an unsafe environment for the children. In order to find a place of safety and to get relief from the cognitive dissonance, which arises from trying to love people who are at war, the children have aligned with one parent and have rejected the other."[1]

"It is quite understandable why H. might have feelings of insecurity. He has stated that he was on his 'mother's team' and that his father, B.B.[,] and A.B. are on a different team. He has internalized that he has to make a choice . . . If he chooses such a relationship the implication is that he will lose his relationship with his mother."[2]

Definition:	The polarized child is aligned with Parent A and resists and/or refuses contact with Parent B. The term is descriptive, without any implication of causation or responsibility.
Reasonable precautions:	Beware that confirmation bias, zealous advocacy, and the adversarial legal system can exacerbate and reify the child's polarized position. Only a comprehensive assessment of the child's development, relationships, needs, and abilities in the context of the larger family dynamics can begin to untangle the unique confluence of relationship pressures and practical exigencies responsible for any particular child's polarized position.

1. P.L.M. v. L.J., [2008] 54 R.F.L. 6th 126 para. 132, http://canlii.ca/t/1zkcg.
2. H.B. v. M.B., [2018] O.N.C.J. 916 para. 164, http://canlii.ca/t/hwwhs.

What to look for:	The polarized child acts and speaks as if the adult conflict is all black and white. She has created this artificially binary position by aligning with one parent and rejecting the other. Family court professionals must look beneath this veneer for inevitable shades of gray evident as mixed feelings about each of the parents, always aware that the child's rejection of Parent B may be based at least in part on valid safety concerns.
How to respond to the adults:	Therapeutic interventions and court orders must singularly emphasize the child's need and right to enjoy a healthy relationship with both parents. Helping parents to separate their feelings about the other adult from the child's feelings about that parent is often part of this process.
How to respond to the child:	A child's polarized position is seldom a response to one cause.[3] Instead, numerous mutually compatible relationship pressures and practical considerations must be carefully assessed in order to fully understand and thus prescribe the unique combination of interventions best suited to help any given child (re-)establish healthy relationships with both (all) caregivers.
Implications for custody-related decisions:	Approaching a child's polarized position within her parents' conflict as necessarily due to competing and mutually exclusive binary causes is to do harm. The polarized child's needs can only be served by understanding and responding to the complex and chaotic confluence of factors compromising her best interests. In some such cases, child custody evaluations and related litigation should be postponed until efforts to repair the polarized dynamics have been tried.

3. "[J]ust because children resist contact with one parent does not necessarily mean that they are alienated . . . . There may be a number of reasons as to why a child is resisting contact, all of which must be carefully considered." M.L.S. v. N.E.D., [2017] S.K.Q.B. 183 para. 181, http://canlii.ca/t/h4pqj.

Not All Molehills Are Mountains

Imagine a family of three that has always functioned well but has recently been disrupted by an apparent alliance between Mother and daughter. Dad catches the pair engaged in secretive, whispered conversations. He notices Mom giving the child unexpected gifts hidden in brown paper bags. He's startled to discover the pair giggling together behind a locked door.

In a healthy family system, Mother takes Father aside to alert him that their 12-year-old began her first period. The child is horrified and embarrassed and excited and needs a lot of coaching, reassurance, and supplies. Relieved, proud, and a bit uncomfortable, Dad offers his support but agrees not to talk about it until their daughter brings it up. All is well and the family resumes its healthy development.

In a conflicted family system, adult biases and beliefs color perceptions and compromise communications. Otherwise innocuous events are distorted by confirmation bias such that relationship molehills quickly become mountains of conflict. If these hypothetical parents were living apart and their daughter began to resist seeing her father once a month without explanation, Dad might allege that Mom is trying to undermine the father-daughter relationship. Mom might respond by alleging that their daughter's resistance was evidence of Dad's insensitivity or misbehavior, a conclusion that not coincidentally validates her own painful choice to leave the marriage. For some families, this is all that it takes to begin filing motions, making reports to child protective services, and obtaining ex parte protection orders.

Polarized Fractals?

The polarized child is a natural and expectable byproduct of the conflicted family system,[4] which itself is the natural and expectable

4. Referring to "reluctant, recalcitrant, and polarized parents." Janet R. Johnston et al., *Therapeutic Work with Alienated Children and Their Families*, 39 Fam. Ct. Rev. 316, 316 (2001).

byproduct of zealous advocates[5] whose polarized positions are, in turn, the natural and expectable byproducts of our adversarial court system.[6] Polarization within the family system will simultaneously spill over into allied systems, tearing neighborhoods and communities and extended families apart. Everyone involved in and connected to the polarized family across allied and superordinate systems—including you, the well-intended, skilled family law professional—is vulnerable to the either/or tug-of-war of the polarized family system. "Polarization between the mother's camp and the father's camp became the norm rather than the exception for family, friends and professionals. People saw things from the perspective of the camp which with they were aligned."[7]

This is not to say that any one system causes the polarization of any other. This is not dominoes falling in a row or even a contagion that can be traced back to its source. This is the emergent and chaotic nature of systems, resonating together in response to relationship pressures. "Being caught in the middle of a parental disagreement places youths in a difficult position in which they may feel pressure to choose between their parents. Choosing to side with one parent may harm their relationship with the other, may lead to resentment of their parent ally . . . ."[8]

Confirmation bias was first introduced in Chapter 4. Recall that confirmation bias is the very human predisposition to perceive what you

---

5. Referring to "polarizing professionals, including overly enmeshed counsel and mental health professionals." John-Paul E. Boyd, Canadian Research Institute for Law and the Family, Alienated Children in Family Law Disputes in British Columbia (2015) (2015 CanLIIDocs 321), http://canlii.ca/t/2863 (last visited July 24, 2021).

6. "Courts and family law professionals need to move beyond polarized and simplistic analyses that not only fail to capture the richness and subtlety of these cases but also mirror the inflexible, 'all or nothing' thinking of alienated children and their parents." Barbara J. Fidler & Peggie Ward, *Clinical Decision-Making in Parent-Child Contact Problem Cases: Tailoring the Intervention to the Family's Needs*, *in* Overcoming Parent-Child Contact Problems: Family-Based Interventions for Resistance, Rejection, and Alienation 13 (Abigail M. Judge & Robin M. Deutsch eds., 2017).

7. P.L.M. v. L.J., [2008] 54 R.F.L. 6th 126 para. 100, http://canlii.ca/t/1zkcg.

8. Gregory M. Fosco & John H. Grych, *Adolescent Triangulation into Parental Conflicts: Longitudinal Implications for Appraisals and Adolescent-Parent Relations*, 72 J. Marriage & Fam. 254, 255 (2010).

expect to perceive, a tendency that increases as emotion increases and calm, clear thinking diminishes.

The polarized child is often a victim of confirmation bias run amok. We previously identified confirmation bias as one among the engines that drives the triangulated child's adaptation of chameleon-like characteristics. The same is true of the polarized child to an even greater extreme. Whereas confirmation bias contributes to the chameleon child's experience of two separate, parallel realities, it contributes to the polarized child's rejection of one of those realities and buy-in to the other.

It may be that most polarized kids were once, at least briefly, chameleon kids intent only on fitting into each of their parents' disparate and warring worlds. For some, this adaptation is sufficient and self-sustaining. For others, however, real-life aversive experiences and practical hurdles and the feedback loop that emerges when the child's chameleon-like behaviors encounter a parent's confirmation bias forces an impossible choice A loyalty bind is created that teaches the child that loving that parent means betraying the other. The result is a child who is strongly aligned with Parent A and resists or refuses contact with Parent B. To illustrate:

> [A] child may say something fairly neutral, but the parent will twist it into a concern about the child. To the child, it is perceived as though the aligned parent is being supportive. As soon as a child begins to define himself as a victim, the other parent begins to be defined as abusive. Once that occurs, the child has been moved into the middle of the conflict taking the lead role in rejecting the other parent, with the aligned parent taking what appears to be a passive, and supporting role.[9]

The dilemma is that each polarized child's polarized position within the conflicted family system is both the result and one among many causes of that family's unique constellation of interwoven dynamics. Some are as benign as the embarrassment of puberty. Others are as toxic as abuse, neglect, and the vicarious experience of adult intimate partner violence.

---

9. M.L.S. v. N.E.D., [2017] S.K.Q.B. 183 para. 181, http://canlii.ca/t/h4pqj.

Our job as family law professionals is to put aside our own confirmation biases in an effort to see beyond the vitriol and black-white binary allegations—to recognize the entirety of the iceberg, not just the part that is obvious above the water—so as to understand the many confluent pressures that contribute to that particular child's polarized position.

The View through a Funnel

We know that a very small minority of children who are sexually abused grow up to become perpetrators.[10] We also know that the majority of sexual abuse perpetrators were sexually abused as children. Together, these facts illustrate the view through a funnel: the world looks very different depending on which end you hold to your eye.

This lesson teaches us to be wary of retrospective research. No matter how well-intended, any study that begins with an outcome phenomenon and attempts to reason backward to identify origins or causes or even correlations (particularly without a matched control group) is likely to be grievously flawed and misleading.[11] Thus, although it may be correct to observe that "severely alienated children express extremely polarized views of their parents,"[12] it is illogical and bad science to thereby assert that all children who express extremely polarized views of their parents have been alienated.

---

10. *See* Matthew Glasser et al., *Cycle of Child Sexual Abuse: Links between Being a Victim and Becoming a Perpetrator*, 179 Brit. J. Psychiatry 482 (2001).

11. Regarding the flaws inherent in backward reasoning particularly among professionals espousing a binary model of alienation see Kimberly Joyce, *Under the Microscope: The Admissibility of Parental Alienation Syndrome*, 32 J. Am. Acad. Matrimonial Law. 53 (2019).

12. Richard A. Warshak, *Severe Cases of Parental Alienation*, *in* Parental Alienation: The Handbook for Mental Health and Legal Professionals 125 (Demosthenes Lorandos et al. eds., 2013).

Enumerating Relationship Pressures and Practical Hurdles

Our understanding of the factors that contribute to the polarized child's position within the conflicted family system has emerged fitfully and painfully over time. The history that created the false dichotomy between alienation and estrangement, the introduction of the hybrid model, and the evolution of an ecological model are detailed in Chapter 15. We offer here a brief overview of the many factors that must be considered in the process of serving the best interests of each unique polarized child.[13] We have identified the 13 factors in five categories.

1. **Temporal, proximal, and environmental variables include**:

(a) **Is the child's position acute and reactive?** Too often, evaluators and the court have little more than a brief snapshot of a family's dynamics. Without an understanding of the family's history and a larger picture of the child's behavior, it can be impossible to distinguish a child's vehement rejection of Parent B in response to a recent punishment from the same behavior associated with a history of insensitive care. Context is just as necessary if one is to distinguish a child's fawning adoration of Parent A immediately after receipt of a gift or bribe from the same behavior associated with a particularly strong affinity, idealization, or enmeshment. With this in mind, the evaluator is reminded that one interview is never sufficient,[14] and advised that a process-oriented observation protocol can further help to make these distinctions.[15]

(b) **Is the child's resistance/refusal event- or time-dependent?** Allegations of alienation, supercharged emotions, and zealous advocates can blind all involved to simple, pragmatic concerns. When court-ordered time with Parent B conflicts with desirable events scheduled in the child's

13. This section is adapted and expanded from Benjamin D. Garber, *Sherlock Holmes and the Case of Resist/Refuse Dynamics: Confirmatory Bias and Abductive Inference in Child Custody Evaluations*, 58 Fam. Ct. Rev. 386 (2019).

14. Daniel J. Hynan, *Interviewing Children in Custody Evaluations*, 36 Fam. & Conciliation Cts. Rev. 466 (1998).

15. Benjamin D. Garber, *Exploring a Process-Oriented Forensic Family Observation Protocol*, 54 Fam. Ct. Rev. 261 (2016).

world (e.g., team practice or a playdate) or in Parent A's home (e.g., family dinner, holiday celebration, time with a beloved half-sibling or step-sibling), a child's transition resistance may have little or nothing to do with either parent. For example:

> [C]hildren might rather stay at one parent's home not because they have an alignment toward that parent, but because their friends or significant other lives in the neighborhood. This is especially important for children who attempt to remove themselves from any ongoing parental conflict by spending more time with friends.[16]

(c) **Is the child clinging to stimuli incidental to Parent A?** Technology should be the first suspect. Some children resist or refuse contact with Parent B not because of Parent B, but more concretely because they are granted greater power, control, and access to resources in Parent A's care. More screen time. More sugary foods. Later bedtimes, curfews, and wake-up calls.

When parents recognize how these factors motivate the child's behavior, some effectively create a bidding war for the child's affections, each trumping the other's latest offer of more technologies, greater freedoms, and more fun.

When parents don't recognize how these factors motivate the child's behavior, confirmation bias can cause one or both to misinterpret the child's behavior as validating larger fears and accusations. It's not unusual, for example, for Billy's wish to spend more time at Mom's because she has the latest, shiniest, megapixelated gizmo to fuel Mom's belief that Billy is avoiding Dad because he's abusive or neglectful.

(d) **Is the child avoiding stimuli incidental to Parent B?** Aversive environmental factors that the child associates with Parent B can motivate contact resistance and easily become confused with resistance of

16. Shely Polak & Mike Saini, *Children Resisting Contact with a Parent Postseparation: Assessing This Phenomenon Using an Ecological Systems Framework*, 56 J. Divorce & Remarriage 220, 237 (2015).

Parent B himself. This includes neighbors, new partners, half-siblings and stepchildren, pets, activities (or the lack of them), and unfamiliar sensory experiences. Most family law professionals have anecdotes about children who resisted contact with one parent and were only discovered later to be scared by that parent's neighbor's dog or avoidant of the unfamiliar smells in a parent's new apartment.[17] Alert to this factor, evaluators are wise to conduct home visits even in the absence of allegations specific to either environment.[18]

(e) **Is the child avoiding "culture shock"?** When homes and parenting practices and family compositions are disparate, transition can induce a kind of culture shock akin to that of the world traveler who wakes up one day in Moscow and the next day in Tijuana. Some children will resist transition because that culture shock can be overwhelming.[19] Distinctly different religious practices, diets, schedules, physical environments, sensory experiences, and languages (to name just a few such variables) don't mean that the child prefers one home over the other, but more simply that the transition is too emotionally taxing.

2. **Individual child variables**. The child's unique history, strengths, weaknesses, and needs must be considered as they contribute to her alignment with Parent A and resistance to/refusal of Parent B.

(a) **How do characteristics of the child contribute to the child's polarized position?** Temperament describes innate differences in how we engage the world and manage stimulation.[20] Temperament—often observed in terms of anxiety and associated differences of resilience, security, and capacity to manage change—have been identified as relevant to

---

17. Benjamin D. Garber, *Conceptualizing Visitation Resistance and Refusal in the Context of Parental Conflict, Separation, and Divorce*, 45 Fam. Ct. Rev. 588 (2007).

18. Daniel J. Hynan, *Parent-Child Observations in Custody Evaluations*, 41 Fam. Ct. Rev. 214 (2003).

19. Carol Smart et al., The Changing Experience of Childhood (2001).

20. Mary K. Rothbart & John E. Bates, *Temperament*, *in* Handbook of Child Psychology: Social, Emotional, and Personality Development 105 (William Damon et al. eds., 1998).

family alliances.[21] For example: "Anxious, fearful, and passive children lack the resiliency to withstand the intense pressures of the custody battle and the aligned parents' alienating behaviors. It might be psychologically easier for them to choose a side to avoid crippling anxiety."[22]

In the same vein: "A child's rigid rejecting stance may reflect, in part, having resources that are too limited or inadequate for navigating shared time with warring parents, particularly when conflicts arise unpredictably during transitions between homes."[23]

(b) **Does the child resist all separations?** Separation anxiety can occur quite typically in the course of development and can be exacerbated under high stress.[24] In some instances, separation anxiety can rise to the level of diagnosable psychopathology. Evaluators must take care not to mistake a child's separation anxiety and her parents' associated misattributions for resistance/refusal specific to relationships at issue. Other diagnosable conditions including depression, agoraphobia, and autistic spectrum disorders can similarly contribute to resist/refuse behaviors.[25]

(c) **Is the child saying what she believes the listener wants to hear?** Children's suggestibility has been thoroughly documented and the corresponding need to conduct non-leading interviews is thoroughly established.[26] We know, for example, that many children who are forced to migrate between warring homes develop extraordinary skills reading and

---

21. Daniel B. Pickar & Robert L. Kaufman, *The Special Needs Child after Separation or Divorce: Involving Both Parents in Treatment and Intervention Planning*, *in* Evidence-Informed Interventions for Court-Involved Families: Promoting Healthy Coping and Development 325 (Lyn R. Greenberg et al. eds., 2019).

22. Joan B. Kelly & Janet R. Johnston, *The Alienated Child: A Reformulation of Parental Alienation Syndrome*, 39 Fam. Ct. Rev. 249, 261 (2001).

23. Marjorie Gans Walters & Steven Friedlander, *When a Child Rejects a Parent: Working with the Intractable Resist/Refuse Dynamic*, 54 Fam. Ct. Rev. 424, 425 (2016).

24. Derrick Silove et al., *Separation Anxiety Disorder*, *in* Mental Disorders Around the World: Facts and Figures from the WHO World Mental Health Surveys 167 (Kate M. Scott et al. eds., 2018).

25. Pickar & Kaufman, *supra* note 21.

26. Michael E. Lamb et al., *A Structured Forensic Interview Protocol Improves the Quality and Informativeness of Investigative Interviews with Children: A Review of Research Using the NICHD Investigative Interview Protocol*, 31 Child Abuse & Neglect 1201 (2007).

responding to adult cues, adapting chameleon-like to their parents and to inquiring adults, alike. The chameleon child is discussed in detail in Chapter 8.

3. **Dyadic variables: The quality of the child's relationship with the rejected parent.**

(a) **Do objective data suggest that the child has ever had a healthy relationship with Parent B?** One would expect many children who have never had a positive relationship with a parent to resist or refuse contact with that parent. Most dramatically, a child's anxiety about contact with a parent who is entirely unknown (e.g., having been incarcerated, deployed on active military duty, or voluntarily missing) is realistic and expectable. Unfortunately, determining whether a child has a healthy relationship with either parent, past or present, remains highly subjective.[27]

(b) **Does the child experience Parent B as a sensitive and responsive caregiver?**[28] A child's resistance/refusal of contact with a parent who is known to be relatively insensitive and unresponsive to their needs and/or who has been vicariously experienced as otherwise anxiety-inducing (e.g., as a result of witnessing acts of violence or destruction) can be often associated with resist/refuse dynamics (Chapter 14 [estrangement]). This includes the child's incidental or vicarious experience or perception of mutual partner violence.[29]

---

27. Daniel J. Hynan, *Observing Parents Interact with Children: All Too Infrequently Asked Questions (and Answers)*, *in* Handbook of Child Custody 49 (Mark L. Goldstein ed., 2016).

28. The publication first introducing these variables asked the question, "Is Parent B a sensitive and responsive caregiver?" Experience (including the preparation of this book) has since taught us that estrangement is in the eye of the beholder. Andrea Danese & Cathy Spatz Widom, *Objective and Subjective Experiences of Child Maltreatment and Their Relationship with Psychopathology*, 4(8) Nature: Human Behaviour 1–8 (2020). Thus, an objective description of the adult caregiver (as might be provided via a parenting capacity evaluation—Chapter 14 [estrangement]) will not be as relevant as an evaluation of how the child experiences that adult. This is particularly important when one recognizes that the child's vicarious experience of adult intimate partner violence can result in estrangement.

29. The policy and research concerning interpersonal violence [IPV] are complex from so many perspectives. For an example of evolving definitions and research, see Mary

4. **Dyadic variables: The quality of the child's relationship with the aligned parent.**

(a) **Is the child expressing developmentally appropriate affinity?** Affinity describes the spontaneous and common bond of affection shared between people who have common interests, opinions, affiliations, and/or practices.[30] Affinities between a child and one or the other parent naturally shift over the course of development. For example: "[T]his case is unlike those situations where adolescents, who have a natural affinity towards one parent due to temperament, gender, familiarity or shared interests, wish to reside primarily with one parent, but do not outright reject the other."[31]

(b) **Is the child resisting separation from Parent A across contexts?** A child's anxiety about separating from Parent A is easily misconstrued as resistance of Parent B. This dynamic often arises when the Parent A–child relationship is enmeshed and particularly when the child is parentified in that relationship, such that separation feels to the child like neglect of her parent whom she fears is at risk in her absence (Chapter 12).[32]

(c) **Is Parent A needlessly undermining the child's relationship with Parent B?** Parent A's (and/or her allies') unwarranted negative words, actions, and expressed emotions about Parent B to and around their child can be associated with the child's resist/refuse behaviors. This is alienation (Chapter 15).

E. Gilfus et al., *Gender and Intimate Partner Violence: Evaluating the Evidence*, 46 J. Soc. Work Ed. 245 (2010). For other examples of the discussion, see Daniel George Saunders, *Research Based Recommendations for Child Custody Evaluation Practices and Policies in Cases of Intimate Partner Violence*, 12 J. Child Custody 71 (2015); Daniel George Saunders et al., *Beliefs and Recommendations Regarding Child Custody and Visitation in Cases Involving Domestic Violence: A Comparison of Professionals in Different Roles*, 22 Violence against Women 722 (2016).

30. *See* Lawrence Ganong et al., *Stepfathers' Affinity-Seeking with Stepchildren, Stepfather-Stepchild Relationship Quality, Marital Quality, and Stepfamily Cohesion among Stepfathers and Mothers*, 33 J. Fam. Psych. 521 (2019).

31. M.L.S. v. N.E.D., [2017] S.K.Q.B. 183 para. 181, http://canlii.ca/t/h4pqj.

32. *See* Benjamin D. Garber, *Parental Alienation and the Dynamics of the Enmeshed Parent-Child Dyad: Adultification, Parentification, and Infantilization*, 49 Fam. Ct. Rev. 322 (2011).

5. **Systemic variables.** This includes factors that require an understanding of how all the relationships within the family bear on the child's polarized position.

(a) **Is the child avoiding the parents' mutual conflict at transition?** For many children, transition between parents means yet again enduring the anxiety that is piqued when the two adults are together. The prospect of being together in the presence of angry combatants understandably triggers a kind of post-traumatic anxiety avoidance. For this reason, the child's transition between caregivers can be supercharged by "[the] stress of witnessing the fights (which often occurred at the time of the exchange), or in dealing with their two opposing parents at the same time."[33] It may not matter whether transition is supervised, is video recorded, or occurs at the local police station. It may not even matter whether the adults are silent and remain in their respective vehicles. For the child, the tension can be palpable and highly aversive. Further:

> [M]ore than two-fifths of all the children [in a particular study] demonstrated some kind of somatic symptom or exacerbation of a physical illness at the time of the transition. Parents complained that their children came home ill and that it was the other parent's neglectful caretaking that was responsible. For this child, resistance and refusal may be acute and transitory, but vulnerable nonetheless to mischaracterization.[34]

(b) **Is the child being identified in either or both homes with the other parent?** When a child is identified by either parent as allied with and/or as physically or behaviorally similar to the other (hated) parent, she can become a target of misplaced tensions. If, for example, Billy happens to have his father's hairline, a similarly shaped jaw, and the same grating habit of chewing with his mouth open, Mom may find herself venting feelings toward the boy that belong to the man. The child caught up in this dynamic has become the surrogate target of a parent's "entrenched

---

33. Janet R. Johnston et al., *Latency Children in Post-Separation and Divorce Disputes*, 24 J. Am. Acad. Child Psychiatry 563, 571 (1985).

34. *Id.*

hatred" of the other parent[35]—that is, she is being scapegoated or made the object of projective identification and, like Cinderella, is driven to escape her mistreatment.[36]

35. Steven Demby, *Commentary on Entrenched Postseparation Parenting Disputes: The Role of Interparental Hatred*, 55 Fam. Ct. Rev. 417 (2017).

36. This "Cinderella effect" is discussed in the literature only in terms of stepchildren (e.g., "The phenomenon at issue is parental discrimination against stepchildren, relative to how parents treat their birth children. It is manifest both in reduced levels of investment in stepchildren and in elevated rates of mistreatment, up to the extreme of lethal abuse."). Martin Daly & Margo Wilson, *Is the "Cinderella Effect" Controversial? A Case Study of Evolution-Minded Research and Critiques Thereof*, *in* Foundations of Evolutionary Psychology (Charles Crawford & Dennis Krebs eds., 2008).

Chapter 10
Enmeshment

"The evidence establishes that [Mother] is currently considerably enmeshed with her daughter [C.H.] and is unable to see her child as a separate individual in her own right. This makes it extremely difficult for [Mother] to consider [C.H.'s] needs or to accurately assess her behaviors. [Mother] is unable to keep the spillover of her own emotional experiences from affecting [C.H.], who is highly susceptible to this influence."[1]

"[Clinical psychologist] Dr. Grossman observed that [Father] and [M.W.] spent all of their time together with very few peer interactions with [Father's] complete attention devoted to [M.W.] at all times. This enmeshed dynamic seem[ed] to have skewed [M.W.]'s perception of what a normal amount of attention [was] from his parents, and, as such, he [felt] neglected by his mother when she engage[ed] in normal activities of daily living. Dr. Grossman expressed concern that [M.W.] [was] not developing age-typical levels of autonomy, independence, and individuation from his parents, particularly [Father], and, if proper intervention [was] not implemented with [M.W.] in this regard, this dynamic could negatively impact his social emotional development for years to come."[2]

1. Harrell v. Harrell, 236 So. 3d 704, 712–13 (La. Ct. App. 2017).
2. Wagner v. Wagner (*In re* Marriage of Wagner), 2017 IL App. (1st) 162261-U, at *1 (Ill. App. Ct. 2017).

Definition:	If healthy development is marked by a child's gradual movement from the newborn's everything-is-me oceanic sense of self to the healthy adult's bounded and autonomous identity, then enmeshment describes those relationship dynamics that impede this process relative to a child's health, age, and cultural norms.
Subtypes:	Adultification (Chapter 11) Parentification (Chapter 12) Infantilization (Chapter 13)
Other usages:	The noun "enmeshment" and the verb "to enmesh" are often misused and misunderstood. The terms are sometimes used generically and without definition or distinction as to type.[3] They are other times conflated with "triangulation." The terms can describe boundary corruption between adults. We restrict our use to describe boundary corruption within parent-child relationships.
Reasonable precautions:	Enmeshment occurs when an adult enlists a child to fulfill his adult needs. Taking every reasonable step to assure that adults have healthy and supportive peer relationships (e.g., friends, family, faith-based and community affiliations, psychotherapy) will sometimes relieve the pressure on the child and free her to resume healthy development.
What to look for:	Socially isolated adults, insular and isolated family systems, children who resist separation from a parent, and/or children whose social and emotional development are delayed without alternative explanation.
Caution:	Children often feel valued and "special" in enmeshed relationships and therefore resist interventions that threaten to "demote" them back into the lesser role of child.

3. For example, "The child was entirely enmeshed, however, in father's belief that mother abused him, and the notion of the abuse was consistently reinforced by father and stepmother." Knutsen v. Cegalis, 137 A.3d 734, 738 (Vt. 2016).

How to respond to the adults:	Parents need to understand the very significant developmental costs paid by the child who is inappropriately enlisted to serve the adult's needs. Communicating this dynamic is often complicated by the child's expressed pleasure and eagerness to fill a role in the enmeshed relationship.
How to respond to the child:	The child must be thanked for taking care of Mom or Dad and reassured that new adult resources are now in place, freeing the child to resume childhood. Specialized social and emotional supports to help the child manage inevitable feelings of anxiety, loss, and rejection may be necessary.
Implications for forensic process:	Burdening a child with adult needs works against the child's best interests. Beware that a child's stated preference to be with Parent A and/or resistance to contact with Parent B may reflect at least in part the child's enmeshed relationship with Parent A.

A Developmental Perspective

No one would argue that the behavioral rules and expectations appropriate for an infant are appropriate for a teenager (or vice versa), and yet much of family law practice, theory, and research ignores development entirely. It's not at all uncommon to read statutes or case law that refer to children generically, with little or no attention to developmental differences. Those few times that development is taken into account, its treated like a singular dimension grossly equated with age. Nothing could be further from the truth.

Perhaps the most common and most egregious illustration of our field's developmental blindness is evident in parenting plans. Courts often go through an excruciating and expensive process to craft detailed plans that allocate parenting rights and responsibilities in the manner that is believed to be best suited to the child's needs. But look closely: these documents seldom anticipate the child's inevitable and largely predictable development.[4]

4. "When the parenting plan anticipates changes and development, the likelihood of future conflict can be reduced and the duration and severity of any conflict that does

The effect is like buying the child a very expensive pair of shoes and expecting that he'll wear them for the rest of his life.

Human Development Is Not Unidimensional

Height and weight and how fast you drive are unidimensional measures. Change in any one of these metrics can only go up or down. Unfortunately, when the law does acknowledge and even try to accommodate development, it treats it like a singular dimension.

Development is a generic concept like *size*. A carpenter would be very confused if he was asked to build a house that was 100 feet. One hundred feet *what*? Height? Depth? Length? Total combined dimensions? The court's reference to development should prompt exactly the same confusion.

Human development occurs simultaneously but seldom synchronously in numerous interwoven subsystems or domains. Like the members of a family or the families that together make up a community, these domains together make up the individual. Nature and nurture conspire to support or impede the child's social, emotional, cognitive, moral, and physical development (to name just a few).

The asynchrony among these developmental subsystems within any given individual can be very misleading. Borrowing a term from developmental psychologist Jean Piaget, we refer to these differences as *decalage*. In Chapter 8, for example, we talked about how chameleon kids often develop precocious social skills that can mislead a parent, teacher, evaluator, or judge into crediting the child with generally precocious development. This is often not the case. Those family dynamics that nurture the rapid early development of social skills often do so at the cost of the child's emotional development, creating very significant decalage.

---

erupt can be contained." Benjamin D. Garber, The Roadmap to the Parenting Plan Worksheet (2015); *see also* Parenting Plan Evaluations: Applied Research for the Family Court (Leslie Drozd et al. eds., 2d ed. 2016).

It's Impossible to Understand Enmeshment outside of Its Developmental Context

We assign very different meanings to many behaviors as a function of development. Thumb-sucking. Masturbation. Clinginess. Bedwetting. The same is true of enmeshment. Whereas the newborn's enmeshed relationship with her parents is necessary and natural and life-sustaining, that same undifferentiated, unbounded relationship is seen as more and more profoundly pathological as the child approaches adulthood.[5]

Recall the drip experiment described in Chapter 3. Dip a finger into a cup of water. Slowly withdraw the finger. A single coherent drip clings to its tip. That drip is bounded and unique. You can see its boundaries, the edges that distinguish the drip from all that surrounds it. Now shake the finger. The drip falls back into the larger pool of liquid and immediately loses its cohesion. It becomes unbounded and entirely indistinct from its environment.

The infant experiences self like the drip before it emerges from the cup. Everything is me, and I am everything. This is enmeshment. An unbounded, undifferentiated sense of self. My needs are the only needs. This is the subjective opposite of autonomy, a state of bounded separateness that supports the child's sense of identity and invites healthy relationships.

Enmeshment is healthy and necessary and entirely natural for the newborn, but less and less so as the healthy child grows through the toddler and school-aged years toward adolescence and is launched into adulthood. Somewhere along this path, culture and biology gradually conspire to determine that an unbounded and limitless identity crosses the blurry line from necessary and natural to pathological and pathogenic.

For all of its simple appeal, the drip analogy fails for at least two reasons. First, the drip is a binary state. It is either whole and bounded or incoherent and diffuse. We perceive nothing in between. The human movement from the infant's diffuse and unbounded sense of self toward healthy, bounded identity or autonomy only emerges gradually, often

5. Claudia Manzi et al., *Cohesion and Enmeshment Revisited: Differentiation, Identity, and Well-Being in Two European Cultures*, 68 J. Marriage & Fam. 673 (2006).

in two-steps-forward, one-step-back fits and starts. The process is often slow and halting and emergent over the course of a lifetime.

Second, whereas every drip is identical no matter who dips their finger, human identity varies tremendously as a function of the interaction of genetics and experience, particularly the child's experience within her particular relationship ecology. Attachment theory captures this reality to some small degree, demonstrating how the child's experience of her parent's care impacts her emergent and responsive sense of self:

> [L]ove, anxiety, and anger are intimately connected in the attachment system. Together they produce the feelings of security that encourage a developmentally appropriate degree of physical independence and also the anxiety and anger that encourage reunion behavior when the child moves outside of the secure range. Neither love nor anxiety nor anger exists independently. They are a part of a system of emotions.[6]

Even Parents Need to Be Refueled

Shift gears. Rather than talking about drips, let's talk about cars. Recall the refueling metaphor introduced in Chapter 3. In short, people are like cars. We all need to get emotionally refueled somewhere, somehow, some more often than others.

Healthy adults get refueled through interaction with allied and superordinate systems: Intimate partners. Extended family. Peers. Friends. Neighbors. Bosses. Therapists. Faith leaders. Having topped off their tanks, these adults are then better prepared to refuel their children. Hierarchies of power, control, and access to resources between systems and within the family system, in particular, require that this emotional fuel flows downhill from those more powerful to those more needy.

We consider this process healthy because those who give have the emotional resources to do so without compromising self. A healthy

---

6. Robert E. Emery, *Families as Systems: Some Thoughts on Methods and Theory, in* Emerging Methods in Family Research 109, 121 (Susan M. McHale et al. eds., 2014) (volume 4 of the National Symposium on Family Issues book series).

therapist, for example, helps to emotionally refuel her client (more so by her sensitive, responsive constancy than by any particular intervention), careful to maintain the ethically mandated boundaries that distinguish professional from client and the psychologically mandated boundaries that distinguish self from other. A therapist who fails to maintain these boundaries is vulnerable not only to licensing board complaints and civil actions, but even more powerfully compassion fatigue, vicarious trauma, and burnout (Chapter 18). These boundary failures are one form of unhealthy enmeshment.

An adult who can't or won't get emotionally refueled by other adults is vulnerable to seek nurturance in other ways. Some escape into drugs and alcohol and other addictions, briefly distracting themselves from a need that grows all the while. Others seek emotional need fulfillment from their children. We see the latter occur in high-conflict divorcing families.[7]

Role Corruption: When Parents Turn to Their Kids for Emotional Fuel

It's easy to imagine how it can happen: exhausted by the demands of an unrewarding job, constant financial challenges, health issues, and parenting, Mom has no time or energy to see her friends, to read a book, or take a walk. She's running on empty, just trying to keep her head above water.

Billy goes to Mom for most of his emotional fuel.[8] She does what she can to hold and reassure him but finds herself clinging to the child at least as much as he clings to her. He brings her his favorite stuffed animal or a cup of tea or he rubs her feet and basks in the glow of her gratitude. She lets him in on some of her adult experiences or needs him to hide

---

7. "A parent in marital conflict may be particularly prone to role reversal, which in turn adversely affects child development." Jenny Macfie et al., *Pathways from Infant Exposure to Marital Conflict to Parent-Toddler Role Reversal*, 29 Infant Mental Health J. 208, 208 (2008).

8. We posit that this normatively shifts across the course of social and emotional development such that younger, less emotionally mature children are more vulnerable to this effect because they have so few other sources of nurturance and support. Any analysis of this point must also include other demographic variables if the research outcomes are to be parsimonious.

the alcohol so she won't drink or to remind her to take her medicine or simply needs him to need her. Billy does these things eagerly. In these subtle ways—none obviously abusive or upsetting or grossly inappropriate—the tables start to turn. Roles shift. The hierarchy of power, control, and access to resources within the family system is corrupted. However much or little the boundaries between parent and child had begun to coalesce before this process begins, stalls, and even reverses. Billy has become Mommy's source of emotional fuel, a role that he cannot possibly fulfill and should never have to, but he does so gladly nonetheless.

This, too, is about adaptation. Fitting into the family system. The process can take as many distinct forms as there are families. For some, this means trying to become a star athlete or the school valedictorian or the most pious among the altar boys. For others, this means trying to win the science fair or struggling to play Beethoven or starting a small business.[9] And for some, winning Mom's or Dad's affection and attention means making sure that Mom wakes up on time to get to work or that Dad doesn't get lonely at night.

Billy's and his mother's roles have been corrupted by misdirected needs. Parents are supposed to be there for their kids, not vice versa. But some life circumstances can leave a parent feeling isolated and empty and inclined to turn to a child for support. It's not healthy, but it is easy. The rationalization sounds like this: "I didn't have anyone else to turn to" or "He's old enough to understand" or "She saw what happened. She knows what I'm going through" or perhaps the most common rationalization we hear when enmeshed parents talk about their kids: "She gets it. No one else does." "Enmeshed subsystems have diffuse boundaries and convey a greater sense of support at the cost of independence and autonomy . . . . Enmeshed parents are loving and caring, but their children tend to be dependent and may have difficulty relating to people outside the family."[10]

---

9. We speak of children "trying" and "struggling" to fill these systemic niches because these efforts often fail, creating youthful identity crises that, when properly resolved, help many people discover their own needs and identities.

10. Joseane De Souza & Maria Aparecida Crepaldi, *Emotional and Behavioral Problems of Children: Association between Family Functioning, Coparenting, and Marital Relationship*, 22 Acta Colombiana de Psicología 82 (2019) (citation omitted).

Enmeshment has often been discussed in the developmental literature as "role reversal," suggesting that the term is only relevant when a child is enlisted to parent a parent.[11] In fact, enmeshment describes a much broader and varied spectrum of dynamics better referred to as "role corruption."[12] This phrase recognizes role reversal as one among several distinct and mutually compatible outcomes possible when a parent turns to a child for need fulfillment.

The Relationship Ecology of Parent-Child Enmeshment

Role corruption can occur in many, varied life circumstances.[13] We encounter some of these in subsequent chapters as they are associated with distinct forms of enmeshment.

High-conflict divorce is one such circumstance. Embroiled in acrimony, allied and superordinate support systems all taking sides, social media amplifying and distorting every breath everyone takes, this parent is likely to feel alone and embarrassed or ashamed or enraged or all of these, and pressured to rationalize a separation despite once having publicly committed to love, honor, and cherish. The adults who may once have been one another's primary source of emotional fuel now can't be in the same room together. These experiences are compounded by

11. Janet R. Johnston, *Role Diffusion and Role Reversal: Structural Variations in Divorced Families and Children's Functioning*, 15 Fam. Rel. 493 (1990).

12. "To the extent that this phrase implies an exchange of roles within a family system (as when a conventional working father becomes a 'stay-at-home-dad' and his wife joins the work force), it fails to adequately capture the breadth or the destructive power of the dyadic dynamics that complement the development of parental alienation. Instead, the phrase role corruption is used here . . . ." Benjamin D. Garber, *Parental Alienation and the Dynamics of the Enmeshed Parent-Child Dyad: Adultification, Parentification, and Infantilization*, 49 Fam. Ct. Rev. 322, 324 (2011). *See also* Benjamin D. Garber, The Dynamics of the Enmeshed Family System Ten Years Later: Growing Our Understanding of Adultification, Parentification, and Infantilization (in press, 2021).

13. Anne Shaffer & L. Alan Sroufe, *The Developmental and Adaptational Implications of Generational Boundary Dissolution: Findings from a Prospective, Longitudinal Study*, *in* Implications of Parent-Child Boundary Dissolution for Developmental Psychopathology 67 (Patricia K. Kerig ed., 2005).

overwhelming anxiety and guilt and fear about the future, about money, about the labyrinthine legal process, and particularly about the children's well-being.

This parent's coffee cup is full to overflowing with emotion, leaving little or no room for clear thinking. In this state she's prone to impulsive choices, fight-or-flight reflex actions, and primitive responses. Of course, this may have always been true of her personality and a cause rather than an effect of the separation and divorce, but the difference is moot.[14] Here and now she's needy and alone. Her familiar supports have abandoned ship. Who gets it? Who really understands and is still there for her? Her child, of course.

The *enmeshed child* enjoys her special status. It feels good to be needed by Mom or to have become Dad's new best friend. The new role feels to the child like a promotion or a battlefield commission, a jump-step investment of trust and privilege and responsibility in the midst of chaos and confusion. The experience of feeling special and valued is deeply rewarding and motivating to the child, even if the burden is daunting and the associated opportunity cost—the missed peer activities, lost developmental experiences, and the anxiety that comes with discovering that you no longer have an emotional safety net; that you have become your parent's emotional safety net—can have devastating long-term consequences.

That's part of the cost that the enmeshed child is forced to pay: missing out on opportunities to explore healthy peer relationships, participating on teams, developing hobbies, interests, and skills, exploring the physical environment and discovering one's own body, and perhaps most powerfully, the loss of security that comes with discovering that there's no one there to pick you up when you fall. There's no one present to kiss the boo-boo, tuck you in at night, give you a hug of reassurance, and send you on your way because those hugs and kisses and pats-on-the-back have suddenly become yours to give to a needy and fallen parent.

---

14. This description suggests character pathology, a long-standing distortion of identity, relationships, and need fulfillment built into some individuals. Character pathology can often be diagnosed using reliable and valid psychometric instruments, but the time, effort, and money associated with these evaluations is seldom worthwhile in the context of contested custody litigation. What matters to legal and mental health professionals, as we have argued, are the dynamics of the system, not the individual's diagnosis.

The enmeshed child dismisses her own needs as baby-like, thriving on the empty emotional calories of her new role. Mom tells me all about her dates. Dad lets me read his e-mails and use his phone. We stay up late to watch the news together and sometimes even R-rated movies. We talk all about court stuff and how Mom is trying to take me away from him and how much he needs me.

Consumed with this special new role and a driving need to take care of a parent, motivated by nothing more strongly than winning that parent's affection and attention, the enmeshed child neglects homework, fails tests, and refuses to go to school. She will decline party invitations and miss sleepovers, and complain of mysterious ailments that coincidentally keep her home when all the other kids go out. Developmental and cultural landmarks like birthdays and graduations and the SATs and driver's ed are bypassed or forgotten or failed with weak rationalizations about those "childish" events, punctuated by an empty insistence that "I don't care." And she actually might not care, because her developmental trajectory has been thrown off track. She's no longer growing toward autonomy. She's stuck in hold-me-tight, her identity still entwined with that of a parent, while her peers are practicing let-me-go steps that help to coalesce boundaries and define a separate self.

Developmental Decalage

The enmeshed child's developmental equilibrium is thrown off-center, nurturing some pockets of development but allowing others to atrophy. If healthy life circumstances feed cognitive, social, emotional, and moral development in more or less equal measure, the dynamics of the enmeshed child's family system feed her social development—the ability to read and respond to interpersonal, nonverbal cues—leaving her cognitive and emotional development far behind. Like the proverbial child prodigy who can do calculus but has never made a friend, the enmeshed child becomes an expert at reading others' posture and vocal tone and facial cues even if she lacks the thinking and feeling skills to cope with the experience.

The experience of enmeshment is self-perpetuating. The deeper the child is invested in serving her parent's needs, the more she misses out on critical separation and peer experiences, and the more she'll invest in her corrupted role within the destructive family system, which, in turn, causes her to miss out on more and more peer experiences. On and on the process goes, reinforcing the boundary that consumes the enmeshed pair and dissolving the boundary that ought to be growing between them.

Never having had to learn how to fall asleep alone in his own bed, never having awkwardly navigated a classmate's birthday party, never having had to manage the terror of the bus ride to summer camp, the enmeshed child relies more and more completely on his role as Mommy's best friend to fuel his emotional needs and define his emerging if distorted sense of self. Mom's half-hearted (and perhaps court-ordered) efforts to urge him to go out with his peers or enroll in soccer camp or join the football team or see his dad fail. She says the words, but he reads her emotions and he knows his place. She needs him at home.

We know that scouts and teams and clubs and just hanging out on the playground are among the culturally endorsed, normative crucibles in which autonomy is tested two-steps-forward and one-step-back, fueling the child's gradual experience of growing up and growing away toward identity. When roles are corrupted and these repetitive, graduated individuation opportunities are missed, the enmeshed child falls further and further behind his peers until the birthday party invitations stop coming. In one author's experience:

> Highly enmeshed families tend to have boundaries that are overly diffuse and permeable, causing family members to become emotionally entangled with one another . . . . Enmeshment can take the form of (a) conditional access to resources (e.g., conditional support) that occurs at the cost of hindering individual autonomy or (b) distress and hostility that seamlessly spills over across subsystems and immerses individuals in the ongoing issues in the family . . . . A main premise is that the high level of interdependency increases children's preoccupation with and sensitivity to family stress . . .[15]

---

15. Jesse L. Coe et al., *Family Cohesion and Enmeshment Moderate Associations between Maternal Relationship Instability and Children's Externalizing Problems*, 32 J. Fam. Psych. 289, 291–92 (2018).

Intergenerational Enmeshment?

Role corruption can be passed down from one generation to the next.[16] In order to explain, we need to use our familiar box of dominoes in a new way: Stand a dozen tiles on end in a single line across a table top, each representing a single generation. Imagine that any given tile is at once the child of the tile to its left and the parent of the tile to its right.

In the succession of healthy generations, the dominoes fall left to right, each parent nurturing his or her child who grows up to nurture his or her child, who grows up to nurture his or her child, and onward across the generations to the right.

But what happens if that left-to-right succession is interrupted? If a parent dies young or is incarcerated or deployed with the military while his child is young or becomes drug addicted and spends years in detox or is otherwise unavailable to meet his child's needs? In these and similar circumstances, one of two outcomes will occur: In a majority of instances, allied systems fill in. An uncle or a grandfather or a coach fills the gap by taking on the job of nurturing the child. Sometimes a superordinate system becomes involved, providing a big brother surrogate, ordering that the remaining parent enroll the child in therapy, or even removing the child to foster care. By no means are all caregivers interchangeable, but these stop-gaps can help to assure that the child grows up feeling nurtured and thereby becomes better able to nurture her children so that the dominoes keep falling forward.

Other times, a parent's physical or emotional absence goes unfilled. Allied and superordinate systems fail. There are no surrogates available or the surrogates who do step up are too little, too late. This unfortunate child falls between the cracks in the foster system, becomes Cinderella among favored half-siblings or stepsiblings or adopted siblings, or otherwise grows up without the benefit of reliable emotional fuel or a secure base. The result can be a needy and angry, depressed and anxious adult incapable of engaging in healthy relationships, vulnerable to seeking nurturance from all the wrong places, including her own child.

16. Skyer W. Roper et al., *The Intergenerational Effects of Parental Divorce on Young Adult Relationships*, 61 J. Divorce & Remarriage 249 (2020).

When parent relies on child, the intergenerational dominoes begin to fall backward, from right to left, raising a succession of distressed and dysfunctional adults.

Enmeshment, Estrangement, and Alienation?

Context is everything.

Systems are, by definition, self-righting constellations of interdependent relationships. Anything that affects one relationship within the system will necessarily affect the others as the entire constellation seeks a new balance.

This is exactly what happens in many conflicted family systems. In the absence of healthy, proactive, and child-centered adult communication, cooperation, and respect, dynamics become deeply entrenched. One court captured this process eloquently:

> Unfortunately what has occurred in the past year, apparently due to the parental conflict, is that there appears to have been increasing polarization between Jaymen's parents' two households. Instead of each parent ensuring a proper balance of love, belonging and acceptance along with structure, expectations, and supervision, each has attempted to compensate with what they see the other parent missing. As a result, a perception has evolved in Jaymen's mind that his mother's home is the "accepting, loving" environment and his father's home has become the "mean, controlling" environment. The more he talks that way with his mother, the more she worries about what goes on at [Father']s home and the more reluctant she is to encourage him to work things out with his father and [Stepmother] and to take responsibility for his behaviour. Jaymen then becomes more avoidant of [Stepmother] and his father to which [Stepmother] and his father react with more authoritative measures. That makes their environment increasingly unpleasant to Jaymen.[17]

17. Daren v. Millen, [2013] S.K.Q.B. 173 para. 14, https://canlii.ca/t/fxhc8.

The dynamics of this system shift over time, each individual and subsystem reacting to and simultaneously causing reactions in allied individuals and subsystems, these shifts resonating among allied and subordinate systems. The enmeshed mother-son dyad pushes away from the father and stepmother, further enmeshing the first and distancing the second. Each is blinded by emotion, needs, confirmation bias, and self-serving myopia. Like the blind wisemen in the ancient parable referenced in Chapter 6, each is certain that the part of the elephant he encountered is the whole beast.

At some point in the rapid evolution of these intrafamilial dynamics, the court becomes involved. A guardian ad litem or evaluator adjusts her orbiting telescope in order to take a snapshot of the family system, generating a still image of a moving, growing target. In this case, that picture captures a child triangulated amidst his parents' conflict, aligned and likely enmeshed with a mother who appears to be alienating her son from a father and stepmother whose resentment and authoritarian manner are contributing to estrangement. The child's resistance to or refusal of contact with Dad is multiply determined by these interwoven and self-perpetuating dynamics.

Is This Enmeshment, Estrangement, or Alienation?

Books are, by definition and physical necessity, sequential presentations bound by a linear succession of pages. It would be nice if this book could define all of the relevant terms before asking you, the reader, to consider their interaction, but our subject refuses to cooperate. Because relationships are neither linear nor sequential, we are forced to ask you to think about subjects that we have yet to introduce.

Feel free to read ahead and come back to this discussion. Estrangement is defined and discussed in Chapter 14. Alienation is defined and discussed in Chapter 15. You may want to review polarization (Chapter 9) and about the emergent, chaotic nature of systems (Chapter 3), as well.

Is the Canadian case excerpted above about a child named Jaymen an example of enmeshment, estrangement, or alienation?

The answer is yes. The little that we know suggests that all three of these dynamics are simultaneously at play. In fact, this co-occurrence or hybrid explanation is more the rule than the exception:

> [P]arents who were alienating were also those who had poor boundaries and engaged in role reversal with their children. They had difficulty distinguishing their own feelings from those of their child, and the child often became the parent's confidante, comforting and admonishing other family members, thus assuming an inappropriate executive or parenting role in the family.[18]

18. Janet R. Johnston et al., *Is It Alienating Parenting, Role Reversal, or Child Abuse? A Study of Children's Rejection of a Parent in Child Custody Disputes*, 5 J. Emotional Abuse 191, 207 (2005).

Chapter 11
Adultification

"Ms. D. has done many things well in parenting S.D. but lacks insight regarding the extent to which she has enlisted her daughter to meet her own needs at the expense of S.D.'s needs . . . children who experience these problems suffer a variety of short-term and long-term deficits in both their individual functioning and their interpersonal relationships. Parents often do not appreciate the extent to which pseudo-maturity is occurring at a significant cost to child development."[1]

"If ever there is an example of a manipulative 'adultified' child, [Suzy] fits the mould. She 'took on' each of the authority figures in this courtroom. . . . At times, she was quite coy and responded 'Well, I'm not sure how much I should tell you.' The clear message was that, 'I'll tell you either what you want to hear or what I think you should hear.'"[2]

Definition:	Adultification is one of at least three distinct and mutually compatible forms of enmeshment. Adultification describes pressures within the enmeshed parent-child dyad that enlist the child as the adult's peer, ally, or companion in contravention of age- and culture-specific expectations and that impede the child's healthy development.[3]

1. J.E.S.D. v Y.E.P., [2017] B.C.S.C. 495 para. 14, http://canlii.ca/t/h2tqx.

2. Family & Children's Servs. of Waterloo Region v. B.Y., [1995] W.D.F.L. 1011 para. 55, http://canlii.ca/t/fn1n3.

3. Regarding cultural differences and adultification, see, for example, Jou-Chen Chen, *The Implications of Childhood Adultification on the Mental Health of Young Adults among Chinese and Taiwanese Immigrant Families*, 78 Dissertation Abstracts Int'l Sec. A: Human. & Soc. Sci. 9-A(E) (2018) (Ph.D. dissertation, Virginia Tech).

Reasonable precautions:	The adultified child feels special and valued by the adult who shares information and experiences that he may not understand and that evoke emotions that he may not be able to manage. He may appear to be entitled, defiant, and resistant to or resentful of age-appropriate limits and interests. He experiences interventions intended to restore the hierarchy of the family system as effectively demoting him from this prized role.
What to look for:	The adultified child's knowledge about specific pockets of experience may seem adultlike and discrepant with his general knowledge and broader functioning. He may use age-atypical words and phrases appropriately without evidence of parroting.[4] He may resent the non-adultifying parent and professionals for talking down to him or otherwise treating him "like a baby." He is likely to attempt to engage with you in a peer-like manner uncharacteristic of others his age.
How to respond to the adults:	The adultifying parent will often praise the child's intelligence and ability and argue that he is mature enough and/or old enough or otherwise deserving of his inappropriate role. These parents sometimes take a quid-pro-quo approach, arguing that the other parent treats the child like an adult; therefore, comparable treatment is warranted and necessary or else the child will refuse contact. This parent's investment in the child may be relieved by investing in other appropriate adult peer supports (e.g., support groups, therapy) and may benefit from education about the developmental costs incurred by the adultified child.

4. "Parroting" or mimicry refers to a child's rote repetition of another person's words, phrases, and/or body language without concomitant experience, emotions, or even meaning. Parroting is often taken as evidence of an adult's intentional acts to script or otherwise shape a child's presentation to an evaluator or a court. For example, "[i]n the wake of a bitter divorce, it is deceptively easy to assume that a child is simply parroting the attitudes, beliefs and behaviors of a spiteful former partner." Janet R. Johnston & Matthew J. Sullivan, *Parental Alienation: In Search of Common Ground for a More Differentiated Theory*, 58 Fam. Ct. Rev. 270, 271 (2020).

How to respond to the child:	Adultification reinforces the child's verbal and social skills and sense of entitlement, often empowering the child's resistance to otherwise age-appropriate interventions. Cognitive/verbal interventions may be least effective as they invite his super-mature social and verbal defenses. Emotional/experiential therapies that allow the child to feel safe while feeling vulnerable and needy and to be reassured by appropriate caregiving may be most effective.
Implications for custody-related decisions:	The opportunity to be treated like an adult can be extremely attractive, contributing to the adultified child's resistance to contact with the other parent and corrupting his stated wishes for custody outcomes. Courts and evaluators must be mindful of the corrosive effects of these unhealthy pressures.

Many and Varied Meanings

Each of the terms defined in this book has been treated in court and in the literature like a projective stimulus—an inkblot that becomes whatever the viewer needs it to be—given whatever idiosyncratic meaning the speaker or writer casts upon it. Creative expression of this sort suits poets but confounds and confuses courts and risks doing harm to children. *Adultification* may be the most variably and creatively defined among them. To illustrate:

1. **Adultification as the treatment of minors as adults under the law.**[5] The legal system has often used the term to describe the treatment of children as if they had reached the age of consent. In the broadest sense, scholars speak of the "adultification of juvenile courts"[6] and refer to "the federal transfer and prosecution of American youth as adults."[7] In

5. Psychology takes a consistent and strong stand against such policies and laws. *See* Thomas Grisso et al., *Juveniles' Competence to Stand Trial: A Comparison of Adolescents' and Adults' Capacities as Trial Defendants*, 27 Law & Hum. Behav. 357 (2003).

6. Riane M. Bolin & Brandon K. Applegate, *Adultification in Juvenile Corrections: Examining the Orientations of Juvenile and Adult Probation and Parole Officers*, 41 Am. J. Crim. Just. 321 (2016).

7. Mae C. Quinn & Grace R. McLaughlin, *Article III Adultification of Kids: History, Mystery, and Troubling Implications of Federal Youth Transfers*, 26 Wash. & Lee J. C.R. & Soc. Just. 523, 523 (2020).

these contexts, the term generally refers to "the practice of trying youth under 18 as adults, detaining them in adult jails, and sentencing them to adult criminal punishments to serve time in prisons."[8]

2. **Adultification as a tool of racism and bias?** The term has appeared more and more frequently in recent years in the context of immigration law to refer to discrimination against non-White immigrants or illegal youths. For example: "Adultification refers to the phenomenon whereby children of color suffer a wide variety of negative outcomes across a diverse range of public systems, including education, juvenile justice, and child welfare, because they are perceived as more adult-like than their white peers."[9]

3. **Adultification as premature autonomy?** For example, homeless youths ages 19 to 21 have been described as adultified by virtue of having been forced to take on the "premature caregiving" of others: "Early adultification complicated participants' experiences with leaving home by imbuing them with premature independence and familial detachment."[10]

4. **Gender identity and adultification.** Transgender status is seen by some as evidence of precocious maturity, which can carry with it burdens and responsibilities identified in this context as adultification: "transgender girls are adultified and sexualized rather than framed as innocent or imperiled."[11]

5. **Adultification as a foil motivating social welfare movements.** Reaction to the treatment of minors as adults under the law has created a political platform for highlighting the distinct needs of children particularly in the courts,[12] provoking an important social welfare response

---

8. Juveniles in Solitary Confinement: Rehabilitation or Torture?, Panel Discussion at the Center for Justice at Columbia University on Life in the Box: Youth in Solitary Confinement (Feb. 13, 2014).

9. Laila Hlass, *The Adultification of Immigrant Children*, 34 Geo. Immigr. L.J. 199, 202–03 (2020).

10. Rachel M. Schmitz & Kimberly A. Tyler, *Growing Up before Their Time: The Early Adultification Experiences of Homeless Young People*, 64 Child. & Youth Services Rev. 15 (2016).

11. Amy L. Stone, *Gender Panics about Transgender Children in Religious Right Discourse*, 15 J. LGBT Youth 1 (2018).

12. "The ethically insupportable feature of the children's liberation movement is its failure to acknowledge that dependent status precludes possession of the full rights of the

among those who recognize that children's needs and abilities can be starkly different than those of adults.[13]

6. **Adultification as a description of a child's behavior.** Closer to the present purpose, *adultification* is sometimes used to describe the outcomes associated with permissive parenting without regard to the quality of the parent-child relationship, as in "Dr. Jordan translated the statement in his initial report that I.P. is a product of early adultification to mean that the parents had given her too much independence to make decisions beyond her age level."[14] Alternately, the term is sometimes used to refer to a child's precocious or adultlike words and actions, as in "both children talked about the mother in speech that was 'brittle, litany-like, with artificial quality, with affect that does not match the words, without conviction, in unchildlike, adultified language, of rehearsed quality.'"[15] Although adultification (in the present sense of the word) can be associated with these behaviors, we prefer the simpler and more self-evident term "adultlike" in this context.

7. **Adultification and parentification are used interchangeably.** Finally, some authors treat these two terms as synonyms or as a distinction of degree when speaking of children's adultlike roles within the family system. For example, Burton refers to four types of *adultification* that differ along a spectrum from triangulation in the form of access to "precocious knowledge" to "peerification" to "parentification."[16]

---

emancipated person." Diana Baumrind, *Reciprocal Rights and Responsibilities in Parent-Child Relations*, 34 J. Soc. Issues 179 (1978).

13. E.g., Nancy E. Dowd, *Children's Equality: Strategizing a New Deal for Children*, 47 Fordham Urb. L.J. 379 (2020).

14. Palazzolo v. Mire, 10 So. 3d 748, 758 (La. Ct. App. 2009); Jacqueline J. Goodnow, *Children's Household Work: Its Nature and Functions*, 103 Psych. Bull. 5 (1988); Jacqueline J. Goodnow & Jeanette A. Lawrence, *Work Contributions to the Family: Developing a Conceptual and Research Framework*, 94 New Directions for Child & Adolescent Dev. 5 (2001).

15. L.A.U. v. I.B.U., [2016] A.B.Q.B. 74 para. 109, http://canlii.ca/t/gn91d.

16. "Childhood adultification involves contextual, social, and developmental processes in which youth are prematurely, and often inappropriately, exposed to adult knowledge and assume extensive adult roles and responsibilities within their family networks." Linda Burton, *Childhood Adultification in Economically Disadvantaged Families: A Conceptual Model*, 56 Fam. Rel.: Interdisc. J. Applied Fam. Stud. 329 (2007).

Parenting Styles?

Some of these various uses of the term *adultification* refer to distinct types of parenting. Baumrind distinguishes four parenting styles representing the quadrants created on a graph contrasting parenting control (high to low) on the Y-axis and parenting support (high to low) on the X-axis.[17] Specifically:

1. **The permissive parent** exercises low control but offers his child a high degree of support. This is the "Disneyland Dad" who is incapable or unwilling to set limits and follow-through, sometimes for fear of eliciting the child's anger and sometimes in an effort to win the child's affection by making the other parent appear to be the "bad cop." Permissive parenting is discussed further as it bears on understanding manipulative estrangement in Chapter 14.

2. **The disengaged parent** exercises low control and offers low support. This parent tends to be distracted, uninvolved, and emotionally distant, behaviors that are sometimes associated with addiction and/or serious psychopathology. The disengaged parent's son or daughter may feel rejected and may, in turn, reject or avoid the parent. Although one might expect that a disengaged parent wouldn't bother to engage in high-conflict custody litigation, some do so for the sake of appearances and/or at the urging of extended family and new partners.

3. **The authoritarian parent** is similarly low on support, but high on control. This parent lacks empathy, may have limited perspective-taking abilities, and beneath his demanding and controlling façade may be particularly anxious. From the outside looking in, the authoritarian parent may appear rigid and harsh.

4. **The authoritative parent** is high on both control and support. This parent establishes child-centered structure (limits and consequences, clear roles, boundaries, and routines) and follows through with compassion, empathy, and nurturance. "Children's growing sense of autonomy is the counterpart to parental authority. Within their boundaries of

17. Diana H. Baumrind, Current Patterns of Parental Authority (1972); *see also* Diana H. Baumrind, *Rearing Competent Children*, *in* Child Development Today and Tomorrow 349 (William Damon ed., 1988).

autonomy, children pretty much get to make their own decisions, albeit with a degree of parental oversight."[18]

Across studies and across cultures, authoritative parenting is associated with the healthiest family dynamics and developmental outcomes: "An authoritative parent displays neither the coercive disciplinary style expected of an authoritarian personality nor the indulgent disciplinary style expected of a democratic personality but in contrast to both is responsive and demanding, confrontive and autonomy supportive, affectionate and power assertive."[19]

Valuable and validated as these distinctions are, they are usually described as if they were static and fixed. Like child and family development, we must understand parenting styles in context. Whether Mom is permissive or Dad is authoritarian is at least in part an emergent and self-organizing function of their relationship within the larger pressures of the system. Consider, for example, a simple parable often used to illustrate how family dynamics can become entrenched in clinical work:

A family goes for a ride in a rowboat. Mom and Dad sit side-by-side, each with one oar. The kids are in the stern. Somewhere in the middle of the lake, Mom begins to worry that Dad is leaning too far to port, so she leans to starboard. Dad feels Mom shift away from him and worries that they'll capsize, so he leans to port. This goes on silently, back and forth, until the parents both fall out and the boat floats away with the kids still onboard.

Mom may have begun a tad more permissive than Dad who was himself just a tad more authoritarian when that boat left the dock. By the time they'd reached the middle of the lake, however, each resonating off the other but neither communicating constructively, they'd adopted extreme positions. If they swim to shore, dry off, rescue the children, and each finds a new partner, will they remain this extreme? Maybe. But more likely they will each retain their initial inclinations exacerbated

---

18. Robert E. Emery, *Families as Systems: Some Thoughts on Methods and Theory*, *in* Emerging Methods in Family Research 109, 117 (Susan M. McHale et al. eds., 2014) (volume 4 of the National Symposium on Family Issues book series).

19. Diana Baumrind, *Is a Pejorative View of Power Assertion in the Socialization Process Justified?*, 17 Rev. Gen. Psych. 13 (2013).

to some degree by this experience. Whether they ever again reach these extremes or otherwise adapt their parenting styles will once again depend on the social ecology of the new system.[20]

We use the term *adultification* exclusively to describe a specific form of parent-child enmeshment that is often fostered, most easily observed, and potentially has its most destructive impact in the crucible of high-conflict divorce.

Many children are triangulated amidst their parents' battles (Chapter 7). Some become polarized, aligning with Parent A and resisting or refusing contact with Parent B (Chapter 9). Within the aligned dyad, some relationships become enmeshed (Chapter 10). That enmeshed parent-child dyad can develop one or more of at least three dynamics depending on how Parent A communicates and the child perceives her self-serving needs. Adultification is the first of these. Parentification and infantilization are discussed in the next two chapters.

Adultification occurs when Parent A more or less intentionally conscripts her son to serve as her ally, peer, companion, or, in some form, an emotional partner.[21] The process can begin as overtly and abruptly and benignly as when a widowed mother advises her grieving son that, "you're the man of the house, now."[22] It can grow unrecognized in a father's well-intended buddy-buddy efforts to take his son into his confidence.[23] It can become evident only slowly and subtly, long after it's become deeply

---

20. We note in this regard that the same is true of attachment security as assessed in the toddler years. Contrary to popular belief, attachment security and insecurity (and the gradations and variations in between) are not immutable traits set in stone early in life but attributes influenced by experience that may adapt and respond to contemporary relationship ecology. *See* Tommie Forslund et al., *Attachment Goes to Court: Child Protection and Custody Issues*, ATTACHMENT & HUM. DEV. (Jan. 11, 2021) (advance online publication), https://www.tandfonline.com/doi/pdf/10.1080/14616734.2020.1840762.

21. *See* Anita Chandra et al., *Children on the Homefront: The Experience of Children from Military Families*, 125 PEDIATRICS 16 (2010).

22. For example, see Patricia Lester & Brenda Bursch, *The Long War Comes Home*, PSYCHIATRIC TIMES, July 13, 2011, https://www.psychiatrictimes.com/view/long-war-comes-home.

23. This has been termed "expressive parentification." *See* Gregory J. Jurkovic, *Destructive Parentification in Families: Causes and Consequences*, *in* FAMILY PSYCHOPATHOLOGY: THE RELATIONAL ROOTS OF DYSFUNCTIONAL BEHAVIOR 237 (Luciano L'Abate ed., 1998).

entrenched, as when a child is confused why his peers don't know their parents' private secrets the same way that he knows Mother's or Father's every thought and action.

Adultification can be associated with parental absence:

> I don't know [if growing up too fast] is good or bad. In some cases it's good and some cases it's kind of sad that your kids are almost forced to grow up a little bit quicker and have to step up to the plate. . . . [I] have young sons and my husband is deployed. . . . [T]hey kind of step up and are the man of the house. A lot of them try to take on that role, which is a great help to us moms. I know that myself. But it's sad in a way too. [It] takes away a little of their youth.[24]

The adultifying parent may feel angry, lonely, abandoned, rejected, and/or depressed. She might be socially isolated (by preference or personality, due to work or religious affiliation, linguistic and/or cultural differences, and/or pressures created by her [former] partner).

Contrary to inferences one might draw reading the literature about adultification without carefully narrowing its definition, parent-child adultification has nothing to do with the justice system. It is not specific to any particular race, culture, language, immigration status, gender identification, socioeconomic status, or housing status. The stresses associated with each of these variables can, however, erode healthy dynamics, leaving children more vulnerable to triangulation and thus forced to adapt in whatever way they can.

Like parentification (Chapter 12), adultification corrupts generational boundaries and the hierarchy within the family system. It prematurely and inappropriately vests children with adultlike power, control, and access to resources thereby needlessly burdening children who don't have the cognitive and emotional resources necessary to cope with the burdens of adult relationships. When these boundaries are breached—when children are prematurely promoted to serve as an adult's friend and ally—the impact on the child is at least two-fold.

---

24. Catherine P. Bradshaw, *School Transitions among Military Adolescents: A Qualitative Study of Stress and Coping*, 39 Sch. Psych. Rev. 84, 96 (2010).

First, it feels good when Dad treats you like his new best friend. The symbiotic and mutually rewarding parent-child relationship at least briefly makes both participants happy. The adult suddenly has a new companion who idolizes and blindly validates his every word and feeling. The child suddenly has all those previously forbidden adult privileges and—best of all—the adultifying parent's undivided affection and attention.

Second, the adultified child feels scared. The hierarchy of power, control, and access to resources within and between systems otherwise acts to reassure even though it's also frustrating. No one wants to be controlled—that's why you seldom comply with the speed limit—but knowing that someone is in charge quells our anxiety. It's calming to think that someone has his hands on the steering wheel, even if we argue about where the car's going. It's reassuring to know that there's a safety net in place just in case we fall down. Adultified and parentified children don't have these protections. The result is terror hidden more or less successfully under the transient glee and pride and arrogance that come with their corrupted roles.

Because pathological enmeshment is about the child serving the adult's needs, the dynamic is self-reinforcing. A parent's gratitude or safety or attention is a powerful reward in and of itself, far greater than any tangible incentive. Whereas healthy parents serve their children's needs ("Hey Mommy, look what I made!"), enmeshed parents reward their children for responding to their needs ("Hey Billy! Look what I need!"). This is backward, of course, asking the emotionally immature child to refuel the adult rather than vice versa.

As with any form of enmeshment, the child's age and emotional maturity are relevant to understanding the risks associated with adultification. All other things being equal, we contend that the longer the child enjoys the benefits of a healthy childhood before becoming triangulated into the adult conflict (or more generally, the later the age of onset), the less destructive the experience may be for the child. This assumes that as the child ages and matures, he simultaneously develops a broader social network so that the loss of Mom's healthy attention extracts somewhat less of a cost later in life.

Thus, at the extremes of age, the parent who treats his three-year-old son like his best friend and buddy is likely doing immeasurably greater harm than the parent who first turns to his 30-year-old son for companionship. The toddler has no resources outside of the family system with which to cope with the emotional pressures of his corrupted role. All he can do is find a way to adapt to the relationship dynamic in an effort to get his affiliation and nurturance needs met. By contrast, the adult child presumably has a lifetime of experience, mature cognitive, social, and emotional skills, and a broad network of social supports that give him perspective on and greater resilience coping with the shifting parent-child dynamic.[25]

Adultification Is More Common in Certain Relationship Ecologies

As the stress on a family system increases, the risk that healthy rules, roles, and relationships will break down increases. We know, for example, that poverty,[26] the experience of and exposure to intimate partner violence,[27] immigrant status,[28] growing up without adequate emotional nurturance,[29] and high-conflict divorce[30] each can dramatically increase

---

25. "Some studies reveal that when the parentification experience and family process happens at an earlier age, the long-term outcomes are more severe and enduring. However, the premise that older children engaged in the role of parentification experience greater and more severe outcomes is seen in literature, as well." Lisa M. Hooper et al., *Characterizing the Magnitude of the Relation between Self-Reported Childhood Parentification and Adult Psychopathology: A Meta-Analysis*, 67 J. Clinical Psych. 1028, 1030 (2011).

26. Burton, *supra* note 16.

27. *See* Debra Lynn Stephens, *Battered Women's Views of Their Children*, 14 J. Interpersonal Violence 731 (1999).

28. *See* Maria Elena Puig, *The Adultification of Refugee Children: Implications for Cross-Cultural Social Work Practice*, 5 J. Hum. Behav. Soc. Env't 85 (2002); *see also* Sophie Walsh et al., *The Role of Parentification and Family Climate in Adaptation among Immigrant Adolescents in Israel*, 16 J. Rsch. Adolescence 321 (2006). See also the discussion of language brokers in Chapter 7.

29. "The role may serve to settle 'accounts due' for parents who were not adequately cared for themselves as children." Genie Burnett et al., *Family Unpredictability, Parental Alcoholism, and the Development of Parentification*, 34 Am. J. Fam. Therapy 181, 182 (2006).

30. Tara S. Peris & Robert E. Emery, *Redefining the Parent-Child Relationship Following Divorce: Examining the Risk for Boundary Dissolution*, 5 J. Emotional Abuse 169 (2005).

the risk that a child will become triangulated into the resulting adult conflict, enmeshed with one parent, and adultified in that relationship. For example, we know that immigrants are often impoverished, that poverty and cultural alienation can increase the risk of domestic violence, and that stresses like poverty, cultural alienation, and domestic violence can together create a recipe for high-conflict divorce.[31] The intersection of these risk factors can leave a child to have to manage a perfect storm of systemic stresses that triangulates, corrupts healthy boundaries, and adultifies, parentifies, and/or infantilizes.

Who Gets Adultified?

Only children are (obviously) at far greater risk than children with siblings, although there are no data addressing whether the presence of half-siblings or stepsiblings reduces the only child's risk. Within sibling groups, first-born children are far more likely to be adultified than later-born children.[32] This may be common sense, particularly if the term is used in its broader sense to include functional adultlike caregiving responsibilities for younger kids. But even within our narrower parent-child definition, the idea that the eldest among two or more siblings is more likely to be conscripted to serve as Mom's partner or Dad's friend still makes sense.

Healthy Adultification?

Growing up requires practicing more-and-more adultlike skills, privileges, and responsibilities over time (that is, the hierarchy gradually shifts to grant the child more and more power, control, and access to resources) commensurate with the child's emerging abilities and cultural expectations. We call it "cute" when Mom allows her four-year-old daughter to make her own breakfast or when Dad allows his ten-year-old son to help paint the house (never mind that we call it oppositional or entitled or

---

31. This convergence of risk factors is known as "intersectionality." *See, e.g.*, Edna Erez & Shannon Harper, *Intersectionality, Immigration, and Domestic Violence*, *in* The Handbook of Race, Ethnicity, Crime, and Justice 457 (Ramiro Martinez et al. eds., 2018).

32. Burnett et al., *supra* note 29.

ungrateful when these same children refuse to do these same chores ten years later). We do not, however, think of these as adultifying behaviors because the parents continue to hold the reins of authority and remain present in case a problem should arise. In effect, the child is allowed or encouraged to experiment with a new degree of autonomy without any loss of felt-security. These are instances of the healthy holding tight/letting go dynamic at work.

The same may be true when the parents hire or otherwise require one child to care for her siblings on occasion. Temporarily delegating caregiving responsibilities to a child is not adultification as long as the parent retains the authority and the child retains his safety net. These are, instead, instances of healthy practicing. This distinction is unfortunately lost when these labels are misused and conflated in the research literature. For example, "[t]emporary parentification is considered normative at times and may even be associated with responsibility, competence, and autonomy in children who are given adequate support and acknowledged for their helpfulness."[33] Indeed, practice exercising adultlike privileges and responsibilities is normative and necessary and associated with later competence and skill. By contrast, eroding the power hierarchy within the family system, corrupting roles, and taking on a minor child as a peer and equal partner is never a healthy dynamic.

Adultification Co-Occurs with Other Destructive Dynamics

When parent and minor child become equal partners, when the two function on the same level of the power and control hierarchy within the family system, adultification is at work. And when that corrupted relationship is built around animosity for the other parent, it may be that both adultification and alienation are at work. Alienation is discussed in Chapter 15. For example:

> Dr. A. found Mother and John to be "in lock step" with their opinion that Father was not a person of merit—a "scoundrel, a

33. *Id.* at 181.

cheater, a fake." In this regard, they have established an enmeshed dynamic wherein they act as one another's "protector." Mother acts as John's protector in that she assumes a gate-keeping position asserting that contact with Father will be dangerous to John and upend his wonderful life. Mother also assumes the role of Father's victim and engages John as her protector.[34]

The costs of adultification are broad and profound and can be lasting. The dynamic can negatively impact not only the individual child, but contribute to that child growing to become a needy parent vulnerable to turn to his child for emotional support. Like a line of dominoes falling backward, children nurturing parents, the dynamic can corrupt serial generations, compromising the emotional well-being of every member of the affected systems.

The adultified child is socially precocious. Because serving as a parent's best friend both increases adult contact and decreases peer contact, these kids develop an impressive ability to engage with anyone of any age. But perhaps most obviously, adultification quickly washes away the intimidation and deference many children feel when engaging adults. Thus, no matter his age, the adultified child can play any room. He appears able to manage any social interaction with poise, without fear, and with skill. No matter the state of his verbal skills (often enhanced through practice and exposure among adults), this child is an excellent listener and very adept at winning adult attention, affection, and acceptance.

The problem, of course, is that underneath the shiny and entertaining or demanding and entitled exterior is an empty shell. The adultified child's emotional development is often much less mature, if not entirely stymied and even regressed. Cheated out of opportunities to differentiate and manage his own unique emotional states, terrified that strong feelings provoke rejection, abandonment, and loss, missing out on playground and backyard lessons in frustration tolerance, delay of gratification, friendship, win-lose, and anger management, the adultified child

34. Proceeding under Article 6 of the Family Court Act W.K. v. J.K., 63 Misc. 3d 1221(A), 107 N.Y.S.3d 817 (table) (N.Y. Fam. Ct. 2018). Note that the last sentence suggests that John has also been parentified in the enmeshed relationship with his mother.

might never outgrow the preschooler's me-here-now emotional maturity. These deficits can undermine the foundation of adult self-regulation and executive functions. Raised in the belief that he is entitled and deserving of every attention but without ever coalescing a bounded sense of self distinct from others, this child will become angry and resentful, lonely, scared, defiant, jealous, and disrespectful. For example:

> Chronic childhood [adultification] is associated with subsequent negative outcomes in adulthood, including depressive symptoms . . . ambivalence about dependency needs . . . characteristics of narcissistic and self-defeating personality styles . . . a sense of personal inauthenticity or "imposter phenomenon" . . . and a tendency to utilize splitting as a psychological defense.[35]

Research teaches us that adultified children are at high risk for "anxiety, hyper-organization, poor relations with others, and poor educational and career achievement."[36] In addition, "[a]dultification was also negatively related to . . . living autonomously in adulthood, transitions of emerging adulthood, number of sexual partners, but positively related to smoking marijuana and binge drinking."[37]

Most powerfully and dramatically, the adultified child, like the parentified and the infantilized child, is at risk of failing to individuate. This refers to the healthy and necessary process of launching away from family and toward autonomy. Enmeshment inhibits this necessary and natural process by definition, often due to the child's fear that growing up and growing away will cost him his parent's love. This child's experience of family dynamics have taught him that physical separation and emotional separateness are to be avoided at all costs.

---

35. These authors used "parentification" although their working definition is much closer to our use of "adultification," thus the substitution of terms. Burnett et al., *supra* note 29, at 182.

36. Burton, *supra* note 16.

37. Julia Margarita Bernard, *Exploring the Predictors and Outcomes of the Adultification of Adolescents*, 72 Dissertation Abstracts Int'l Sec. A: Human. & Soc. Sci. 5-A (2011) (Ph.D. dissertation, Purdue University).

Remedies for the adultified child's systemically acquired social and emotional dysfunctions must be systemic if they are to be real and lasting. These include:

1. Relieving the pressure on the child by helping the adultifying parent get her needs met elsewhere.[38] For example, anecdotal reports strongly suggest that community interventions intended to assure that stressed caregivers' logistic and emotional needs are fulfilled can reduce the risk of adultification and parentification on their children.[39]
2. Demoting the adultified child in a sensitive, supportive manner, emphasizing the relief and greater freedoms of the new role and teaching her new and healthier ways of winning affection, attention, and acceptance at home and in the peer community.[40] We see these dynamics play out, for example, among children who have been adultified in the wake of one parent's military deployment when the family roles shift back upon the soldier-parent's return.[41]
3. When the goal is establishing age-appropriate roles and relationships, targeted cognitive-behavioral interventions may be necessary. These tools can help an adultified youth to begin dating, get a driver's license, spend time with her other parent, or simply move out on her own. But even after these goals are achieved, larger issues about identity and separation and loss and emotion regulation, are likely to persist and need insight-oriented therapies, group therapies (e.g., dialectical behavior therapy (DBT)),

38. *See* Cliff Yung-Chi Chen & Andrea Panebianco, *Physical and Psychological Conditions of Parental Chronic Illness, Parentification, and Adolescent Psychological Adjustment*, 35 Psych. & Health 1075 (2020).

39. *See* Elizabeth Krumrei et al., *Post-Divorce Adjustment and Social Relationships: A Meta-Analytic Review*, 46 J. Divorce & Remarriage 145 (2007).

40. *See* Helen W. Coale, *Therapeutic Rituals and Rites of Passage: Helping Parentified Children and Their Families*, *in* Burdened Children: Theory, Research, and Treatment of Parentification 132 (Nancy D. Chase ed., 1999); *see also* Helen W. Coale, *Therapeutic Use of Rituals with Stepfamilies*, 2 Fam. J. 2 (1994).

41. *See* Amy Reinkober Drummet et al., *Military Families under Stress: Implications for Family Life Education*, 52 Fam. Rel. 279 (2003).

and healthy, corrective emotional relationships. The success of these therapies may require that the adultifying parent participate in simultaneous supportive and educational therapies of her own so as to learn to genuinely give the child permission to separate, individuate, and enjoy healthy age-appropriate relationships.

Chapter 12
Parentification

"I think it's very sad, the parentification of [this little boy]. He has been parent and it's kind of hard to give up that role. He's been the parent for . . . [his] siblings and [his] mother, to protect."[1]

"[T]he child grew up 'parentified,' that is, he essentially functioned as defendant's parent rather than the other way around, and he placed her needs ahead of his own."[2]

Definition:	Parentification is one of at least three distinct and mutually compatible forms of enmeshment. Parentification describes pressures within the dysfunctional family system that enlist the child as the adult's caregiver in contravention of age- and culture-specific expectations and at a grave cost to the child's healthy social and emotional development.
Subtypes:	Instrumental parentification describes a dynamic within which a child is enlisted to care for practical matters in a parent's life. By contrast, emotional parentification describes the dynamic within which a child is enlisted to care for the adult's emotional needs

1. Contra Costa County Children & Family Servs. Bureau v. C.S. (*In re* X.V.), 2019 WL 1353492, at *7 (Cal. Ct. App. Mar. 26, 2019).
2. N.J. Div. of Child Prot. & Permanency v. Y.Z. (*In re* Guardianship of D.Z.), 2015 WL 1237829, at *1 (N.J. Super. Ct. App. Div. Mar. 19, 2015).

Reasonable precautions:	The parentified child (more so the emotionally than the instrumentally parentified child), like the adultified child, feels special and valued by the adult who relies upon him for his well-being. The parentified child may appear to be entitled, defiant, and resistant to or resentful of age-appropriate limits, activities, and interests. Unlike the adultified child, the parentified child has learned to win attention, acceptance, and affection by caring for others. As a result, this child often does not know how and/or cannot comfortably receive others' caring.
What to look for:	The parentified child, like the adultified child, is likely to have specific pockets of precocious and/or inappropriate adult information, awareness, and sensitivities. Having been enlisted as one parent's caregiver, the parentified child may be hypervigilant in matters concerning that parent's welfare such as medication compliance, substance abuse, medical illness, self-harm, and/or suicidality. The parentified child may resist or refuse contact with his other parent in the belief and/or having experienced that the parentifying parent cannot function while they are apart.
How to respond to the adults:	The parentifying adult has misdirected his need for care on to the child. This may be due to real needs that are not otherwise fulfilled and/or a manipulative need to keep the child close. Comprehensive social, emotional, intellectual, addictions, financial, housing, nutrition, and medical assessments (among others) may be necessary in order to assure the adult's proper care. Psychotherapy and psychoeducation will be necessary to help the adult reassure the child that she has adequate supports and that the child can therefore safely separate.

How to respond to the child:	The parentified child has learned to win attention, affection, and acceptance by serving as a parent's parent at a terrific cost to her own development, well-being, and happiness. She needs both reassurances that the parent with whom she is enmeshed is safe and corrective experiences to help her learn how to engage in healthy, reciprocal relationships. This child is particularly poor at self-care and thereby at high risk for engaging in non-reciprocating (coercive, controlling, exploitative) adult relationships and developing compassion fatigue, vicarious trauma, and burnout in the workplace.
Implications for custody-related decisions:	The parentified child needs time away from the parentifying adult, so as to experience healthy, reciprocal relationships and to develop appropriate interpersonal boundaries, but may regress or decompensate if wrenched away from the parent for whom she cares. Recognizing this dilemma, the court must simultaneously implement remedies for both the parentifying parent and the parentified child so as to give both permission to separate and individuate safely. In some extreme instances, it is only when the parentifying adult has been hospitalized that the child can begin to discover healthier ways of relating elsewhere.

Definitions (Again)

The words and phrases used to distinguish the various manifestations of enmeshment are generally awkward, polysyllabic mouthfuls referencing vaguely defined thoughts, feelings, and/or relationships. Chapter 11 argued for a carefully circumscribed definition of adultification as a specific parent-child relationship dynamic distinct from its many alternate uses and its commonly conflated, if not conjoined twin, parentification.

Defining parentification is a bit easier given that the term is used far less frequently across disciplines. In general, *parentification* is used to describe a child's age and culturally atypical caregiving role within the family system. For example: "Parentification has been defined as a distortion of, disturbance in, or lack of appropriate boundaries between family subsystems, resulting in a functional or emotional role reversal in which the child takes on adult responsibilities that are inappropriate for his or her developmental stage and age."[3]

Unfortunately, this definition and others like it prove to be overly broad. It glosses over a single, critically important variable that arises in the relevant literature in two distinct ways. This variable not only bears on how we define parentification but is strongly associated with its developmental outcomes.

At issue is the child's emotional security or subjective experience of care and containment.[4] No matter the nature, longevity, or severity of family stresses, no matter the variation of rules and roles within the family system, children prove to be emotionally healthier, more resilient, and enjoy better developmental outcomes when they feel continuously cared for and contained by their caregivers.[5] We often refer to this as felt-security and the sources of this felt-security as emotional anchors.

More specifically, the security of the parent-child relationship and the breadth of the child's subjective experience of emotional support within the family system, across allied systems (e.g., neighborhood, extended family, faith organization), and superordinate systems (e.g., case manager, therapist, principal, probation officer) help to mitigate the otherwise

---

3. Lisa M. Hooper et al., *Parentification in Military Families: Overlapping Constructs and Theoretical Explorations in Family, Clinical, and Military Psychology*, 39 Child. & Youth Services Rev. 124, 124 (2014).

4. "The parentified child's future development and the possible outcomes may depend on how the child feels about, and makes meaning of, the parentification experience." Judyta Borchet et al., *We Are in This Together: Retrospective Parentification, Sibling Relationships, and Self-Esteem*, 29 J. Child & Fam. Stud. 2982, 2982 (2020).

5. "War acquires comparatively little significance for children so long as it only threatens their lives, disturbs their material comfort, or cuts their food rations. It becomes enormously significant the moment it breaks up family life and uproots the first emotional attachments of the child within the family group." Anna Freud & Dorothy T. Burlingham, War and Children 37 (1943).

deleterious impact of parentification.[6] This essential truth is evident time and again as we consider two distinct types of parentification, the experience of the child-as-parent-to-siblings and the instrumental versus emotional responsibilities incurred by the child-as-parent-to-parent.[7]

Children as Their Siblings' Caregivers?

The developmental and family law literature often uses the term *parentification* as an umbrella term to capture two very different dynamics in need of differentiation: child-as-parent-to-siblings and child-as-parent-to-parent. Unfortunately, a great deal of research using the term *parentification* fails to make this distinction, creating a morass of often contradictory observations and confusing empirical findings.

For want of better labels, child-as-parent-to-siblings describes those family systems in which a child (usually first-born and more often than not female) takes on a surrogate caregiving role for her sibling(s). This is often seen in high-stress families when adults are impoverished, linguistically or culturally isolated, overwhelmed with work responsibilities, chronically ill, and/or substance dependent.

By contrast, we reserve the term *parentification* to refer to child-as-parent-to-parent. The literature teaches us that this can occur in one or both of two distinct ways. *Instrumental parentification* describes a child's role providing practical assistance to a parent (e.g., making sure Mom takes her medications on time or Dad gets up for work). *Emotional parentification* describes a child's role serving the adult's emotional needs (e.g., reassuring, providing affection, attention, acceptance). Among these three distinct but mutually compatible uses of the term (i.e., child-as-parent-to-siblings, instrumental parentification, and emotional parentification), we know that emotional parentification is most likely to negatively impact the child's social and emotional development.

6. Borchet et al., *supra* note 4.

7. Noting that others frame this distinction differently. For example, see Peter Jankowski, *Parentification and Mental Health Symptoms: Mediator Effects of Perceived Unfairness and Differentiation of Self*, 35 J. Fam. Therapy 43 (2013).

Parentification Occurs across Relationship Ecologies

None of these dynamics are restricted to a particular type of family system or circumstance. We know that triangulation and enmeshment in their various forms are more likely to occur as family stresses increase in number and severity and that family systems with fewer resources (i.e., those that are less resilient) are more vulnerable. Beyond that, it's important to understand that these dynamics can occur across socioeconomic strata, zip codes, cultures, races, religions, genders, and with no regard for the legal status of the relationships within the family unit. The literature describes parentification (broadly defined) occurring when parents are chronically, acutely, and/or terminally ill, when parents are addicted, deployed in the military, and incarcerated.

Parentification (broadly defined) has been noted among immigrant families,[8] impoverished families,[9] and intact families in which both parents work full time.[10] The phenomenon is frequently discussed as it pertains to single-parent families "in which the mother becomes so overburdened that she begins to rely too much on her 'right-hand man.' The parentified child often becomes parent to the parent in this situation. This structure is maintained at the cost of the child's normal, age-appropriate thrust toward interaction with his peer group."[11] A child is more likely to face parentification if that child is female[12] and her mother is ill, single, or out of work.[13]

---

8. Olga Oznobishin & Jenny Kurman, *Parent-Child Role Reversal and Psychological Adjustment among Immigrant Youth in Israel*, 23 J. Fam. Psych. 405 (2009).

9. Thomas J. McMahon & Suniya S. Luthar, *Defining Characteristics and Potential Consequences of Caretaking Burden among Children Living in Poverty*, 77 Am. J. Orthopsychiatry 267 (2007).

10. Earl A. Groomsman & Gerri L. Sweder, The Working Parent Dilemma (1986).

11. Nancy Boyd-Franklin, Black Families in Therapy: A Multisystems Approach 623 (1989).

12. Deborah Jacobitz et al., *Cross-Sex and Same-Sex Family Alliances: Immediate and Long-Term Effects on Sons and Daughters*, *in* Burdened Children: Theory, Research, and Treatment of Parentification 34 (Nancy Chase ed., 1999).

13. *See* Jo Aldridge, *The Experiences of Children Living with and Caring for Parents with Mental Illness*, 15 Child Abuse Rev. 79 (2006).

Research suggests that chronically, critically, and terminally ill parents may be more likely to engage their child in both instrumental and emotional parentification: "Ill parents' energy/fatigue level was not related to adolescent distress, but ill parents' emotional well-being was directly associated with adolescent distress. Adolescents' household responsibilities were not linked to their distress level; however, higher levels of emotional parentification appeared to affect their psychological adjustment."[14]

Parentification may be most frequently studied in the context of adult substance dependence. For example:

> [C]hildren in inconsistent environments may create their own systematic patterns as a way to cope. This facet of parentification is likely to be operating in alcoholic families as well. When parents drink and children feel frightened and helpless, they may care for their parents [in order] to bring some sense of control to an otherwise uncontrollable situation.[15]

Indeed, parents with chronic and critical illnesses,[16] who are substance dependent,[17] and who are diagnosed with character pathology[18] may be most likely to parentify their kids.

---

14. Cliff Yung-Chi Chen & Andrea Panebianco, *Physical and Psychological Conditions of Parental Chronic Illness, Parentification, and Adolescent Psychological Adjustment*, 35 Psych. Health 1075, 1087 (2020).

15. Genie Burnett et al., Family Unpredictability, *Parental Alcoholism, and the Development of Parentification*, 34 Am. J. Fam. Therapy 181, 186 (2006).

16. Marie M. Duryea, *Mothers with Chronic Physical Illness and the Parentification of Their Children*, 69 Dissertation Abstracts Int'l Sec. B: Sci. & Engineering 714 (2008), https://repository.unm.edu/dspace/bitstream/1928/3608/1/Duryea_Dissertation.pdf; *see also* Tanya L. Tompkins, *Parentification and Maternal HIV Infection: Beneficial Role or Pathological Burden?*, 16 J. Child & Fam. Stud. 113 (2007).

17. Marolyn Wells et al., *Codependency: A Grass Roots Construct's Relationship to Shame-Proneness, Low Self-Esteem, and Childhood Parentification*, 27 Am. J. Fam. Therapy 63 (1999).

18. Monica M. Fitzgerald, *Child Sexual Abuse, Early Family Risk, and Childhood Parentification: Pathways to Current Psychosocial Adjustment*, 22 J. Fam. Psych. 320 (2008).

Mothers are more likely to parentify their children than fathers.[19] Adults who do not find their adult partners nurturing and supportive[20] and those who report that their own parents were not adequately nurturing are more likely to parentify their children.[21] With regard to the latter, one author hypothesizes that

> emotionally deprived parents may unconsciously regard their children as parental figures . . . it is plausible that some type of deprivation, abuse, or serious boundary violation in the parent's background (primary determinant) leads to parentifying attitudes and cognitions (mediators), which in turn result in the destructive parentification of one of the children.[22]

Developmental Outcomes

Parentification (broadly defined) is often construed as deleterious to the child's development, particularly as it impedes the child's willingness and ability to separate.[23] Numerous studies associate parentification (broadly defined) with diagnosed pathology including eating disorders, affective

---

19. Tara S. Peris & Robert E. Emery, *Redefining the Parent-Child Relationship Following Divorce: Examining the Risk for Boundary Dissolution*, 5 J. Emotional Abuse 169 (2005); *see also* Tara S. Peris et al., *Marital Conflict and Support Seeking by Parents in Adolescence: Empirical Support for the Parentification Construct*, 22 J. Fam. Psych. 633 (2008).

20. Boyd-Franklin, *supra* note 11.

21. Refer to Chapter 10 and the idea of intergenerational transmission. *See also* Wells et al., *supra* note 17.

22. Gregory J. Jurkovic, *Destructive Parentification in Families: Causes and Consequences, in* Family Psychopathology: The Relational Roots of Dysfunctional Behavior 237 (Luciano L'Abate ed., 1998).

23. "Over the past four decades, the parentification discourse has focused largely on associations with pathology, such as the following conditions and disorders: trauma, distress, and adversity; eating disorders; mood disorders; substance use disorders; dissociative disorders; and personality disorders." Lisa M. Hooper et al., *Characterizing the Magnitude of the Relation between Self-Reported Childhood Parentification and Adult Psychopathology: A Meta-Analysis*, 67 J. Clinical Psych. 1028, 1028 (2011).

disorders, substance abuse, and characterological disorders,[24] noting that the child's age and duration of the child's service in the parentified role may be related to the severity of its impact.[25] "A considerable body of evidence suggests that the consequences of parentification are often destructive, crippling, traumatic, and negative . . . . Furthermore, experiencing parentification during adolescence may engender unique pernicious outcomes."[26]

Upon a thorough review of the research, one author found the negative developmental sequelae of parentification so pervasive and profound that she recommends that every healthcare professional must screen for childhood parentification.[27] This is likely because,

> [p]arentified children often suffer from depression, suicidal feelings, shame, excessive guilt, unrelenting worry, social isolation, and other internalizing symptoms, such as psychosomatic problems . . . . Parentification during a youngster's formative years is often the prologue to an adult life characterized by interpersonal distrust . . . an inability to function independently, and—perpetuating the cycle—a tendency to misuse parental authority.[28]

---

24. "Parentification is associated with both masochistic and narcissistic personality styles in adults and that individuals who have been parentified have diminished capacities for object relations under conditions of separation and disappointment in others." Marolyn Wells & Rebecca Jones, *Relationship among Childhood Parentification, Splitting, and Dissociation: Preliminary Findings*, 26 Am. J. Fam. Therapy 331, 332 (1998).

25. Kim Shifren & Lauren V. Kachorek, *Does Early Caregiving Matter? The Effects on Young Caregiver's Adult Mental Health*, 27 Int'l J. Behav. Dev. 338 (2003).

26. Lisa M. Hooper, *Parentification, in* Encyclopedia of Adolescence 2023 (Roger J.R. Levesque ed., 2012). Note that this observation goes contrary to our general belief that the impact of destructive family dynamics diminishes as the child's early history of healthy family dynamics increases. This author's statement suggests that the impact of enmeshment may be specific to the child's developmental needs.

27. "It is important for clinical psychologists and other mental health care providers to assess for level and duration of the parentification roles and responsibilities carried out in the family of origin." Hooper et al., *supra* note 23, at 12.

28. Gregory J. Jurkovic, Lost Childhood: The Plight of the Parentified Child xiv (1997).

Reports of the developmental costs that the parentified child incurs are deeply concerning, but must be interpreted with caution, due to failures to distinguish effects as a function of the specific dynamic, confirmation bias on the part of researchers,[29] and race/culture differences.

On balance, taking on instrumental caregiving roles in the family (including child-as-parent-to-siblings) can be a positive experience particularly for older children, as long as the parent remains emotionally present and responsive in the child's life. Recall that our review of enmeshment more generally and adultification in particular reached a similar conclusion.

Instrumental parentification has been shown to have its developmental and systemic benefits, including promoting the development of the child's resilience[30] and social skills.[31] "In some circumstances, such as when caring for a sibling (as distinct from caring for a parent), parentification may engender feelings of self-efficacy, competence, and other positive outcomes."[32] One overview suggests that parentification (broadly defined) can be associated with improved problem-solving and coping skills, personal growth, competence, decreased risk of substance abuse and dependence, and overall positive mental health.[33]

We note finally that culture and race may be very important mediators of the effect of parentification within the family system: "Emotional parentification was associated with positive outcomes among African American youth in the form of increased parent-child relationship quality."[34]

---

29. Lisa M. Hooper, *Predictors of Growth and Distress Following Childhood Parentification: A Retrospective Exploratory Study*, 17 J. Child & Fam. Stud. 693 (2008).

30. Antonietta DiCaccavo, *Working with Parentification: Implications for Clients and Counseling Psychologists*, 79 Psych. & Psychotherapy: Theory Rsch. & Prac. 469 (2006).

31. Alison Thirkield, The Role of Fairness in Emotional and Social Outcomes of Childhood Filial Responsibility (2002) (unpublished Ph.D. dissertation, Georgia State University).

32. Borchet et al., *supra* note 4, at 2987.

33. Hooper, *supra* note 26.

34. Tamar Y. Khafi, *Ethnic Differences in the Developmental Significance of Parentification*, 53 Fam. Process 267 (2014).

Chapter 13
Infantilization and the Helicopter Parent

"This child is not a porcelain doll. We actually harm the ability of children to develop independence to assist in their own protection by over-protecting them."[1]

"[T]he overall pattern of her behaviours suggest that at times K uses her children to fulfill her own personal needs for attention, to elicit support and services from others, and to receive affection and approval from professionals. Such behaviour can be damaging to her children and may lead to the children receiving misdiagnoses or unnecessary treatment."[2]

Definition:	Infantilization is one of at least three distinct and mutually compatible forms of enmeshment. Infantilization describes pressures within the family system that impede a child's otherwise healthy development in the service of a parent who needs to be needed.

1. Morwald-Benevides v. Benevides, [2017] O.N.S.C. 539 para. 120, http://canlii.ca/t/h5cs8.
2. D. v. K., [2015] A.B.P.C. 121 para. 85, http://canlii.ca/t/gjgx9.

Subtypes:	**Four mutually compatible subtypes are discussed:** • *Adaptive or relationship-specific infantilization* describes an otherwise healthy child's regressed or delayed functioning exclusively in relationship to one parent or context and not elsewhere in the child's life. The infantilization is adaptive to the specific relationship ecology even though it is maladaptive and inappropriate to the child's development generally. • *Permissive infantilization* describes an otherwise healthy child's regressed or delayed functioning in one or more relationships associated with excessively permissive, enabling, and conflict-avoidant parenting practices. • *Opportunistic infantilization* describes an otherwise healthy child's regressed or delayed functioning that serves an instrumental purpose outside of the infantilizing dyad. • *Infantilization as factitious disorder imposed on another* describes the dynamic in effect when a parent intentionally injures or induces an illness in his child so as to personally benefit from the resulting sympathy and emotional support.
Reasonable precautions:	Infantilization poses two immediate and potentially dangerous dilemmas that family law professionals must carefully assess: (1) the infantilizing parent may appear to be a model caregiver when the child is very young, injured, ill, or otherwise needy and thereby very difficult to recognize, and (2) in the extreme, infantilization can do lasting harm to the child who is deprived of the opportunity to develop toward autonomy, who is taught to be dependent, and who suffers real psychological and physical trauma up to and including death.

What to look for:	Children who are dependent on care in a manner and/or to a degree that is atypical of age and cultural norms and not otherwise attributable to medical, cognitive, psychological, or sensory difficulties. The child's neediness may be exclusively or primarily evident in the care of one parent and greatly diminished or absent in other relationship environments.
How to respond to the adults:	Infantilization, like adultification and parentification, occurs when an adult inappropriately enlists a child to fulfill the adult's needs. In the case of infantilization, the best response once again helps the parent to establish healthy alternate means of fulfilling those needs so as to explicitly give the child permission to be healthy and to develop toward autonomy.
How to respond to the child:	The infantilized child's developmental delays, illnesses, injuries, and disabilities have been rewarded with adult attention, affection, and acceptance. His natural drive for separation and autonomy have been inhibited, ignored, or punished by withholding, withdrawal, or outright rejection. Remedies call for reversing these dynamics so as to allow and encourage the child's cautious movement toward age- and culture-appropriate independence one step at a time.
Implications for custody-related decisions:	Identifying and responding to infantilization in the context of contested custody litigation requires deference to experts who are able to confidently determine that the child's developmental deficits are not the result of genuine medical, psychological, developmental, or sensory impairments/delays and are due, instead, to the pressures within the enmeshed parent-child relationship. Chronic and recalcitrant infantilization is abusive and can put the child in immediate physical danger, thus requiring prompt and certain responses from child protective services, medical personnel, and the courts.

Definitions (One More Time)

Whereas the terms *adultification* and (less so) *parentification* are often assigned overly inclusive and misleading meanings, the term *infantilization* has seldom been heard in the context of family law. Indeed, when the term is used at all, it most often carries a pejorative sense of condescension and even sexism or racism, as in "a progressive loss of initiative and the kind of submission to a situation in which there is no autonomy, which has no opportunity for independent action or decision."[3]

Much as the term *infantilization* may be unfamiliar in the context of family law, the concept it communicates is commonplace. Look no further than the latest edition of any parenting magazine or blog to discover dramatic descriptions of this dynamic disguised under one or another synonymous colloquialisms including "helicopter parenting,"[4] "overparenting,"[5] and "the cosseted parent." These pop-culture monikers are inevitably jam-packed with adjectives like "overprotective," "overbearing," "permissive," "intrusive," and "overindulgent," which then leak into psychological research and the legal record. For example:

> Dr. Meeske testified that it was evident that [Mother] clearly loves her boys and wants to do what she can to help the children. However, her intentions are "misplaced" and she assumes the role of the helicopter parent and then it's very difficult for the boys to

---

3. Morales Feliciano v. Romero-Barcelo, 672 F. Supp. 591, 611 (D.P.R. 1986). In the context of gender bias, see *Verdu v. Trs. of Princeton Univ.*, 2020 WL 1502849, at *4 (D.N.J. Mar. 30, 2020) ("the infantilization of women plays into archaic gender stereotypes about women as chaste, sexually innocent, naive, lacking sexual autonomy, and needing protection").

4. *See* Wendy M. Rote et al., *Helicopter Parenting and Perceived Overcontrol by Emerging Adults: A Family-Level Profile Analysis*, 29 J. Child & Fam. Stud. 3153 (2020).

5. One hypothesis is that the excessive control involved in overparenting may increase the likelihood that children are unable to regulate emotions or relationships. *See* Nathan A. Winner & Bonnie C. Nicholson, *Overparenting and Narcissism in Young Adults: The Mediating Role of Psychological Control*, 27 J. Child & Fam. Stud. 3650 (2018).

> take direction from [staff] because the boys act as the victim. And then [Mother] comes in and tries to act as the rescuer.[6]

Infantilization is the term used in psychology to describe those parent-child relationships in which the adult enjoys, benefits from, and/or nurtures the child's dependent neediness and thereby inhibits her healthy development. Although the infantilizing parent may indeed be overprotective, overbearing, permissive, intrusive, and overindulgent, these are elements of a much larger pathological and abusive systemic dynamic that is both chronic and progressive, escalating by degrees over time as the child's maladaptive dependence causes him to fall further and further behind the development of his age-mates.

It's easy to think about this concept in terms of learning to ride a bike.[7] Good parenting means being able and willing to take the training wheels off at some point, running alongside as the child finds her confidence, and then making the excruciating decision to let go even though you know that she's going to fall. She might even get hurt. A parent who can give her child this confidence, who has the emotional maturity to let go, and who has the fortitude to be there to kiss the boo-boo and encourage her to try again is supporting healthy development.

An infantilizing, overcontrolling, or "helicopter parent" can't or won't let go. This adult's primitive and misplaced need to feel needed and in control far supersedes his ability to support his child's drive toward autonomy. As a result, the training wheels stay on or the bike is taken away altogether. This parent experiences the child's natural experimentation with separation as threatening and unacceptable. In its place, an infantile neediness is nurtured and reinforced. The result is a deeply enmeshed and pathological dynamic.

---

6. Schriner v. Schriner, 903 N.W.2d 691, 700 (Neb. Ct. App. 2017).

7. With credit to Benjamin D. Garber, Holding Tight/Letting Go: Raising Healthy Kids in Anxious Times (2016).

Is the parent who inhibits a child's separation in response to objective and immediate danger infantilizing? If so, then most of the world's parents spent more than a full year infantilizing their children during the COVID-19 pandemic. Schools shut down. Playgrounds were emptied. Families interacted with no one but themselves.

No, this is not infantilization, overprotection, or helicopter parenting. This is keeping your children safe. However, the motivation doesn't matter if you're concerned with the impact on the child. There is growing evidence that the year or more of quarantine has taken a very significant toll on the social, emotional, and academic development of an entire generation,[8] most especially minority children.[9]

Resting this distinction on an assessment of danger highlights two important points. First, the risk of danger is ultimately in the eye of the beholder even when the Centers for Disease Control and Prevention and local, state, and federal governments issue safety advisories. One of the many lessons learned during the pandemic is how little consensus there is among well-educated and intelligent people about what is real and what is dangerous. Parents still argue that COVID-19 is a hoax and that those who kept their children home from school and away from the playgrounds are overprotective.[10]

Second, it's important to recognize that the same ambiguous distinction about objective danger is often used to distinguish two other family system dynamics: alienation and estrangement. We address this matter in detail in Chapters 14 and 15.

---

8. Shannon L. Stewart et al., *Child and Youth Mental Health Needs and Service Utilization during COVID-19*, Traumatology (advance online publication) (2021), https://doi.org/10.1037/trm0000345.

9. Amanpreet Bhogal et al., *Are the Kids Really Alright? Impact of COVID-19 on Mental Health in a Majority Black American Sample of Schoolchildren*, 304 Psych. Rsch. (2021), https://doi.org/10.1016/j.psychres.2021.114146.

10. Personal Communication with Dr. Laura M. Landerman (Apr. 9, 2021), disclosed with permission.

The infantilizing parent allows hold-me-tight and forbids any degree of its otherwise healthy counterpart, let-me-go. The result is a child who never learns how to tolerate frustration, delay gratification, or manage adversity. He is never given the opportunity to learn to regulate his own emotional states, never mind his sleep-wake cycle, his bowels, or his bladder. This means that he never has the opportunity to develop any separateness from the infantilizing parent who takes perverse pleasure in managing the child's body and emotions and needs.

This child's experience of peers or friendships is typically extremely limited and brief. Unable to function independently, the infantilized child's neediness and infantile state elicit peer rejection, bullying, and ridicule, which reinforces his avoidance and his retreat into the infantilizing cocoon. Further:

> The infantilized child may be home-schooled or chronically truant. He or she will be more or less explicitly discouraged from making friends and made to feel guilty or simply forbidden from participating in age-appropriate activities. By the middle of grade school, this child may be labeled as school resistant, developmentally delayed, agoraphobic, or asocial in a manner this author has seen misdiagnosed as an autistic spectrum disorder. In fact, infantilized children frequently suffer from anxiety disorders, depression, and various developmental delays due to isolation, lack of developmentally appropriate experience, and guilt and may require treatment, but the conventional regime of individual psychotherapy and medication will fail. The primary cause of this child's challenges resides not in his or her biology, but within the family's dynamics.[11]

11. Benjamin D. Garber, *Parental Alienation and the Dynamics of the Enmeshed Parent-Child Dyad: Adultification, Parentification, and Infantilization*, 49 Fam. Ct. Rev. 322, 327 (2011).

A Case Example from Our First Author (Garber)

I'll never forget an evaluation I provided to the court many years ago. A young woman had had four children, each by a different father. The first died under mysterious circumstances in her care at age three. The second and third had each been removed from her care by child protective services (CPS) in their toddler years due to the mother's well-documented abuse, one with two broken legs. The fourth child, ten months old at the time of the evaluation, had been removed from her care and placed in long-term foster care at birth as a precaution, although the pair had maintained weekly supervised visits. By law, CPS had to attempt to reunify Mother and toddler before terminating her parental rights to the fourth child and allowing his foster parents to adopt him.

My job was to evaluate Mother's parenting capacity and the quality of the parent-child relationship.

I spent six hours with this mother and infant across several days in a variety of conditions. Time and again, she proved to be wonderfully sensitive and responsive to the child. She carried him and rocked him and fed and clothed him. She was kind and supportive. She was ready with a diaper or a lullaby or a distracting toy when he needed it. She was patient and generous and understanding. I saw nothing at all to criticize or even recommend. Although these observations were diametrically opposed to the vast and compelling documentation of her abuse of her first three children, my job was to report what I observed.

I prepared my report and was subpoenaed to testify. The state's attorney asked me to explain the obvious discrepancy between my observations and this woman's unambiguous history of horrific child abuse. Was she putting on a show because she knew that she was being observed? Maybe, but the alternate hypothesis was that this young mother needed to be needed. She provided excellent care as long as her child was needy and dependent. She had only become abusive of her older children (and had perhaps even murdered the first) when each had become mobile and begun to separate from her. Each child's shaky first tiny steps so threatened this woman that she decompensated in rage.

Who Infantilizes?

The incidence and impact of overparenting varies by gender, culture, immigration status, race, and religion.[12] The literature suggests that mothers are more often seen as more overinvolved in their child's lives than fathers. First time parents are seen as more overprotective than their more experienced peers, and parents who have suffered losses due to miscarriage, sudden infant death, and other fatal tragedies understandably struggle with letting go.

"Helicopter parents" are commonly identified as anxious[13] and perfectionistic by nature.[14] The effects of these behaviors differ by the parents' gender, such that intrusive fathering has been associated with children's poorer *emotional* adjustment, while intrusive mothering has been associated with poorer *social* adjustment (especially for sons) in young adulthood.[15]

Several studies have at least speculated that overprotective, helicopter, and infantilizing parenting practices reflect the adults' "psychological control practices, which involve emotional and psychological manipulation of children (e.g., inducing guilt, withholding love as a form of control)."[16]

---

12. Melanie M. Domenech Rodríguez et al., *Parenting Styles in a Cultural Context: Observations of "Protective Parenting" in First-Generation Latinos*, 48 Fam. Process 195 (2009).

13. Ryan J. Gagnon, *Examining Overparenting, Socioeconomic Status, and Parental Out-of-Time Experience: Does Socioeconomic Status and Out-of-School-Time Experience Matter?*, 1010 Child. & Youth Services. Rev. 181 (2019).

14. Chris Segrin et al., *Overparenting Is Associated with Perfectionism in Parents of Young Adults*, 9 Couple & Fam. Psych. 181 (2020).

15. Sofie Rousseau & Miri Scharf, *"I Will Guide You" The Indirect Link between Overparenting and Young Adults' Adjustment*, 228 Psychiatry Rsch. 826 (2015).

16. Winner & Nicholson, *supra* note 5. As this book is being written, we are all observing and experiencing the impact of the COVID pandemic on families and institutions. Some of this research may have to be reconsidered in that context as to its impact on children and adverse childhood experiences, for example, or the impact across child development phases. *See* Daniel Bryant et al., *The Rise of Adverse Childhood Experiences During the COVID-19 Pandemic*, 12.S1 Psychol. Trauma: Theory, Rsch., Prac. & Pol'y S193 (2020).

Who Is Most Likely to Be Infantilized?

We don't know. We find no reliable data suggesting differences that one might expect on the basis of gender; age; gestational, perinatal, or infant health; developmental course; or family composition, although we do know that the likelihood of infantilization diminishes as the number of children in a sibling group increases.[17]

We venture that children who have survived any number of high-risk variables from complicated pregnancy to emergency delivery, neonatal intensive care needs, and early injuries and those with older siblings who have survived similar events are at higher risk of being overprotected. This is different, however, from infantilization in that overprotection is adaptive because it is associated with a real past or continuing threat while infantilization is about the adult's need to feel needed.

The Effects on the Child

At the broadest level, infantilization interrupts or reverses the development of the healthy boundaries that define self as distinct from other. Although the mechanics of how the process plays out can take several different forms, the result is a child who is unable to explore her social, emotional, and developmental potential.[18] The infantilized child is unable to separate from the enmeshed caregiver, is socially and emotionally (if not physically) dependent on that caregiver, and is weak or entirely lacking in the skills necessary to successfully engage with same-age peers.[19]

Later in life, children who were infantilized are more likely to struggle academically and in the workplace.[20] The experience of infantiliza-

17. *See* Jill C. Bradley-Geist & Julie B. Olson-Buchanan, *Helicopter Parents: An Examination of the Correlates of Over-Parenting of College Students*, 56 Educ. & Training 314 (2014).

18. Aaron M. Luebbe et al., *Dimensionality of Helicopter Parenting and Relations to Emotional, Decision-Making, and Academic Functioning in Emerging Adults*, 25 Assessment 841 (2018).

19. Richard L. Munich & Matthew A. Munich, *Overparenting and the Narcissistic Pursuit of Attachment*, 39 Psychiatric Annals 227 (2009).

20. Bradley-Geist & Olson-Buchanan, *supra* note 17.

tion has been associated with higher levels of young adult anxiety and depression,[21] entitlement,[22] and with lower levels of self-efficacy among college students.[23] Children who identify their parents as intrusive and overcontrolling tend to demonstrate weaker empathy and overall moral development,[24] and an increased likelihood of engaging in substance abuse.[25]

Observations of benefits associated with intrusive and infantilizing parenting suggest moderating factors. Some of these contradictory findings may be due to inconsistent definitions, gender differences, and the mediating effects of parental warmth or affection.[26] For example, it appears that college-age daughters are more negatively impacted by helicopter parenting than sons[27] even though "higher levels of helicopter parenting were indirectly linked to better psychological adjustment (fewer

---

21. Jaerim Lee & Sieun Kang, *Perceived Helicopter Parenting and Korean Emerging Adults' Psychological Adjustment: The Mediational Role of Parent-Child Affection and Pressure from Parental Career Expectations*, 27 J. CHILD & FAM. STUD. 3672 (2018).

22. Holly H. Schiffrin & Miriam Liss, *The Effects of Helicopter Parenting on Academic Motivation*, 26 J. CHILD & FAM. STUD. 1472 (2017).

23. Veronica Darlow et al., *The Relationship between Helicopter Parenting and Adjustment to College*, 26 J. CHILD & FAM. STUD. 2291 (2017).

24. "[H]elicopter parenting could undermine empathic and prosocial outcomes by negatively impacting self-regulatory behaviors and promoting narcissistic tendencies." Meredith McGinley, *Can Hovering Hinder Helping? Examining the Joint Effects of Helicopter Parenting and Attachment on Prosocial Behaviors and Empathy in Emerging Adults*, 179 J. GENETIC PSYCH.: RSCH. & THEORY ON HUM. DEV. 102 (2018).

25. "[H]elicopter parenting was associated with higher levels of alcohol use through lower levels of psychological needs satisfaction and self-control." Ming Cui et al., *Helicopter Parenting, Self-Regulatory Processes, and Alcohol Use among Female College Students*, 26 J. ADULT DEV. 97, 97 (2019); *see also* Jie Xu & Xiaoxia Cao, *Young Adults' (Mis)use of Prescription Opioid Drugs: An Exploratory Study*, 35 HEALTH COMM. 1407 (2019).

26. Larry J. Nelson et al., *Is Hovering Smothering or Loving? An Examination of Parental Warmth as a Moderator of Relations between Helicopter Parenting and Emerging Adults' Indices of Adjustment*, 3 EMERGING ADULTHOOD 282 (2015), https://doi.org/10.1177/2167696815576458.

27. "[P]arents' behavior continues to predict their child's well-being even in emerging adulthood, and that parenting may differentially predict male and female college students' mental health outcomes." Chrystyna D. Kouros, *Helicopter Parenting, Autonomy Support, and College Students' Mental Health and Well-Being: The Moderating Role of Sex and Ethnicity*, 26 J. CHILD & FAM. STUD. 939 (2017).

depressive symptoms, greater satisfaction with life) through higher levels of parent-child affection."[28]

Our reading of the literature in developmental psychology, relevant legal and medical cases, and our experience as clinicians and family law professionals suggests the value of distinguishing four types of infantilization:

1. **Adaptive or relationship-specific infantilization.** In one presentation, infantilization is associated with a child's regressed or delayed functioning in the context of one parent-child dyad but not in any other social environment (e.g., with the other parent or at school). This child is adapting chameleon-like to fit into very different environments, one of which implicitly rewards developmental dysfunction. The discrepancy between her presentations can confound evaluators and inflame litigation because the two parents sound as if they are describing completely different children.

Dad describes ten-year-old Billy as independent and skilled and confident and successful. The child toilets well, feeds and dresses himself, and enjoys many healthy friendships. Mom describes the same child as needy and demanding and regressed. He soils himself, needs help with basic self-care, and insists on sleeping with her when they're together. The linear, sequential reasoning of the legal process demands that one of these parents must be lying or delusional when, in fact, the child is simply adapting to fit into each of two distinct relationship dynamics.

2. **Permissive infantilization.** Healthy caregivers recognize that anger is part of the natural and necessary palette of human emotions. They teach their children how to tolerate and express their strong emotions by their example and through experience. This is how most people learn to tolerate frustration and delay gratification.

In sharp contrast, some people are terrified of anger and confrontation in any form in any setting. Whether this is the residue of early trauma, the experience of their parents' anger ending love, and/or other causes doesn't matter. What matters is that as parents, these adults will do anything to keep their children happy. They can never say no, they can

28. Lee & Kang, *supra* note 21.

never set limits and follow through, they can never discipline or scold or correct for fear of eliciting anger.

The result is a permissive type of infantilization that cheats a child out of the opportunity to learn to manage her own emotional experiences. Unlike the infantilized child who is cloistered and socially isolated, this child may be free to engage the world but utterly lacks the skills to do so. Never having had to wait or take turns or lose at a game, never having had to share or come in second place, this child can't manage any relationship but the one in which his every whim and wish is immediately fulfilled.

Parenting Priorities?

This discussion of permissive infantilization highlights the value of assessing parents' parenting priorities. We find this very useful in any number of clinical and forensic contexts. Responses often provide valuable insight into parenting beliefs, practices, and overall family functioning.[29] The task is simple and quick. It is easily repeated across time in the interest of tracking change or completed simultaneously but independently by parenting partners in the interest of assessing and addressing caregiving consistency.

The participating parent is asked to rank order 15 statements from 1 = most important to 15 = least important. No items should be skipped and no numbers should be repeated.

Item (priority ratings where 1 = highest priority and 15 = lowest priority)	Parent A's rankings	Parent B's rankings
A successful co-parenting relationship with my child(ren)'s other parent		
Finding a new partner or spouse for myself		

(continued on next page)

29. Copied with permission from Benjamin D. Garber, Ten Child-Centered Forensic Family Evaluation Tools: An Empirically Annotated Users' Guide (2015).

Item (priority ratings where 1 = highest priority and 15 = lowest priority)	Parent A's rankings	Parent B's rankings
My ability to provide for my child(ren) financially		
My child(ren)'s happiness		
My child(ren)'s other parent's happiness		
My child(ren)'s other parent's physical and mental health		
My child(ren)'s physical and mental health		
My own happiness		
My own physical and mental health		
The amount of time that I'm with my children each week/month		
The comfort of the home that I provide for my child(ren)		
The quality of my child(ren)'s relationship with me		
The quality of my child(ren)'s relationship with my new/future partner or spouse		
The quality of my child(ren)'s relationship with their other parent		
The quality of my child(ren)'s relationship with their other parent's new/future partner or spouse		

Results must be interpreted with each parent by comparison to that parent's documented choices (e.g., "if you value your child's health more than your own, why do leave him at daycare every day while you go to the gym?"). More powerfully, Parent A's priorities are contrasted with Parent Bs priorities as one means of working toward greater co-parenting consistency or as part of a family system evaluation process.

3. **Opportunistic infantilization.** The term *infantilization* most often appears in case law when a child's real illness, injury, pain, and/or disability is neglected, needlessly prolonged, or exacerbated (but not created) by a parent who hopes for or enjoys associated financial gain and other practical benefits.[30] These cases appear most frequently as Social Security Disability appeals, malpractice torts, special education disputes, and divorce-related child support litigation.[31]

Opportunistic infantilization is evident in a parent's failure to adequately work to relieve, reduce, or remedy a child's real, preexisting medical and/or psychiatric needs so as to win a lawsuit, be granted government benefits, or to gain access to services and service providers. This infantilizing parent prioritizes practical rewards more than her child's pain. Opportunistic infantilization can be seen, for example, in the mother who repeatedly misses her son's physical therapy appointments because the greater the child's handicap, the greater the likelihood of a settlement from the insurance company of the driver who hit him. It's evident, as well, in the divorcing dad who neglects his son's insulin injections and then lies to the divorce court so as to make the child's mother look neglectful. Opportunistic infantilization is evident in the court's ruling about a seventh-grade boy who was seriously injured in his gym class at school:

> [Father] has effectively infantilized his son and this dynamic has contributed both to the development and persistence of his ongoing disability . . . [Father's] own overly protective and overly solicitous attitudes and actions have played a role in creating

30. If the goal is only external (e.g., financial gain, insurance payout, or paid leave from work), the fifth edition of the Diagnostic and Statistical Manual (DSM-5) would identify this as *malingering* (V65.2) (i.e., the intentional manufacture or exaggeration of illness or injury in order to earn external incentives).

31. We recognize the flipside of this pathological coin: those caregivers who ignore or deny a child's real injury, illness, or disability. This is (medical) neglect. It is not infantilization and is not diagnosable as factitious disorder imposed on another: "Caregivers who lie about abuse injuries in dependents solely to protect themselves from liability are not diagnosed with factitious disorder imposed on another because protection from liability is an external reward." American Psychiatric Association, Diagnostic and Statistical Manual of Mental Disorders (DSM-5) 300.19 (5th ed. 2013).

> Devon's original vulnerable mental state, his reaction to the head injury, and the reinforcement of the somatoform complaints which followed. His continued obsessive attending on Devon has only reinforced this disability.[32]

4. **Infantilization as factitious disorder imposed on another?** Factitious disorder imposed on another (FDOA) (formerly known as Munchausen syndrome by proxy and factitious disorder by proxy and elsewhere known as "fabricated and/or induced illness in children"[33]) is a Diagnostic and Statistical Manual Fifth Edition (DSM-5) condition diagnosable in a caregiver who induces or alleges an illness, injury, or disability in her child so as to selfishly benefit from responding professionals' attention and the child's resulting neediness.[34] These responses "can be seen in schools, churches, the legal system, child protection agencies, the home, and the community at large."[35]

Whereas opportunistic infantilization takes advantage of a real and pre-existing illness, injury, or disability so as to gain practical benefits (especially

---

32. Hussack v. Sch. Dist. No. 33 (Chilliwack), [2009] B.C.S.C. 852 paras. 245–46, http://canlii.ca/t/2464z.

33. Anne Lazenbatt & Julie Taylor, *Fabricated or Induced Illness in Children: A Rare Form of Child Abuse?* (Univ. of Edinburgh Research Briefing 2011), https://www.research.ed.ac.uk/files/12941026/K201118.pdf.

34. We contend that the DSM diagnosis of the parent in this *folie à deux* is artificially constrained by the medical model of individual psychopathology. Like the arguments made (and rejected) in favor of diagnosing an alienating parent (Chapter 15), the description may be accurate but is insufficient. At issue is the relationship or the system. The DSM notably says little about the child "victim" of FDOA. Very much like the enmeshed parents described here, the FDOA parent is observed to be lacking in healthy, proper social and emotional supports and turns her needs inappropriately on her child. For example:

> Poor relationships with relatives and a poor social network appear to be environmental risk factors for FDIA [FDOA] conditions. The mothers, in both cases, were very isolated individuals with symbiotic links with their children. Also, conflictual relationships were reported in the parents' couples that were separated or experienced a conflictual marriage.

Noemi Faedda et al., *Don't Judge a Book by Its Cover: Factitious Disorder Imposed on Children—Report on 2 Cases*, 6 Frontiers Pediatrics 110 (2018).

35. *Id.*

money), infantilization via FDOA requires that the parent induce an illness, injury, or disability so to fulfill the adult's need for emotional gain.[36] In both cases, the infantilizing parent is using the child's pain for personal gain.

Infantilization, FDOA, and Sexual Abuse Allegations

In the context of contested custody litigation, serial unfounded allegations of child sexual abuse are occasionally identified as FDOA.[37] In these cases, one parent's (typically the mother's) repetitive and unsupported allegations are described as infantilizing efforts to win attention at grave cost to the child's well-being. For example:

> Dr. England also opines that Ms. A. may be suffering from Factitious Disorder Imposed on Another. She points to Ms. A.'s persistence that the children have been or are being sexually abused by their father, noting that: [Ms. A] is reporting that the children are experiencing a number of symptoms which if correct would warrant mental health diagnoses. This was most notable with [her son] where the severity level of [Ms. A.'s] presentation was at a level previously unseen by the writer. In the writer's opinion [Ms. A.'s] perception of the children is distorted by the lens of her mental health issues, with the result that she lacks an accurate grasp of the needs of the children. Most notably this relates to the children's relationship with their father.[38]

(continued on next page)

36. Noting that the DSM-5 criteria for FDOA (300.19) (1) require that "[t]he deceptive behavior is evident even in the absence of obvious external rewards"; and (2) contrary to our discussion, "[w]hile a preexisting medical condition may be present, the deceptive behavior or induction of injury associated with deception causes others to view such individuals (or another) as more ill or impaired, and this can lead to excessive clinical intervention."

37. UNICEF, Action to End Child Sexual Abuse and Exploitation: A Review of the Evidence (2020).

38. T.E.A. v. R.L.H.C., [2019] B.C.S.C. 1042 para. 146, http://canlii.ca/t/j16wn.

Or even more egregiously:

> Ms. Skriver noted that [Mother]'s insistence on having O participate in multiple medical sexual abuse examinations and her perceiving O as having been sexually abused was also reflective of a need for [Mother] to present O as impaired or abused. [Mother]'s lack of insight and her tendency to reconstruct reality to fit her beliefs, suggest that she truly believes O and [her sibling] to be displaying their identified behaviours and may even be unwittingly inducing some behaviours in her children.[39]

39. D. v. K., [2015] A.B.P.C. 121 para. 84, http://canlii.ca/t/gjgx9.

Chapter 14
Estrangement or Justified Rejection

"[M]other's volatile conduct and displays of temper, which, over the years, have been a source of deep emotional upset to the children and, at least in the case of Telly, have led to emotional estrangement from the mother."[1]

"Despite the father's assertions to the contrary, I find that the breakdown of the girls' relationship with their father is the result of the father's own actions, and not the result of any influence or alienating behaviours on the part of the mother."[2]

Definition:	Estrangement is a family systems dynamic characterized by a child's resistance to or refusal of contact with a parent whom the child reasonably associates with insensitive, unresponsive, inappropriate, abusive, neglectful, violent, and/or destructive words, actions, and expressed emotions.
Subtypes:	**Five mutually compatible subtypes are distinguished**: *Incidental avoidance* describes a child's resistance to and/or refusal of contact with one parent due to either the child's anxiety about unfamiliar and/or aversive stimuli proximally associated with that parent (e.g., a noxious odor, a threatening noise from a neighbor's apartment, that parent's needy new baby) and/or incidental rewards associated with the contact resistance/refusal (e.g., participating in a desired activity that might otherwise have been missed).

1. Webb v. Knudson, 582 A.2d 282, 287 (N.H. 1990).
2. Nduwayo v. Muhonga, [2018] O.N.S.C. 6730 para. 36, http://canlii.ca/t/hw3bt.

	Direct estrangement describes a dynamic characterized by a child's resistance to/refusal of contact with a parent who has previously directed insensitive, unresponsive, inappropriate, abusive, neglectful, violent, and/or destructive words, actions, and expressed emotions at the child. *Vicarious estrangement* describes a dynamic characterized by a child's resistance to/refusal of contact with a parent whom she has incidentally witnessed as having directed insensitive, unresponsive, inappropriate, abusive, neglectful, violent, and/or destructive words, actions, and expressed emotions at another person, animal, and/or toward property. *Traumatic estrangement* describes the child's anticipatory trauma-like response (e.g., dissociation, panic, hypervigilance, hyperreactivity) associated with the future prospect of contact with a parent who was previously experienced (directly or vicariously) as insensitive, unresponsive, inappropriate, abusive, neglectful, violent, and/or who used destructive words, actions, and expressed emotions. *Instrumental estrangement* describes the child's unassisted manufacture or intentional exaggeration of experiences with Parent B for the conscious purpose of rationalizing resist/refuse behaviors.
Reasonable precautions:	Findings of estrangement call first and foremost for an assessment of the child's safety in the care of the rejected parent. Distinctions among the types discussed here will help guide assessment and intervention. Evaluators and courts are cautioned that estrangement (of any type) is seldom the only dynamic causing the child's resist/refuse behavior. (See "Enumerating Relationship Pressures and Practical Hurdles" in Chapter 9.)
What to look for:	The estranged child is likely to credibly and consistently find contact with and the prospect of contact with the rejected parent anxiety-inducing if not traumatic. Changing the setting and time of proposed contacts and arranging for trusted others to be present or to supervise may quell

	some of this anxiety and help differentiate among types. The congruence of the child's words, emotions, and behaviors can help to rule out the hypothesis that others have scripted, prompted, bribed, and/or threatened the child, thereby inducing or exacerbating the resistance. The child may secretly harbor emotional ambivalence about the rejected parent.[3] The child may additionally experience a degree of guilt or otherwise feel responsible for causing the rejected parent's inappropriate behaviors.
How to respond to the adults:	The child's physical and emotional safety must be established as the first priority at all times. The aligned parent must be enlisted to both monitor the child's safety and support the child's cautious and therapeutically directed engagement or *reunification* with the rejected parent.[4] The rejected parent must (1) understand how his words, actions, and expressed emotions impact the child, (2) develop alternative and child-appropriate means of managing those same feelings and urges in the future, and (3) learn to patiently comply with court-ordered and therapeutic approaches intended to repair the formerly destructive family dynamic.[5]

3. "[Estranged] children can be distinguished from alienated children by their ability to acknowledge that they love the other parent but are not interested in pursuing much contact at the moment." Milanizadeh v. Zeinali, [2011] O.N.S.C. 870 para. 113, http://canlii.ca/t/ht4qc (quoting Nicholas Bala et al., *Alienated Children and Parental Separation: Legal Responses in Canada's Family Courts*, 33 Queen's L.J. 79 (2007)).

4. Benjamin D. Garber, Mending Fences: A Collaborative, Cognitive-Behavioral Reunification Protocol Serving the Best Interests of the Post-Divorce, Polarized Child (2021).

5. "By realising the impact that violent behaviour can have on children's wellbeing and fathers' interpersonal relationships with them, it is argued that intervention programmes can support men to develop more appropriate ways of relating to their children, and thus safeguard children from potential long-term consequences of domestic abuse." Timothy R. Broady et al., *"I Miss My Little One a Lot": How Father Love Motivates Change in Men Who Have Used Violence*, 26 Child Abuse Rev. 328 (2017).

How to respond to the child:	The child's strong feelings must be validated and her safety assured.[6] Any intervention intended to repair her relationship with the rejected parent must be cautiously paced to her needs and abilities and overtly supported by the aligned parent and others whom the child trusts.
Implications for custody-related decisions:	When the court determines that interventions to attempt to repair the schism between a parent and child are appropriate, it is often best to suspend concurrent evaluations and litigation while this process progresses. The outcome of a properly conducted "reunification" intervention will provide the court with data critically important to the future allocation of parenting rights and responsibilities.

Estrangement in its colloquial usage describes an individual's subjective experience of social distance, rejection, isolation, or detachment. As a verb, the term is often reflexive, referring to an individual's actions that effectively exclude or alienate himself from others.[7]

In the fifth edition of the Diagnostic and Statistical Manual (DSM-5), *estrangement* is used to describe trauma survivors' common feeling that no one can understand their experience.[8] The term is most notably used in the DSM-5 description of parent-child relational problem (V61.20), a nonclinical/nondiagnostic state characterized by "unwarranted feelings of estrangement." This aspiring diagnosis is, of course, the DSM-5 category that parental alienation syndrome (PAS)/parental

6. "[P]arental rights of access to offspring should not take precedence over child safety." American Professional Society on the Abuse of Children, ASPAC Position Paper on Allegations of Child Maltreatment and Intimate Partner Violence in Divorce/Parental Relationship Dissolution, https://2a566822-8004-431f-b136-8b004d74bfc2.filesusr.com/ugd/4700a8_c364609c272443a9942591a84ea97c6e.pdf.

7. For example: "Charlotte saw too clearly into her husband's intentions, through the disguise. For the first time she felt how far he had estranged himself from her." Johann Wolfgang von Goethe, Elective Affinities ch. XVI (J.G. Cottaische Buchhandlung, Berlin 1854).

8. For example, post-traumatic stress disorder is characterized in relevant part by "[f]eelings of detachment or estrangement from others." American Psychiatric Association, Diagnostic and Statistical Manual of Mental Disorders (DSM-5) (5th ed. 2013).

alienation disorder advocates rely upon as a backdoor means of asserting that alienation is, after all, included in the nosology.[9]

In family law, *estrangement* carries a very distinct but often misunderstood definition. Advising against the redefinition of common language for specialized purposes, Warshak advises, "The conceptual distinction between realistic and unrealistic aversion is useful, but the terms *alienated* and *estranged* to denote this distinction create confusion when communicating with the legal profession and the general public, for whom these terms carry different meanings. In standard usage, both terms refer to a distance in relationships, but neither term connotes whether or not the distance is rationally based."[10] Unlike its mainstream uses, in this context the verb is usually transitive and used to describe an action one might do to another, as in "the mother's harsh language estranged her son from her."

As a family systems dynamic, estrangement describes the breakdown of a parent-child relationship due to the child's realistic and warranted insecurity with, fear of, or resistance or refusal to engage that parent. "Realistic and warranted" refers to the child's direct and/or vicarious experience of that adult's insensitive, unresponsive, abusive, neglectful, and otherwise inappropriate words, actions, and expressed emotions.

> In the interest of brevity, we rely on a number of shorthand phrases throughout these chapters. For example:
>
> 1. In order to describe a child's resistance of and/or refusal to contact one parent, we refer to "resist/refuse dynamics" (RRD).
> 2. We commonly refer to generic parents identified as Parent A and Parent B without implications of their marital status, gender, or other demographic, geographic, or identity variables,

(continued on next page)

9. William Bernet, *Parental Alienation, DSM-V, and ICD-11*, *in* PARENTAL ALIENATION: THE HANDBOOK FOR MENTAL HEALTH AND LEGAL PROFESSIONALS 125 (Demosthenes Lorandos et al. eds., 2013).

10. Richard A. Warshak, *Family Bridges: Using Insights from Social Science to Reconnect Parents and Alienated Children*, 48(1) FAM. CT. REV. 71n2 (2010).

acknowledging that we arbitrarily describe hypothetical children whom we call Billy or Sally and their parents whom we refer to generically as Mother and Father. These conventions facilitate discussion and must not be construed as excluding same-sex, multigenerational, or never-married couples.

3. In the context of discussing estrangement, in particular, we use "inappropriate behavior" to refer generically to the full spectrum of insensitive, unresponsive, abusive, neglectful, and destructive words, actions, and expressed feelings that can contribute to a child's resist/refuse behaviors.[11]
4. We refer to "felt-security" to describe any individual's subjective state of comfort in a relationship with a second person. We take care not to confuse attachment security in this context.[12]

In recent history, estrangement has been inaccurately portrayed as the mutually exclusive polar opposite of alienation.[13] That is, family law experts often took the binary position (and a minority still do, albeit

11. "When attempting to differentiate alienation from realistic estrangement, it is important to recognize that lapses in good parenting are common and expected; there are no perfect parents. Incidents of poor parenting by the rejected parent may occur in some and even most cases of child alienation, although not necessarily all cases. In other cases, rejected parents are good or perfectly appropriate parents, both before and after the alienation surfaces." Barbara Jo Fidler & Nicholas Bala, *Children Resisting Postseparation Contact with a Parent: Concepts, Controversies, and Conundrums*, 48 Fam. Ct. Rev. 10, 16 (2010).

12. Further regarding attachment security and resist/refuse dynamics, see Benjamin D. Garber, *Parental Alienation in Light of Attachment Theory: Consideration of the Broader Implications for Child Development, Clinical Practice, and Forensic Process*, 1(4) J. Child Custody 49 (2004).

13. "Unfortunately, the responses of these realistically estranged children following separation are commonly and incorrectly interpreted and played out in custody disputes as PAS cases. The deficient, abusive, or violent parent frequently accuses the other parent of alienating the child against him or her." Joan B. Kelly & Janet R. Johnston, *The Alienated Child: A Reformulation of Parental Alienation Syndrome*, 39 Fam. Ct. Rev. 249 (2001).

under more sophisticated and misleading labels) that if a child is refusing contact with Parent B, but Parent B has not been found to have been abusive or neglectful, then Parent A must be alienating.[14] This sophistry is dissected in Chapter 15.

In fact, the science shows us clearly that RRD is a cake made of many distinct ingredients, each of which catalyzes and potentiates the others, each of which is baked in for a different period under its own unique pressures, ultimately yielding a product that is unique to the particular family's dynamics. Estrangement is only one among these many comingling ingredients.

Estrangement Is NOT a Dyadic Dynamic

Estrangement is manifest and too often assessed or attempted to be remedied exclusively within the artificial boundaries of the fractured Parent B–child dyad. Although the obvious working parts of the estranged parent-child relationship can be ascribed either to the rejected parent or the child, to imagine that allied and superordinate others within and outside the family system have no influence on the creation, maintenance, and resolution of this relationship is naïve and contrary to the systemic model.[15]

When a child resists or refuses contact with Parent B, there is nothing that Parent A can do or feel or say—including doing and saying nothing at all—that will *not* contribute to the dynamic. This is the nature of systems and particularly the nature of parent-child relationships. Children's desperate need for emotional fuel trains them, particularly under the stresses of relationship conflict, to become emotional

14. "[I]n cases when abuse or neglect have not occurred, it is highly probable—to 99% clinical certainty—that alienation is the cause of the rejection." Linda J. Gottlieb, Reunification Therapy for Severe Parental Alienation or for an Unreasonably Disrupted Parent-Child Relationship (2019), http://endparentalalienation.weebly.com/uploads/3/1/0/9/31091731/12-22-2019_tpff_treatment_protocol_x_4_6_18_ent_protocol_for_severe_alieantion_rejection.pdf.

15. Benjamin D. Garber, *The Dynamics of the Enmeshed Family System Ten Years Later: Growing Our Understanding of Adultification, Parentification, and Infantilization*, J. Am. Ass'n Matrimonial Law. (in press 2022).

barometers, reading and responding to the system's relational climate. This is the skill that allows many of these children to adapt chameleon-like to their very disparate relationships (Chapter 8). This is also why it is naïve to imagine that a child's rejection of Parent B can exist independent of the child's relationship with Parent A and with allied (siblings, peers, neighbors, extended family) and superordinate (teachers, faith leaders, therapists) others.

Even in the most egregious cases of documented child abuse and diagnosis of the child's resulting trauma, Parent A's most thoughtful, cautious, and well-intended support for her child invariably compounds the ongoing dynamic. Her valid condemnation of Parent B serves to entrench the child's resistance and solidify his model of Parent B as dangerous. This is, of course, necessary and defensible in the interest of safety, but it can also create an insurmountable confound when the court orders the child to engage in supervised visits or "reunification" therapy with Parent B.[16]

What Can Parent A Do?

Her rage at the former partner who harmed her child and her fear that he would do it again are justified, human, and even evolutionarily predetermined, but may put her in jeopardy with the courts. Should she endure findings of contempt, jail time, and even loss of the child's custody or somehow send her beloved child back into the lion's den?

Her tongue-biting restraint, validation of the child's pain, and great care to damn Parent B's *behavior* but not the man himself may feel like a betrayal to the child, fueling his anxiety and potentially compromising his trust in Parent A's ability to protect him. Her efforts to make sure that he has a cell phone with him at all times and remembers how to call 9-1-1, and to secretly tuck a GPS tracker in his backpack, may feel like necessary but not sufficient protections and surely will become fodder for future litigation.

---

16. Benjamin D. Garber, Mending Fences: A Collaborative, Cognitive-Behavioral Reunification Protocol Serving the Best Interests of the Post-Divorce, Polarized Child (2021).

Her minimization or denial of the child's very real experience and empty reassurances that all is well is a form of gaslighting likely to fuel the child's confusion, fear, rage, and mistrust. This is *misalignment*, the dynamic at work when Parent A exposes the child to unwarranted positives about Parent B, thereby putting the child in harm's way.[17]

There is no best answer when parenting instincts and safety run headlong into legal mandates. What these and similarly impossible dilemmas have taught us is that estrangement and alienation are not mutually exclusive opposites. They must never be pitted against one another as a binary, either/or choice. Estrangement and alienation are complementary and frequently co-occurring family system dynamics. The two co-exist with enmeshment within the family system as described by the hybrid model.[18] These three are more often than not all in effect to various degrees, bootstrapping off one another toward a terribly destructive crescendo of intractable polarization and all that that means for the child of such a dysfunctional system.

Estrangement and Enmeshment Are Opposites

This proposal likely jars your thinking. It asks you to move beyond the familiar but misleading alienation versus estrangement argument to really understand the nature of these destructive relationship patterns. Think about it: enmeshment blurs interpersonal boundaries. Estrangement rigidifies relationship boundaries. Enmeshment pulls parent and child together. Estrangement pushes parent and child apart. Enmeshment inhibits the child's movement toward autonomy. Estrangement forces it prematurely. Enmeshment demands *hold-me-tight*. Estrangement forces *let-me-go*. Enmeshment is the mother bird who won't risk allowing the fledgling to learn to fly. Estrangement is the mother bird who forces the fledgling out of the nest prematurely to protect herself.

---

17. Garber, *supra* note 12.

18. Steven Friedlander & Marjorie Gans Walters, *When a Child Rejects a Parent: Tailoring the Intervention to Fit the Problem*, 48 Fam. Ct. Rev. 98 (2010).

Confusing Labels

Nuanced scientific distinctions trickle down from theory and science into the courts and common parlance only as the need emerges. Who ever heard of an "N95" mask before COVID? This trickle-down process is slowed even further when experts disagree about these terms and their meanings. It is only today, as we write, that the critical distinctions among these words are slowly becoming important. Unfortunately, until the distinctions between family system dynamics become as clear and familiar as the distinctions between gasoline, hybrid, and electric vehicles, we're left with confusing and misleading distinctions such as these:

"[Mother] has alienated the children and is responsible for the children's estrangement from [Father]. . . ."[19]

"There can be little dispute that parental alienation exists as a dynamic in some divorcing families, involving the estrangement of a child from a parent."[20]

Are we to understand *alienation* in the professional sense but *estrangement* in the colloquial sense, or vice versa? Are these two courts suggesting that Parent A caused her child's estrangement from Parent B or that Parent B's inappropriate acts constitute alienation? We suspect that both courts are inelegantly confirming that Parent A's unwarranted negative words, actions, and expressed emotions about Parent B can needlessly undermine the child's relationship with Parent B.

Types of Estrangement

Our experience and reading of the literature suggest that estrangement is usefully distinguished as five distinct but mutually compatible types:

1. **Incidental estrangement** describes the dynamic associated with a child's resistance or avoidance of aversive relationships, events, and sensory stimuli that are incidental to Parent B. Those incidental factors may be within Parent B's control (e.g., a noxious cologne) or beyond his control (e.g., his new baby's crying, the ferocious dog in the apartment next door). In these and countless similar instances, the child may have little

19. *In re* Miller, 20 A.3d 854, 859 (N.H. 2011).

20. Snider v. Laszlo, [2009] CanLII 65367 para. 45, http://canlii.ca/t/26s65.

or no wish to avoid Parent B himself, and indeed may eagerly engage with him via distance media, outdoors, and away from his home. These incidental causes may seem to be trivial to others and are often quite easily fixed when they are identified early on. In the context of high-conflict divorce, however, failures of communication and confirmation bias can quickly turn these molehills into mountains. Witness, for example, how incidental estrangement can evolve into direct estrangement when Parent B proves to be insensitive and unresponsive to his daughter's pleas that he wear a different cologne, hire a babysitter, or visit someplace far away from the scary dog.

2. **Direct estrangement** describes the dynamic associated with a child's direct experience as the direct victim of Parent B's abusive, neglectful, insensitive, unresponsive, violent, and destructive acts. The mother who locks her five-year-old daughter in her bedroom for hours on end. The father who is drunk and unresponsive or passed out while his kids are in his care. The supercritical and demanding parent for whom nothing is ever good enough. These are among the prototypes most professionals think of when estrangement is discussed.

3. **Vicarious estrangement** describes the dynamic associated with the child's indirect experience of Parent B's abusive, neglectful, insensitive, unresponsive, violent, and destructive acts directed elsewhere including, for example, witnessing domestic violence between the parents, Parent B's abuse of the child's sibling or a pet, and/or Parent B's destruction of property.[21] For example: "Among this group are children who are estranged as a cumulative result of observing repeated violence or explosive outbursts of a parent during the marriage or after separation. . . . But unlike alienated children, the estranged children do not harbor unreasonable anger and/or fear."[22]

---

21. For example: "Children who have been exposed to intimate partner violence may identify with and show affection toward the abusive parent. Some children may show no obvious reactions while still struggling with exposure to intimate partner violence. Some resilient children may be minimally or not affected by their exposure." Association of Family and Conciliation Courts, Guidelines for Examining Intimate Partner Violence: A Supplement to the AFCC Model Standards of Practice for Custody Evaluation item 9 (2016).

22. Kelly & Johnston, *supra* note 13.

Do direct and vicarious trauma[23] affect the child similarly? They can. Certainly we know that "[i]ntimate partner violence in the presence of children is psychological child abuse. Childhood experience of and exposure to interpersonal violence constitute child welfare, public health, and legal problems, with lifelong physical health, mental health, and behavioral consequences . . . ."[24]

> Acknowledging that vicarious experience can motivate estrangement puts us on a slippery slope. Can indirect exposure to trauma result in estrangement, as when Parent A tells the child horror stories about Parent B? At first glance, the answer would seem to be no, that this constitutes alienation. But what if the horror story is valid and Parent A is acting in good faith to protect the child? Alienation, as defined in the next chapter, occurs when Parent A's message about Parent B is unwarranted and invalid. What of the parent who honestly tells her son that Daddy used to hit her? Or sliding further down the slope, what if Parent A truthfully told Billy that Parent B isn't paying child support? Does differentiating between estrangement and alienation in these cases depend at all on the minor child's age? Emotional maturity? On the impact of the message on the child's behavior and the family dynamics? On the speaker's motivations? These are among the many questions that we hope that this book will help motivate others to begin to answer.

4. **Traumatic estrangement** can co-occur with and be a result of either direct or vicarious estrangement. Traumatic estrangement describes the dynamic at work when a child's direct and/or vicarious experience of Parent B's inappropriate behavior is associated with contact resistance or refusal *and* very significant anxiety symptoms consistent with the diagnosis of post-traumatic stress disorder (PTSD). Consider the story of six-year-old Chance: "Chance began to show alarming signs of neglect

23. Chapter 18 touches on the effects of vicarious trauma on family law professionals.
24. American Professional Society on the Abuse of Children, *supra* note 6.

when returning from weekends with his father, and he became extraordinarily resistant to going on access visits with him on Fridays. When he saw his father arrive at school, he would start yelling, screaming and try to run away from him."[25]

PTSD-like symptoms include, for example, the child's hypervigilant and distracted preoccupation with whether Parent B is nearby or can hear or see her, disproportionate or hyperreactive responses to stimuli that she associates with Parent B, episodes of dissociation under high stress causing the child to feel like she is outside of herself looking in on the interaction with Parent B, and extreme anxiety up to and including panic in anticipation of contact with Parent B.

5. **Instrumental estrangement** describes the child's unassisted manufacture or intentional exaggeration of experiences with Parent B for the conscious purpose of rationalizing resist/refuse behaviors. This is splitting writ large on the canvas of high-conflict divorce, the child's selfish and manipulative capitalization on the conflicted family dynamics for personal gain. The goal may be to spend more time with peers, not to miss preferred activities in and around Parent A's home, greater access to technology and preferred foods and comforts, an effort to remain loyal to Parent A in support of her rejection of Parent B, and/or simply an effort to resolve the ambiguity and avoid the physical burdens of migrating back and forth between homes. In our experience, instrumental estrangement is often associated with adultification and parentification to the extent that the child needs an excuse to remain in Parent A's care so as to fill her needs.

Remedies Require Evaluations of Both Type and Risk

Safety first. Before the professional gets caught up in the distinctions between alienation, enmeshment, and estrangement, or the distinctions among these several types of estrangement, a thorough systems evaluation is necessary to clarify the nature and severity of the child's risk.[26]

---

25. Nduwayo v. Muhonga, [2018] O.N.S.C. 6730 para. 46, http://canlii.ca/t/hw3bt.
26. *E.g.*, Association of Family and Conciliation Courts, *supra* note 21.

But isn't an evaluation of the child sufficient? Wouldn't assessment of the child most efficiently answer these questions?

No. We emphasize again that the questions asked by the family courts are about relationships, not individuals. Dynamics, not diagnoses. The polarized child might eagerly and fluently dictate a dissertation on why Dad is bad and they should never meet again. That information is important, but it is never sufficient. It must be understood in the larger context of interviews with each parent and observations of the relationships in action whenever that is safe and legally permissible. Children are notoriously poor reporters,[27] vulnerable to leading questions,[28] confirmation and allegiance biases,[29] and the proximal and recency influences associated with adults' prompting, scripting, bribes, and threats. A developmental and systemic perspective requires that we understand that every child's presentation is necessarily shaped by her relationships.

Assessment can occur in one of at least three ways:

1. **Individual adult risk assessment** is an individual psychometric evaluation conducted by a qualified mental health professional intended to advise the court whether and how a particular adult's documented history, presentation in interview, third-party reference data, and psychometric (i.e., diagnostic) profile may be consistent with those of others known to be violent and/or abusive in the belief that such similarities are predictive of future risk.[30]

---

27. Kyle Hubbard et al., *Children's Recall Accuracy for Repeated Events over Multiple Interviews: Comparing Information Types*, 23 Psychiatry Psych. & L. 849 (2016).

28. "Children can be quite accurate witnesses at times. However, they can also incorporate information from misleading and suggestive questions into their recall, and once their event memory has been changed, children may be unable to provide accurate reports." Kelly L. Warren & Carole Peterson, *Exploring Parent-Child Discussions of Crime and Their Influence on Children's Memory*, 32 Behav. Sci. & L. 686 (2014).

29. Monica Lawson et al., *A Systematic Review of the Reliability of Children's Event Reports after Discussing Experiences with a Naïve, Knowledgeable, or Misled Parent*, 49 Developmental Rev. 62 (2018).

30. Acknowledging that "[t]he accuracy of screening instruments to identify children who will be abused or neglected has not been established." Julie Taylor et al., *Predicting Child Abuse and Neglect: Ethical, Theoretical, and Methodological Changes*, 17 J. Clinical Nursing 1193 (2008).

Of course, psychological risk assessment is familiar in other areas of the law.[31] In the context of conflicted family systems, such an evaluation presumes that certain measurable human qualities or attributes (e.g., impulse control, frustration tolerance, empathy, anger management) can be objectively assessed and are predictive of future risk.[32] This assumption is often challenged. For example: "Standard psychological testing is not useful for the purpose of identifying whether intimate partner violence has occurred and/or whether a given parent has committed or been subjected to intimate partner violence."[33]

2. **Parenting capacity evaluation** (PCE) often incorporates some or all of the same individual assessment methods characteristic of the individual adult risk assessment but adds other areas of inquiry intended to address the individual's abstract knowledge of and capacity for caregiving (e.g., perspective taking, empathy, willingness and ability to set limits and follow through). PCE is distinct from individual adult assessment on one hand and from child custody evaluation on the other, in that it intends to advise the court about an individual's *general* skills, knowledge, experience, and expectations as a caregiver. PCE pointedly does not look at the quality of the specific parent-child relationship in the belief that the evaluation is a necessary precondition before the child and parent can be seen together safely.

PCE is most commonly ordered in child protective litigation as a necessary antecedent to returning a child into the care of an abusive or neglectful parent.[34] The reliability and validity of both its constituent measures and the process overall have often been challenged.[35] In particular, instruments purported to be able to detect or predict child abuse

31. *See* N. Zoe Hilton, Domestic Violence Risk Assessment: Tools for Effective Prediction and Management (2d ed. 2021).

32. Edwin Megargee, *Using the Algebra of Aggression in Forensic Practice*, 13 Brit. J. Forensic Prac. 4 (2011), https://doi.org/10.5042/bjfp.2011.0045; *see also* Angela Moreland Begle et al., *Predicting Child Abuse Potential: An Empirical Investigation of Two Theoretical Frameworks*, 39 J. Clinical Child & Adolescent Psych. 208 (2010).

33. Association of Family and Conciliation Courts, *supra* note 21, at 10.

34. Stan Houston, *Assessing Parenting Capacity in Child Protection: Towards a Knowledge-Based Model*, 21 Child & Fam. Soc. Work 347 (2016).

35. *See* Karen S. Budd & Michelle J. Holdsworth, *Issues in Clinical Assessment of Minimal Parenting Competence*, 25 J. Clinical Child Psych. 1 (1996); Karen S. Budd et al.,

potential must be recognized for their limitations.[36] This point is particularly important when the concern is whether a child is likely to be subject to the vicarious trauma associated with intimate partner violence.[37]

3. **Contextual dyadic assessment (CDA)** refers to assessment of an adult's risk in the context of a larger systems-focused evaluation. We note that this approach is consistent with some authorities' recommendations,[38] but may be inconsistent with others'.[39] Within the limits of safety and always respecting the court's protective orders, we advocate strongly for CDA in the belief that dyadic relationships are seldom adequately understood when they are artificially removed from the larger context in which they function.[40] In particular, we recommend a process-oriented model of family systems evaluation that specifically allows evaluation of each subsystem within the larger relationship ecology.[41]

Clinical Assessment of Parents in Child Protection Cases: An Empirical Analysis, 25 Law & Hum. Behav. 93 (2001).

36. A number of standardized assessment instruments are available. *E.g.*, Ko Ling Chan, *Evaluating the Risk of Child Abuse: The Child Abuse Risk Assessment Scale (CARAS)*, 27 J. Interpersonal Violence 951 (2011). The reader is advised to review all psychometric instruments via the Buros Center for Testing, at https://buros.org. *See* Tony Carr et al., *The DAS24: A Short Form of the Derriford Appearance Scale DAS59 to Measure Individual Responses to Living with Problems of Appearance*, 10 Brit. J. Health Psych. 285 (2005).

37. "Risk factors included: (a) contextual characteristics of partners (demographic, neighborhood, community and school factors), (b) developmental characteristics and behaviors of the partners (e.g., family, peer, psychological/behavioral, and cognitive factors), and (c) relationship influences and interactional patterns." Deborah M. Capaldi et al., *A Systematic Review of Risk Factors for Intimate Partner Violence*, 3 Partner Abuse 231, 231 (2012).

38. "Screening is an ongoing process rather than a one-time event." Association of Family and Conciliation Courts, *supra* note 21, at 5 (item 2).

39. "In situations of marital/relationship dissolution, the allegation of interpersonal violence needs to be addressed before issues of custody and visitation can be addressed." American Professional Society on the Abuse of Children, *supra* note 6.

40. Acknowledging the opposing view as voiced here about "reunification" therapies: "Instead of possibly dealing directly with abuse that may have occurred and rather than providing for their best interests, the mental health professionals are potentially seriously harming children even further." Toby Kleinman, *Family Court Ordered "Reunification Therapy:" Junk Science in the Guise of Helping Parent/Child Relationships?*, 14 J. Child Custody: Rsch. Issues & Pracs. 296, 296 (2017).

41. Benjamin D. Garber, *Exploring a Process-Oriented Forensic Family Observation Protocol*, 54 Fam. Ct. Rev. 261 (2016).

Priorities Again

Estrangement in the context of divorce forces the court to weigh the child's presumed risk of exposure to inappropriate adult behavior against the child's need to enjoy a healthy relationship with both (all) caregivers. Although this balancing act will be unique to each child's particular circumstance, we endorse Johnston's plan for how the court should prioritize competing factors,[42] ever mindful that parent-child contact can become a platform for a violent adult to continue to perpetrate violence.[43] This plan establishes the following priorities in sequence:

- Priority 1: Protect children
- Priority 2: Protect the safety and well-being of the victim parent
- Priority 3: Respect the right of adult victims to direct their own lives
- Priority 4: Hold perpetrators accountable for their abusive behavior
- Priority 5: Allow children access to both parents

42. As cited in Nancy Ver Steegh & Clare Dalton, *Report from the Wingspread Conference on Domestic Violence and Family Courts*, 46 Fam. Ct. Rev. 454 (2008).

43. Marisa L. Beeble, *Abusive Men's Use of Children to Control Their Partners and Ex-Partners*, 12 Eur. Psych. 54 (2007).

Chapter 15
Alienation

"Parental alienation at one level or another . . . is effectively supporting the child in cruel, unempathic behavior towards another human being. . . . [T]he child is being supported in oversimplified, polarized, black-and-white thinking, which undermines critical-thinking skills . . . these kinds of adverse effects can persist long-term and can have adverse effects on adult capacity for intimate relationships and on adult capacity for emotional self-regulation."[1]

"[Father] has been determined to win the children to his side of this high-conflict divorce by repeatedly finding ways to make his household seem nurturing, fun, and safe, while making [Mother's] household seem neglectful, boring, and dangerous. I predict he will continue to engage in the same campaign at every opportunity. With that in mind, I believe the children should be protected from his toxic influence."[2]

Definition:	Alienation is a family systems dynamic characterized by the child's alignment with Parent A and resistance to or refusal of contact with Parent B due to his experience of Parent A's and/or her allies' unwarranted negative words, actions, and expressed emotions about Parent B.

1. McClain v. McClain, 539 S.W.3d 170, 205 (Tenn. Ct. App. 2017).
2. Duke v. Duke, No. M2013-00624-COA-R3-CV, 2014 WL 4966902, at *7 (Tenn. Ct. App. Oct. 3, 2014).

Reasonable precautions:	The concept of alienation as it occurs in the context of high-conflict divorce has been extremely controversial for decades. Family court professionals are strongly advised to remain current in and be critical consumers of the rapidly evolving literature and case law. Binary theories ("if it's not X, it must be Y") by any name and binary orders ("evaluate whether the child's behavior is due to alienation") no matter how well intended must be eschewed in favor of language that recognizes the many mutually compatible dynamics that can and routinely do contribute to these dynamics.
What to look for:	A triangulated child who has become polarized within the adult conflict, taking a rigid and consistent position in favor of one parent and against the other without proportionate and objective reasons. Elements of enmeshment are likely to be evident within the aligned dyad and estrangement within the rejected dyad. Incidental factors (e.g., the child's sensory preferences, peer group, missed opportunities) and practical factors (e.g., travel time between homes) must be factored into a comprehensive formulation.
How to respond to the adults:	All concerned adults must act to support the child's opportunity to enjoy a safe and healthy relationship with all of her caregivers. The aligned parent and her allies must be educated about the social and emotional harm they are causing the child by exposing her to unwarranted damning messages about her other parent. The rejected parent must be assisted to pick his battles carefully, communicating his affection, attention, and acceptance to the child without further triangulating her by responding to her parroted, exaggerated, and manufactured rationalizations.
How to respond to the system:	A coordinated family systems intervention may be necessary with the goal of rebalancing the quality of the child's relationships, simultaneously repairing her role in her enmeshed relationship with Parent A and (re-) establishing a healthy, age- and culture-appropriate role

	with Parent B. This complex collection of interventions, often referred to as "reunification therapy," is less a talking, insight-oriented process than it is a corrective emotional experience.
Implications for custody-related decisions:	A parent's intractable and selfish choice to expose her child to unwarranted negative words, actions, and expressed emotions about another parent is tantamount to abuse. Timely, incisive, systemically informed, and developmentally attuned orders are necessary and can include, at the extreme, abrupt placement of the child in the care of the rejected parent.

A Very Brief History of Alienation in the Context of Family Law[3]

Although the concept of *alienation* is as old as the concept of family itself,[4] it became a focus of the family law community's shared consciousness in the 1980s due to the very aggressive advocacy of psychiatrist Richard Gardner. Gardner applied the common law tort known as "alienation of affections" brought by men against their wives' adulterous lovers to child custody litigation. He coined the phrase "parental alienation syndrome" (PAS) to describe in very gender-specific language an illness ("syndrome") that he believed arose within a child when a child rejects his father as a result of his mother's "campaign of denigration."[5]

3. There are many sources available that provide a more detailed history of the concept. Among these, the court's ruling in *M.M.B. (V.) v. C.M.V.*, [2017] O.N.S.C. 3991, https://www.canlii.org/en/on/onsc/doc/2017/2017onsc3991/2017onsc3991.html, provides a very practical, readable, and applied summary.

4. For example, "[i]n 1949, psychoanalyst, Wilhelm Reich observed that certain personality types amongst divorced parents psychologically defend themselves from narcissistic injury by fighting for custody of their child and defaming their partner in an effort to rob the other parent of the pleasure of the child." Barbara Jo Fidler & Nick Bala, Best Practice Guide: Responding to Emotional Harm of Children in High Conflict Separation 16 (2013). As further example, see Jay Haley, *Toward a Theory of Pathological Systems*, *in* The Interactional View 31 (Paul Watzlawick & John Weakland eds., 1977).

5. Richard A. Gardner, *Recommendation for Dealing with Parents Who Induce a Parental Alienation Syndrome in Their Children*, 28 J. Divorce & Remarriage 1 (1998); *see also*

Although PAS and its conjoined twin "parental alienation disorder" (PAD) have since been rejected by the scientific community after years of heated debate,[6] those painful decades of conflict yielded at least three important and continuing outcomes relevant to contemporary family law.

The first and most important but least often recognized of these outcomes is an awakening to the role of systemic dynamics. Prior to Gardner and the PAS debate, custody evaluation and litigation amounted to a contest to determine which of two parents had the most florid pathology, the more destructive addiction, the longest arrest record, the most money, and the more compelling influence with the courts. The PAS fiasco forced the field to begin to think about the quality of relationships—that is, to focus on dynamics, not diagnoses. Indeed, this book is one of the many products born of that painful birthing.

The second and much more obvious outgrowth of the PAS controversy is a schism that persists to this day in the family law community. On one side is a relatively small but extremely vocal group of professionals who once advocated for PAS and, failing that, subsequently advocated for the inclusion of PAD in the fifth edition of the Diagnostic and Statistical Manual (DSM-5).[7] Failing that, this faction has since largely (but not consistently) dropped the "syndrome" and "disorder" labels in order to argue that *alienation* is indeed incorporated by reference in the DSM-5 and to persist in advocating for Gardner's model, albeit using less provocative and more politically correct language.[8]

Richard A. Gardner, *Parental Alienation Syndrome vs. Parental Alienation: Which Diagnosis Should Evaluators Use in Child Custody Disputes?*, 30 Am. J. Fam. Therapy 93 (2002).

6. For the contrary view, see, for example, William Bernet, *Parental Alienation and Misinformation Proliferation*, 58 Fam. Ct. Rev. 293 (2020).

7. William Bernet & Amy J.L. Baker, *Parental Alienation, DSM-5, and ICD-11: Response to Critics*, 41 J. Am. Acad. Psychiatry & L. 98 (2013); *see also* William Bernet et al., *Parental Alienation, DSM-V, and ICD-11*, 38 Am. J. Fam. Therapy 76 (2010).

8. "[E]fforts to surreptitiously cloak the theory in the disguise of something benign cannot hide the theory's syllogistic components and nature. Whether the label is mere 'parental alienation' or 'alienation' or 'parental alienation disorder' or some other term, the best interests of children and the interests of justice require that lawyers, judges, and other legal professionals look behind the label being used and determine exactly what version of 'parental alienation' is being applied." Kimberly Joyce, *Under the Microscope:*

On the other side of this contemporary schism is the majority of the scientific community. These are professionals who span the full gamut of roles, cultures, training, and experience who recognize alienation as one among a host of systemic dynamics that must all be weighed in the process of understanding any particular child's polarized position within his family system. This is the third and most important outcome of the developmental process unknowingly jump-started by Gardner. Whereas the neo-Gardner advocates' position comes replete with very appealing if misleading and empirically questionable lists of behaviors, symptoms, and formulaic remedies, the majority opinion is weighted down by the plodding pace of science-done-well, control groups, representative samples, hypothesis testing free of confirmation bias, successive reformulations, the gray areas associated with statistical probabilities, and the absence of one-size-fits-all answers.[9]

As authors, we are proud to speak on behalf of the latter group and openly acknowledge that we eschew the positions advocated by the post-Gardner minority position as defying common sense, illogical, ill-founded, scientifically invalid, and as often causing harm to the child whose well-being we are all committed to serve.

Alienation Is a Dynamic, Not a Diagnosis

Advocacy against recognition of PAS/PAD rests on a number of critical arguments. Central among these is the assertion that alienation is a relationship dynamic that exists *between individuals*, rather than a diagnosis

---

The Admissibility of Parental Alienation Syndrome, 32 J. Am. Acad. Matrimonial Law. 53, 72 (2019).

There is no small irony in the fact that the professional community concerned with divorce is, in one manner of speaking, itself enduring a divorce. Given the fractal nature of nested systems, it's reasonable to expect that all of the dynamics discussed here are being played out at this superordinate level. Indeed, organizations and agencies such as the American Psychiatric Association and the World Health Organization have become polarized in this conflict, each aligned with one side and rejecting the other. *See, e.g.*, World Health Organization, Organizational Memo re: Inclusion of "Parental Alienation" as a "Caregiver-Child Relationship Problem" Code QE52.0 in International Classification of Diseases 11th Revision (ICD-11) (2020).

9. *E.g.*, Joan B. Kelly & Janet R. Johnston, *The Alienated Child: A Reformulation of Parental Alienation Syndrome*, 39 Fam. Ct. Rev. 249 (2001).

that exists *within an individual.* This position is diametrically opposed to the minority view that alienation "is a mental condition in which a child, usually one whose parents are engaged in a high-conflict separation or divorce, allies himself strongly with one parent (the preferred parent) and rejects a relationship with the other parent (the alienated parent) without legitimate justification."[10]

This distinction is important at least to the extent that it bears on evaluation and intervention. Depression, by counterexample, is a valid form of psychopathology that can be diagnosed and treated within the individual, even when it is triggered or exacerbated by relationship upsets. Depression is manifest as a distinct constellation of cognitive, affective, and behavioral symptoms catalogued in the DSM that can be assessed and tracked over time as a measure of treatment progress. One-on-one individual psychotherapy and/or medication treatment can diminish these symptoms and thereby the severity and impact of the illness.

Alienation meets none of these criteria. Alienation cannot be identified or treated *within* the individual. Despite frequent claims to the contrary, we do not know whether alienation is manifest as a distinct constellation of symptoms.[11] The chief behavior of concern—the child's alliance with Parent A and rejection of Parent B—is not in and of itself pathognomonic. Like a cough, the visible outcome can be the result of a wide variety of underlying causes.[12]

---

10. Bernet & Baker, *supra* note 7, at 99.

11. Amy J.L. Baker & Douglas C. Damall, *A Construct Study of the Eight Symptoms of Severe Parental Alienation Syndrome: A Survey of Parental Experiences*, 47 J. Divorce & Remarriage 55 (2007). Inter-rater reliability does not in and of itself convey validity. Thus, although "[t]he cluster of symptoms or behaviors indicating the presence of alienation in the child can also be reliably identified," Michael Saini et al., *Empirical Studies of Alienation, in* Parenting Plan Evaluations: Applied Research for the Family Court 76 (Kathryn Kuehnle & Leslie Drozd eds., 2012), agreement must not be mistaken for meaning. "Agreement and consistency of participants in response patterns are the foundations of reliability in statistical terms . . . . But this is different than validity or the ability to differentiate from other causes." Interview with Michael Saini (Jan. 4, 2021).

12. Gardner originally described eight "symptoms" of PAS. Baker has more recently endorsed the same list as constituting "manifestations" (a creative way of avoiding the medical connotations of "symptoms"). Both are critically flawed by the illogic inherent in retrospective research. If you begin with a pool of people with broken arms, you might find that most sustained the injury in motor vehicle accidents. Prospective study,

> Of course, there are those who adamantly disagree. In this minority view, alienation should be a diagnosable condition in children.[13] Given that the DSM and the International Classification of Diseases (ICD) have both rejected PAS and PAD, these professionals recommend identifying pathology-by-association.
>
> In one line of thinking, the child subject to alienation is likely to qualify for identification of child psychological abuse (DSM V995.51) and child affected by parental relationship distress (DSM V61.29).[14] Whether or not alienation constitutes abuse,[15] we note that these are *not* diagnoses. They are listed in the DSM as "Other Conditions That May Be a Focus of Clinical Attention," which are explicitly described as "not mental disorders."[16]

---

however, will find that only a minority of motor vehicle accident victims have broken arms. By starting with a pool of adults who self-identify as victims of a parent's alienation and reasoning backward (particularly without control groups), it's easy to be misled into believing that those adults' common childhood experiences are unique to the outcome. This is plainly fallacious. For example: "Adjustment of a retrospective analysis for observer bias is difficult . . . . The analysis identifies an association that *might* be true. The only way to know, for certain, is to perform a prospective trial, ideally using a double-blind randomized design." Steven L. Shafer & Franklin Dexter, *Publication Bias, Retrospective Bias, and Reproducibility of Significant Results in Observational Studies*, 114 Anesthesia & Analgesia 931 (2012).

13. Not incidentally, "[d]iagnosis may bring with it shame and have a chilling impact on parents['] report of domestic violence." Lenore E.A. Walker & David Shapiro, *Parental Alienation Disorder: Why Label Children with a Mental Diagnosis?*, 7 J. Child Custody: Rsch. Issues & Pracs. 266 (2010).

14. *See* Jennifer J. Harman et al., *Parental Alienation: The Blossoming of a Field of Study*, 28 Current Directions Psych. Sci. 212 (2019).

15. Kathleen Coulborn Faller, *Commentary on the American Professional Society on the Abuse of Children's Position Paper on Allegations of Child Maltreatment and Intimate Partner Violence in Divorce/Parental Relationship Dissolution*, 13 J. Child Custody: Rsch. Issues & Pracs. 307 (2016); *see also* Edward Kruk, *Parental Alienation as a Form of Emotional Child Abuse: The Current State of Knowledge and Directions for Future Research*, 22 Fam. Sci. Rev. 141 (2018); Jennifer J. Harman et al., *Parental Alienating Behaviors: An Unacknowledged Form of Family Violence*, 144 Psych. Bull. 1275 (2018); Wilfrid von Boch-Galhau, *Parental Alienation (Syndrome)—A Serious Form of Psychological Child Abuse*, 13 Mental Health & Fam. Med. 725 (2018).

16. American Psychiatric Association, Diagnostic and Statistical Manual of Mental Disorders (DSM-5) 715 (5th ed. 2013).

The Single-Factor Model

Occam misled us all.[17] A systemic perspective teaches that simple answers are not more likely to be correct, even if they are very appealing. Thus it is that an either/or binary approach to determining that a child's polarized position within the family system is due to alienation is both powerfully appealing and risks doing tremendous harm.

In its typical form, this single-factor approach reasons that if a child is aligned with Parent A and rejecting Parent B *and* Parent B has not been found to be abusive or neglectful, then de facto Parent A must be alienating.[18] In one dramatic example, one family law professional is quoted as declaring that, "in cases when abuse or neglect have not occurred, it is highly probable—to 99% clinical certainty—that alienation is the cause of the rejection."[19] We find this as illogical and misleading as saying that if it has four legs and doesn't bark, it must be a cat.

---

17. Occam's razor is the principle of parsimony—that is, that simpler and more direct explanations are more likely than complex and indirect explanations. The principle is associated with William of Ockham (1285, England).

18. At the least, cases that are purported to be due exclusively to alienation commonly fail to consider the likely co-occurring role of enmeshment. For example:

> There is no doubt that the Applicant Father has struggled to successfully communicate with the children for many years. However, I do not find that his conduct played a part in damaging the children. In other words, his conduct did not constitute justified estrangement. Because of the poisoning by the Respondent Mother of the children, they wanted nothing to do with the Applicant Father, but his shortcomings were not the issue. Issues identified by the children (for example his driving, ants and rats in his house, and physical abuse) were not grounded in reality. They were figments planted by the Respondent Mother or created by the children themselves. This is not a hybrid situation. It is a unilateral, deliberate and successful alienation by the Respondent mother alone.

A.M. v. C.H., [2019] O.N.C.A. 764 para. 17, https://www.ontariocourts.ca/decisions/2019/2019ONCA0764.pdf.

19. Linda J. Gottlieb, Reunification Therapy for Severe Parental Alienation or for an Unreasonably Disrupted Parent-Child Relationship (2019), http://endparentalalienation.weebly.com/uploads/3/1/0/9/31091731/12-22-2019_tpff_treatment_protocol_x_4_6_18_ent_protocol_for_severe_alieantion_rejection.pdf.

Indeed:

> A Single Factor model rests on the fallacy that abuse or poor parenting on the part of either parent have been, or are able to be, ruled out as sufficient reason for the child's rejecting stance. By contrast, multi-factor models of [alienation] make more useful, valid, differentiated clinical predictions of children's rejection of a parent, informed by basic and applied research on children and families. However, multi-factor models are complex and difficult to argue in court and to use in assessment and interventions.[20]

A Shell Game of Labels

The former advocates of PAS and PAD engage in a type of verbal *legerdemain* that can be very misleading. This is most easily observed in the terminology used to refer to the alienation dynamic itself. Having lost the battle over inclusion in contemporary nosologies, these professionals have simply dropped the words "syndrome" and "disorder" even while they hawk their models entirely unchanged.[21] "The label is fluid because it allows the expert to reason backwards to any intersection of the facts that fits the outcome sought by the client."[22]

In the face of strong criticisms of the single-factor model,[23] these same professionals now advocate a "four-factor model"[24] or a

(continued on next page)

20. Janet R. Johnston & Matthew J. Sullivan, *Parental Alienation: In Search of Common Ground for a More Differentiated Theory*, 58 Fam. Ct. Rev. 270, 270 (2020).

21. "Though she has previously used the word 'syndrome' . . . [Dr. Baker] suggests that using that word had not been her 'choice,' instead attributing that word choice to her publisher, and says that she has stopped using it . . . because the term is 'not necessary.'" Joyce, *supra* note 8, at 72.

22. *Id.* at 60 (alerting attorneys that "expert opponents will be well prepared and relentless in proselytizing and using language that sounds like research or evidence-based studies").

23. For example: "the overly simplistic focus on the brainwashing parent as the primary etiologic agent." Kelly & Johnston, *supra* note 9, at 250.

24. Amy J.L. Baker, *Reliability and Validity of the Four-Factor Model of Parental Alienation*, 42 J. Fam. Therapy 100 (2018).

"five-factor model."[25] Each of these parses the binary choice between alienation and estrangement differently so as to appear to be more inclusive. They are not.

The five-factor model says that alienation must be at work if there is or was

1. Contact refusal
2. A positive relationship prior to contact refusal
3. Absence of abuse or neglect on the part of the alienated parent
4. Alienating behaviors of the preferred parent
5. Child manifesting symptoms of parental alienation (PA)

Upon closer inspection, these turn out to be precisely the same either/or formula broken down into smaller, sequential bits. By analogy, our "if it has four legs and doesn't bark, it must be a cat" example of binary illogic can also be made into a superficially more impressive five-factor model.

With apologies to genets, fossas, falanoucs, and civets (to name just a few),[26] it must be a cat if

1. It is an animal
2. It has four legs
3. It doesn't bark
4. It is not a dog
5. It manifests behaviors associated with cats

Pieces of the Pie

In order to move beyond binary thinking, we need language with which to describe the phenomenon at issue without conflating cause and effect. This means focusing on visible behaviors without implying underlying motives or needs. We also need a means of discussing the relative

25. Demosthenes Lorandos & William Bernet, Parental Alienation—Science and Law (2020).

26. The order of *Carnivora* has two suborders; Caniformia includes dogs as well as skunks, bears, raccoons, seals, and walruses. The other is Feliformia, which includes the family *Felidae*, which is cats. It also includes hyenas and the four relatively unfamiliar species we've named.

contribution of the factors relevant to understanding any particular child's family dynamics.

Several phrases have emerged to describe the phenomenon, notably including "parent-child contact problems" and "strained parent-child relationships." We prefer the behavioral description inherent in the phrase resist/refuse dynamics (RRDs) and speak of the child who has become aligned with Parent A and resists or refuses contact with Parent B as triangulated (Chapter 7) and polarized (Chapter 9). Thus, one can identify the behavior at issue without implying good or bad, guilt versus innocence.

The *hybrid model* recognizes that the RRD pie is commonly cut into three pieces, each of which accounts for some unknown degree of the child's behavior. These are alienation, estrangement, and enmeshment. The model is derived from empirical reviews of high-conflict divorce actions,[27] has been discussed in peer-reviewed published case studies,[28] and is considered in terms of associated outcomes and interventions.[29]

In short, the hybrid model calls for "a multi-factor explanation of children's rejection of a parent with both the aligned and rejected parents contributing to the problem, together with role reversal in parent-child relationships."[30] In one author's view:

> With more research and experience, legal and mental health practitioners have noted that pure or "clean" cases of child alienation and realistic estrangement (those that only include

27. Janet R. Johnston et al., *Is It Alienating Parenting, Role Reversal, or Child Abuse? A Study of Children's Rejection of a Parent in Child Custody Disputes*, 5 J. Emotional Abuse 191 (2005).

28. Barbara Fidler et al., *What Am I Supposed to Do with These Cases? Working with Families Struggling with Entrenched Parent-Child Contact Problems: A Hybrid Case*, *in* Evidence-Informed Interventions for Court-Involved Families: Promoting Healthy Coping and Development 227 (Barbara J. Fidler et al. eds., 2019).

29. Lyn Greenberg et al., *Early Intervention with Resistance/Refusal Dynamics and Hybrid Cases*, *in* Evidence-Informed Interventions for Court-Involved Families: Promoting Healthy Coping and Development, *supra* note 28; *see also* Steven Friedlander & Marjorie Gans Walters, *When a Child Rejects a Parent: Tailoring the Intervention to Fit the Problem*, 48 Fam. Ct. Rev. 98 (2010); Marjorie Gans Walters & Steven Friedlander, *When a Child Rejects a Parent: Working with the Intractable Resist/Refuse Dynamic*, 54 Fam. Ct. Rev. 424 (2016).

30. Johnston et al., *supra* note 27.

> alienating behavior on the part of the favored parent or abuse/neglect on the part of the rejected parent, respectively) are less common than the mixed or "hybrid" cases, which have varying degrees of enmeshment and boundary diffusion between the aligned parent and the child and some degree of ineptness by the rejected parent . . . .[31]

The binary model asks us to focus our infinitely powerful telescope on the child so as to diagnose PAS or PAD. The hybrid model asks us to focus more broadly on the family system. The *ecological model* pulls back even further, asking us to focus on the child's experience within the family system, which, in turn, must be considered in the larger context of community and other allied and superordinate systems. In this perspective, alienation, estrangement, and enmeshment are only three among more than a dozen possible pieces of the pie. This super-systemic perspective acknowledges that RRDs can only be adequately understood in the context of a comprehensive examination of the many mutually compatible dynamics at play, including, for example, the child's experience of separation from siblings and peer group, the child's experience of the parents' respective physical environments, and the child's experience of the transition between caregivers.[32] The full range of factors that must be considered are detailed in Chapter 9 and represented graphically on page xii.

Who Alienates?

The answers to this and many similar questions are identical: we don't know. The field is too young; it has been mired in the politics of controversy; the research is too limited; the prospect of studying families

31. Barbara Jo Fidler & Nicholas Bala, *Children Resisting Postseparation Contact with a Parent: Concepts, Controversies, and Conundrums*, 48 Fam. Ct. Rev. 10, 15 (2010).

32. Benjamin D. Garber, *Sherlock Holmes and the Case of Resist/Refuse Dynamics: Confirmatory Bias and Abductive Inference in Child Custody Evaluations*, 58 Fam. Ct. Rev. 386 (2019).

embroiled in high-conflict litigation is empirically, ethically, and procedurally daunting; and—most critically—it's impossible to characterize a population that engages in any particular behavior unless and until that behavior is carefully defined. Thus, the handful of published accounts purporting to distinguish parents who engage in alienation from those who do not are at the very least in need of replication.

We do know, for example, that Gardner originally asserted that only mothers engage in alienating behaviors.[33] More conservatively, some have suggested that mothers are twice as likely to alienate than fathers.[34] It's interesting to note that Gardner's contemporary successors have eschewed gender-specific language entirely,[35] although there is no way to know how much this change represents an acknowledgement that the dynamic is not gender-specific, the implications of demographic data not yet circulated, or a shameless effort to win public acceptance. Of course, the gender politics of family law are already enormously complex and volatile.[36]

Do alienating parents share an identifiable form of psychopathology? That is, if one were to compare 1,000 parents known to have engaged in alienation with 1,000 parents matched for demographics (e.g., age, culture, child's age), would the alienators prove to have significantly more diagnosable psychopathology? In search of an answer to this question, advocates of the binary model recommend a list of preferred adult

---

33. Richard A. Gardner, The Parental Alienation Syndrome: A Guide for Mental Health and Legal Professionals (1992); Richard A. Gardner, True and False Accusations of Child Sex Abuse (1992).

34. Judith S. Wallerstein & Joan Berlin Kelly, Surviving the Breakup: How Children and Parents Cope with Divorce (1980).

35. "Research does not yet provide support for there being gender differences in who alienates their children; mothers and fathers appear similarly likely to be perpetrators." Harman et al., *supra* note 14.

36. "[F]amily court professionals appear to make different decisions as to PA and child abuse, favoring fathers over mothers." Deborah Goldfarb et al., *International Comparison of Family Court Professionals' Perceptions of Parental Alienation and Child Sexual Abuse Allegations*, 2 Int'l J. Child Maltreatment 323 (2019).

assessment instruments.[37] Unfortunately, most of these instruments lack reliability and validity, thus making data obtained using them suspect.[38]

We note findings that suggest that parents who engage in alienating behaviors have been shown to be highly defensive on individual adult psychometric instruments.[39] In the absence of a control group, it's impossible to know what this means, particularly given that custody litigants generally tend to be defensive on testing.[40]

We note one older study of parents of fourth graders enrolled in one school. Alienating parents identified within this rather cloistered and small sample were characterized as "single, unemployed female parents, whose child was a female with few perceived friends. The degree of alienation was not related to the race, achievement, or attendance of the [fourth-grade] student."[41]

Other studies find that alienating parents demonstrate personality disorder characteristics and diagnoses, including Munchausen syndrome

---

37. William Bernet, Psychological Tests That Are Helpful in Identifying and Diagnosing Parental Alienation (2020), https://pasg.info/app/uploads/2020/02/Bernet-Tests-for-PA-2020-02.pdf, and publicized broadly across social media, such as the Parental Alienation Facebook group, https://www.facebook.com/permalink.php?id=426462547479021&story_fbid=2070099346448658.

38. For example, the Bricklin Perceptual Scales are touted as likely able to distinguish estranged from alienated children despite the fact that "the Scales really have no more than face validity." M.B. Shaffer, *Test Review of Bricklin Perceptual Scales*, *in* The Eleventh Mental Measurements Yearbook (J.J. Kramer & J.C. Conoley eds., 1992) (retrieved from http://marketplace.unl.edu/buros/).

39. For example: "PAS parents are more likely to complete [Minnesota Multiphasic Personality Inventory-2] MMPI-2 questions in a defensive manner, striving to appear as flawless as possible. It was concluded that parents who engage in alienating behaviors are more likely than other parents to use the psychological defenses of denial and projection. . . ." Jeffrey C. Siegel & Joseph S. Langford, *MMPI-2 Validity Scales and Suspected Parental Alienation Syndrome*, 16 Am. J. Forensic Psych. 5 (1998); *see also* Robert M. Gordon et al., *MMPI2 Findings of Primitive Defenses in Alienating Parents*, 36 Am. J. Fam. Therapy 211 (2008).

40. *See, e.g.*, Elizabeth M. Ellis, *Allegedly Alienating Parents Cannot Be Distinguished from among Custody Litigants in General*, 9 J. Child Custody 179 (2012).

41. Raymond L. Calabrese, *The Identification of Alienated Parents and Children: Implications for School Psychologists*, 24 Psych. Schs. 145 (1987).

by proxy,[42] *folie à deux*,[43] or delusional disorders.[44] This proposition continues to be advocated in the present, albeit without reliable empirical support. For example, one very outspoken family law professional describes alienating parents as manifesting severe mental illness, particularly personality disorders. He refers to these parents in print as "disturbed" and "delusional" and describes their thinking as "psychotic."[45] Another writer concerned with alienation refers to "the pathology of a narcissistic-borderline personality parent surrounding divorce"[46] and opines that "[t]he ex-spouse is essentially 'killing' the other parent's child in revenge for the failed marriage and subsequent divorce."[47]

While some or all of these assertions may eventually prove to be true, none are as yet validated and therefore have no place in court. We infer, however, from these numerous and weak or baseless observations that the PAS and PAD advocates have not really changed at all. Where once they sought to identify alienation as an illness residing within the child, in this context they are seeking to identify alienating behaviors as residing within the aligned parent. This flies in the face of the central message of this book and our thinking—that is, that the whole is greater

---

42. Deirdre Conway Rand, *Munchausen Syndrome by Proxy: A Complex Type of Emotional Abuse Responsible for Some False Allegations of Child Abuse in Divorce*, 5 Issues Child Abuse Accusations 135 (1993); *see also* Richard Meadow, *False Allegations of Abuse and Munchausen Syndrome by Proxy*, 68 Archives Disease Child. 444 (1993).

43. Hollida Wakefield & Ralph Underwager, *Personality Characteristics of Parents Making False Accusations of Sexual Abuse in Custody Disputes*, 2 Issues Child Abuse Accusations 121 (1990).

44. Martha L. Rogers, *Delusional Disorder and the Evolution of Mistaken Sexual Allegations in Child Custody Cases*, 10 Am. J. Forensic Psych. 47 (1992). See the discussion of these diagnoses and factitious disorder imposed on another (FDIA) in Chapter 13.

45. Steven Miller, *Clinical Reasoning and Decision-Making in Cases of Child Alignment: Diagnostic and Therapeutic Issues*, *in* Working with Alienated Children and Families: A Clinical Guidebook (Amy J.L. Baker & S. Richard Sauber eds., 2013).

46. Craig Childress, The APA: Ethical Violations & Complicity with Child Abuse (2018), https://apaethicalviolations.com.

47. Letter to the Government of Puerto Rico, House of Representatives, from Craig Childress, Licensed Clinical Psychologist, re: Proposal to Amend Articles 7 and 9 of Law 223-2011 (Nov. 12, 2019), https://drcachildress.org/wp-content/uploads/2019/11/Puerto-Rico-Amicus-Opinion-Childress-2019.pdf.

than the sum of its parts. That chaotic systems spawn self-organizing new identities composed of but qualitatively distinct from component lesser systems. Thus, we believe that it is much less likely that there is an individual profile describing a prototypical alienating parent than a constellation of relationships—an identifiable but not yet catalogued type of system—associated with these behaviors.

What Is the Developmental Impact of Alienation?

Despite volumes of dire predictions, tragic and compelling anecdotes,[48] and heart-rending retrospective accounts, once again we simply don't know.[49] Differences of definition, assessment measures, and research methods cripple what little data we have. Published research tends to be biased, weak, cross-sectional, retrospective, based on small, self-selected, and/or biased samples, and usually without comparison control groups.[50] "[T]he unmerited rejection of a parent can lead to low self-esteem, depression, anxiety and addictions. It can limit [the children's] ability to process information and lead to a pattern of simplistic and rigid thinking. Developmental stages that are being interfered with cannot be recovered."[51]

Certainly, there is reason for grave concern. Losing a caregiver for any reason can itself be traumatic. Living with the tug-of-war loyalty bind that these children endure and managing the stresses associated with

---

48. *See* Pamela Richardson, A Kidnapped Mind: A Mother's Heartbreaking Memoir of Parental Alienation (2006).

49. "The overall lack of empirical quality of individual studies necessitates restraint in making inferences based on a limited number of known studies." Saini et al., *supra* note 11.

50. For example, contrary to her published claims and frequent testimony, "Dr. Baker's parental alienation research is retrospective, based on adult memory of childhood experiences and lacking in research controls." Collective Memo of Concern from 352 Concerned Family Law Academics et al., to World Health Organization, re: Inclusion of "Parental Alienation" as a "Caregiver-Child Relationship Problem" Code QE52.0 in the *International Classification of Diseases 11th Edition* (ICD-11) (July 10, 2019), http://www.learningtoendabuse.ca/docs/WHO-September-24-2019.pdf; *see, e.g.*, Amy Baker, *The Long-Term Effects of Parental Alienation on Adult Children: A Qualitative Research Study*, 33 Am. J. Fam. Therapy 289 (2005); Amy Baker, Adult Children of Parental Alienation Syndrome: Breaking the Ties That Bind (2007).

51. M.L.S. v N.E.D., [2017] S.K.Q.B. 183 para. 83, http://canlii.ca/t/h4pqj.

prolonged parental conflict, serial therapies, interviews, assessments, hearings, trials, and relocations (not to mention the implicit lost opportunities and financial costs) is bound to compromise a child's well-being. We know this because we understand the cumulative effect of adverse childhood experiences (ACEs)[52] even if we have thus far failed to associate these outcomes with the specific parenting behaviors and systemic dynamics presently at issue.

One line of research finds that alienation (referred to by these authors as "denigration") "boomerangs." These authors find that Parent A's efforts to undermine his child's relationship with Parent B often results in the child's rejection of Parent A in adulthood.[53]

Alienation by Degree?

The idea that the alienation dynamic exists by degree from mild to moderate to severe[54] is very appealing even in the absence of reliable and valid means of measuring or distinguishing these groups. Distinctions of this sort—no matter how subjective—have the appeal of simplicity and familiarity. We know how to order soft drinks at the drive-up so why not apply the same familiar language here? The result is research that concludes without empirical foundation that "[i]f the level of alienation is mild or moderate, and if there is appropriate treatment, the consequences [presumably for the child], in the long run, may be negligible. In more severe cases, the impact of alienation on a young child can be profound."[55] Among many other problems, these reports confuse cause and effect. The variable being measured (notably without any established

52. David Finkelhor, *Trends in Adverse Childhood Experiences (ACEs) in the United States*, 108 Child Abuse & Neglect article 104641 (2020).

53. Jenna Rowen & Robert Emery, *Parental Denigration: A Form of Conflict That Typically Backfires*, 56 Fam. Ct. Rev. 258 (2018).

54. *E.g.*, Richard A. Warshak, *Severe Cases of Parental Alienation*, *in* Parental Alienation: The Handbook for Mental Health and Legal Professionals 125 (Demosthenes Lorandos et al. eds., 2013).

55. Pamela S. Ludolph & James N. Bow, *Complex Alienation Dynamics and Very Young Children*, 9 J. Child Custody 153, 163 (2012).

instrument or inter-rater reliability) is not alienation, per se, but actually the longevity and rigidity of the child's rejection of Parent B.[56]

A number of authors make very dramatic claims about the long-term effects of alienation, despite these many and crippling problems of definition, reliability, and validity. For example, one retrospective study of self-identified adult victims of alienation using a yet-to-be-validated instrument reports "significant associations between perceived exposure to parental alienation as a child and lower self-sufficiency, higher rates of major depressive disorder, lower self-esteem, and insecure attachment styles as adults."[57]

Even if this sample had been randomly selected, even if a matched control group had completed the same instruments, even if the subjects' reports were concurrent or prospective rather than retrospective and thereby subject to selective memory and confirmation bias, the researcher's question presupposes its outcome. This study asked yes-or-no questions about alienation. It left no room to consider whether and what interwoven dynamics might simultaneously have been at work.

Or consider a retrospective and qualitative (interview) study of ten self-identified adult victims of childhood alienation. A review of interview transcripts led the authors to associate the participants' self-report of childhood alienation with "anxiety, depression, low self-worth, guilt, attachment problems, difficulty in other relationships, and reduced or delayed educational and career attainment."[58]

---

56. For example:

> Severe cases of a child's alienation from a parent are distinguished from mild and moderate cases by the extent of the child's rejection of a parent and the degree of negativity in the attitudes and behavior toward the rejected parent. Severely alienated children express extremely polarized views of their parents; they have little if anything positive to say about the rejected parent and often rewrite the history of their relationship to obscure positive elements.

Warshak, *supra* note 54.

57. Naomi Ben-Ami & Amy J.L Baker, *The Long-Term Correlates of Childhood Exposure to Parental Alienation on Adult Self-Sufficiency and Well-Being*, 40 Am. J. Fam. Therapy 169 (2012).

58. Caitlin Bentley & Mandy Matthewson, *The Not-Forgotten Child: Alienated Adult Children's Experience of Parental Alienation*, 48 Am. J. Fam. Therapy 509 (2020).

A larger study conducted with more than 500 self-identified adult survivors of PA and relying on at least one instrument with no established reliability or validity[59] found that "exposure to PA was associated with higher ratings of anxiety and depression."[60] Curiously, a contemporaneous publication using the same or a very similar Italian sample phrased their findings much more conservatively, acknowledging that triangulation, not alienation, may be the dynamic at work: "[It] is not simply the degree of parental conflict that seems to affect youth detrimentally following the divorce of their parents, but rather the degree to which they are drawn into their parents' conflict (and hence likely to be exposed to PA behaviors)."[61]

Yet one further study riddled with the same procedural and psychometric problems addressed the impact of childhood alienation on men's health specifically:

> [The] long-term effects of parental alienation include low self-esteem, depression, drug/alcohol abuse, lack of trust, alienation from own children, divorce, problems with identity and not having a sense of belonging or roots, choosing not to have children to avoid being rejected by them, low achievement, anger and bitterness over the time lost with the alienated parent.[62]

---

59. The Baker Strategy Questionnaire. *See* Amy J.L. Baker & Jaclyn Chambers, *Adult Recall of Childhood Exposure to Parental Conflict: Unpacking the Black Box of Parental Alienation*, 52 J. Divorce & Remarriage 55 (2011). Noting a reference elsewhere declaring without evidence that "[t]he measure demonstrated high internal consistency (a = 0.94)." Maria Cristina Verrocchio et al., *Associations between Exposure to Alienating Behaviors, Anxiety, and Depression in an Italian Sample of Adults*, 61 J. Forensic Sci. 692 (2016), https://doi.org/10.1111/1556-4029.13046.

60. Amy J.L. Baker & Maria Cristina Verrocchio, *Exposure to Parental Alienation and Subsequent Anxiety and Depression in Italian Adults*, 44 Am. J. Fam. Therapy 255 (2016).

61. Maria C. Verrocchio et al., *Perceived Parental Functioning, Self-Esteem, and Psychological Distress in Adults Whose Parents Are Separated/Divorced*, 6 Frontiers Psych. 1760 (2015), https://doi.org/10.3389/fpsyg.2015.01760.

62. Leo Sher, *Parental Alienation: The Impact on Men's Mental Health*, 29 Int'l J. Adolescent Med. & Health (2015).

Remedies?

Once again, the conscientious family law professional's hands are tied. As often as experts opine about remedies for alienation,[63] as many court-ordered interventions as we might review,[64] definitional ambiguities, procedural limitations, bad science, political agendas, and misleading analyses undermine our ability to draw broad conclusions.

Imagine, by analogy, that you are hosting a prestigious soup-judging contest but you never set any limits on the recipe or establish any criterion for success. You end up tasting an incredible range of porridges and potages and puddings, broths and borschts, chowders and bisques, and consommés. RRDs come in at least as many types. Until we have established consensual definitions and empirically sound assessment tools, a discussion of how best to respond to alienation will be at least as idiosyncratic as determining which soup is best.

---

63. Demosthenes Lorandos, *Legal Interventions in Cases of Parental Alienation*, *in* Parental Alienation: The Handbook for Mental Health and Legal Professionals 232 (Demosthenes Lorandos et al. eds., 2013).

64. In the case of *W.C. v. C.E.*, [2010] O.N.S.C. 3575 para. 129, the court noted that when allegations of PA are made, there are essentially four possible courses of action:

> 1) Do nothing and leave the child with the alienating parent; 2) Do a custody reversal by placing the child with the rejected parent; 3) Leave the child with the favoured parent and provide therapy; or 4) Provide a transitional placement where the child is placed with a neutral party and therapy is provided so that eventually the child can be placed with the rejected parent.

SECTION III
At the Intersection Where the Family System Meets the Legal System

*"The very nature of a divorce in a family is disrupting in the lives of the children involved. The strictures of the legal system should not operate to cause more chaos. The standard against which all actions must be measured in all custody cases, both by the trial court and the appellate court, should be the best interest of the child."**

* Carroll v. Carroll, 382 N.E.2d 7, 10 (Ill. App. Ct. 1978).

Chapter 16

Ipse Dixit and the Language of Experts

"Allowing mental health professionals to testify as expert witnesses does not give them special powers to discern the truth, otherwise expert witnesses always would agree and could serve as lie detectors in all kinds of trials."[1]

"In an atmosphere of mutual suspicion and contempt, neither side is willing to learn what the other has to teach."[2]

A number of high-profile experts converged on an impressive marble courthouse prepared to testify on opposing sides of a very complex and highly contentious child custody matter. Their accomplishments and affiliations were all impressively displayed on their curricula vitae and more-or-less humbly acknowledged from the witness stand as each was qualified to testify.

The judge noticed that all of the experts from both sides of the case claimed the exact same title and university affiliation, so he asked the fifth among them in as many days whether everyone who worked at that institution received the same credential. The sober, bearded, and bespectacled man looked chagrined but answered truthfully: "Yes, your honor." In fact, the university in question distributed assistant professorships far more freely than parking permits.[3]

1. Robert E. Emery, *Parental Alienation Syndrome: Proponents Bear the Burden of Proof*, 43 Fam. Ct. Rev. 8, 10 (2005).

2. J.R. Lucas, The Concept of Probability (1970).

3. On the flip side of this coin, opposing counsel once tried to disqualify the first author (Garber) in a high-profile custody case by inquiring about his "Yelp rating."

This humorous anecdote highlights the challenge that the court faces when expert testimony is introduced into the legal process. Who should be heard, on what topics, in what circumstances, and the weight that should be assigned to the learned (and time-consuming and expensive) opinions thus elicited can determine the outcome of a case and the life of the child whose future is being contested.

In 2009, the National Academy of Sciences studied the harm suffered by the poor and unprivileged in the United States when meritless forensic sciences are admitted into the criminal and civil courts.[4] They concluded, "Courts do not typically review testimony after finding the underlying methodology reliable and permitting the forensic analyst to take the stand" and "the legal system is ill-equipped to correct the problems of the forensic science community."[5] We take from this a single imperative: legal standards may admit an expert's testimony but must never be mistaken as automatically endorsing that expert's words as true or the expert's recommendations as valid. "Non-researchers need not understand in depth what each aspect of methodology means in regard to particular studies or outcomes. However, they should seek to understand enough to know what questions to ask in order to find out whether a study is relevant to or representative of their particular circumstances."[6]

We are all guilty of ordering restaurant meals without inquiring about the ingredients and purchasing household products without reading their

---

4. National Research Council, Strengthening Forensic Science in the United States: A Path Forward 112 (2009), https://www.ojp.gov/pdffiles1/nij/grants/228091.pdf; *see also* Suzanne Bell et al., *A Call for More Science in Forensic Science*, 115 Proc. Nat'l Acad. Sci. 4541, 4541 (2018) ("As science—and forensic science more specifically—continues to advance, it becomes increasingly absurd to ask or expect lawyers, judges, and juries to take sole responsibility for critically evaluating the quality and validity of scientific evidence and testimony."); Joëlle Anne Moreno, *C.S.I. Bulls#!t: The National Academy of Sciences,* Melendez-Diaz v. Massachusetts, *and Future Challenges to Forensic Science and Forensic Experts*, 2010 Utah L. Rev. 327, 327 (2010) ("Good law depends on good science. The February 18, 2009, National Academy of Sciences report, *Strengthening Forensic Science in the United States: A Path Forward* ('NAS Report'), reveals that, for the most part, forensic science is bad science. The NAS Report also suggests that when confronted with forensic science, most courts make bad law.") (citation omitted).

5. National Research Council, *supra* note 4, at 112.

6. Association of Family and Conciliation Courts (AFCC) Task Force, *Guidelines for the Use of Social Science Research in Family Law*, 57 Fam. Ct. Rev. 193, 196 (2019).

labels and sleeping in hotels without interviewing the cleaning staff or looking under the mattress. These are personal choices we can make usually at no risk to anyone but ourselves. By contrast, to accept expert testimony without examining the ingredients, looking under the mattress, investigating its foundations, and challenging its purveyors is to risk doing great harm to others.

This chapter intends to polish the lens through which you view research and family system dynamics, helping to sharpen your critical eye as a consumer of theory and statistics and the experts who presume to bring these abstractions to bear on the particular families who have placed their futures in the able hands of the courts.[7] To this end, we will discuss the dilemma of *ipse dixit*, research methods, and peer review.

The Dilemma of Ipse Dixit

This header sounds like the title of a southern ballad, a twangy, tearful story full of love lost played on a banjo in a honky-tonk over cold beers. It is not. In fact, it's the weakest part of any expert's testimony, the part that a well-informed advocate or trier of fact must know how to poke and prod until it falls apart.

Guild-specific specialty guidelines, ethical codes,[8] and the law[9] require that expert opinions be couched in consensually endorsed

---

7. We are certainly not the first to address these topics. *See, e.g.*, John A. Zervopoulos, Confronting Mental Health Evidence: A Practical PLAN to Examine Reliability and Experts in Family Law 70–71 (2d ed. 2015); John A. Zervopoulos, How to Examine Mental Health Experts 43–51 (2013).

8. *See* American Academy of Psychiatry and the Law, *Ethics Guidelines*, https://aapl.org/ethics.htm (last visited July 24, 2021); American Psychological Association, *Specialty Guidelines for Forensic Psychology*, 68 Am. Psych. 7 (2013), https://www.apa.org/pubs/journals/features/forensic-psychology.pdf; National Organization of Forensic Social Work, Draft Speciality Guidelines for Values and Ethics (2020), https://4251f553-c8e8-439c-83bb-61068f7fb2c6.filesusr.com/ugd/f468b9_8a8f7984aa8a494fa625c1bd4114641e.pdf; National Academy of Neuropsychology, *Forensic/Ethics On Demand*, https://www.nanonline.org/NAN/_ContinuingEducation/_DistanCE/Forensic_Ethics.aspx (last visited July 24, 2021).

9. *See* Robert P. Archer & Dustin Wygant, *Child Custody Evaluations: Ethical, Scientific, and Practice Considerations*, 17 J. Psych. Prac. 1, 21 (2012) ("The *Daubert* 1993 Supreme Court decision, and its subsequent refinements, generally created a legal

theories, peer-reviewed publications, and substantiating data. This is nowhere more important than when an expert attempts to bring statistically gilded group observations to bear on the very real and statistically immune life of any particular person.[10]

As the U.S. Supreme Court held in a case that, for child custody matters, is a much more worthy test of scientific reliability and ethics than *Daubert* or *Frye*,

> nothing in either *Daubert* or the Federal Rules of Evidence requires a district court to admit opinion evidence that is connected to existing data only by the *ipse dixit* of the expert. A court may conclude that there is simply too great an analytical gap between the data and the opinion proffered.[11]

In case you missed Latin class that day, ipse dixit is every exhausted parent's answer to every defiant child's challenge of every family rule ever made. It is that blunt, dogmatic, and authoritarian, but entirely empty insistence that it is what it is, "Because I said so!"

Ipse dixit might be enough to get an oppositional five-year-old in bed (although probably not), but it will never suffice in court where even the most expert opinion must be grounded on demonstratable, reproduceable, and relevant facts. Witness, for example, two unrelated courts' rulings. In one, an expert opinion that lacks scientific reliability may "be excluded if it is fundamentally flawed or unsupported" because an expert who relies on "a number of 'guesstimations' and speculations" allows the

---

environment that favors testimony based on scientific instruments and procedures with established reliability and validity. Scientific reliability and validity is established, in turn, by research findings that have been subjected to peer-reviews in professional journals, techniques that have quantifiable error rates, as well as having gained general acceptance in the field.").

10. Statistical analysis is a process of determining the meaningfulness of similarities and differences between individuals (or systems when concerned, for example, with choosing a company to invest in). While one can compare a particular variable observed in one individual to measures of that same variable derived from larger samples, it is not possible to apply statistics to one individual. *See* Eric York Drogin, Science for Lawyers (2008); Michael O. Finkelstein & Bruce Levin, Statistics for Lawyers (2001).

11. Gen. Elec. Co. v. Joiner, 522 U.S. 136, 146 (1997).

court to conclude that, like "a house of cards, once those foundations are disproved, the whole analysis collapses."[12]

In the second, "a supremely qualified expert cannot waltz into the courtroom and render opinions unless those opinions are based upon some recognized scientific method and are reliable and relevant under the test set forth by the Supreme Court in *Daubert*."[13]

As widespread and well-known as rulings of this sort are, the ipse dixit—*because I said so!*—problem runs rampant through family law. For example, research has documented the efficacy of eye-movement desensitization and reprocessing (EMDR, a particular type of trauma therapy) as a means of reducing anxiety among victims of interpersonal violence.[14] The bridge from these findings to assert that EMDR is an effective treatment for combat veterans with post-traumatic stress disorder (PTSD) is statistically shaky at least until the studies have been done demonstrating efficacy in this particular population. But the bridge from these findings to assert that EMDR is appropriate and likely to be effective for Fred Smith, a particular combat veteran diagnosed with PTSD seated in the courtroom and desperate to maintain a relationship with his son, rests largely on his lawyer's expert's assertion of ipse dixit.

Inherent in this problem is the general-to-the-individual, or G2i, dilemma, an issue that haunts every expert's efforts to apply population-based norms and sample-specific statistics to Billy or Sally and their high-conflict family system. Statistical means sum across disparate observations to produce a weighted average score. Averages identify the central tendency within a more-or-less diverse pool. That diversity is expressed as its standard deviation.

For example, the average efficacy of EMDR may be statistically better than a placebo among victims of interpersonal violence, but those averages gloss over large individual differences. In a study of this kind, it's often the case that some subjects had powerfully positive responses while

---

12. Ellipsis, Inc. v. Color Works, Inc., 428 F. Supp. 2d 752, 760 (W.D. Tenn. 2006).

13. Jonathan M. Dunitz & Nancy J. Fannon, Daubert *and the Financial Damages Expert*, 26 Me. B.J. 62, 65 (2011).

14. *E.g.*, Runsen Chen, *The Efficacy of Eye Movement Desensitization and Reprocessing in Children and Adults Who Have Experienced Complex Childhood Trauma: A Systematic Review of Randomized Controlled Trials*, 9 Frontiers Psych. 534 (2018).

others had moderate or negative responses. Taken together, the average response across observations is positive. Where any particular patient about to engage in EMDR is likely to fall along this continuum is impossible to predict, even though the group averages are promising.

Of course, prediction is improved when the individual at issue shares relevant characteristics with the research subjects. Even so, matching for variables like age, gender, zip code, race, religion, height, weight, and shoe size is never a guarantee that a statistically meaningful remedy will be well-suited to any particular child or family.[15] Or more concisely:

> A fundamental divide exists between what scientists do as scientists and what courts often ask them to do as expert witnesses. Whereas scientists almost invariably inquire into phenomena at the group level, trial courts typically need to resolve cases at the individual level. In short, scientists generalize while courts particularize.[16]

More pointedly, "a common problem in court practice concerns the risk of invalid inferences for individual cases made based on trends and averages from group-level research."[17]

Question the Research and the Experts Carefully

The universal mandate to do no harm has at least two applications. The first and most easily acknowledged is the choice not to engage in any action that might induce damage or distress. A second, less often recognized but more relevant application in the present context calls for affirmative, positive action to stop another person from doing harm.

(continued on next page)

15. "[F]amily justice practitioners should be clear that while the group data may support a specific conclusion, it does not guarantee that same behavior or outcome for particular persons or family circumstances." AFCC Task Force, *supra* note 6, at 197.

16. David L. Faigman et al., *Group to Individual (G2i) Inference in Scientific Expert Testimony*, 81 U. Chi. L. Rev. 417, 417 (2014).

17. Tommie Forslund et al., *Attachment Goes to Court: Child Protection and Custody Issues*, Attachment & Hum. Dev., Jan. 2021, at 5 (advance copy).

> As family law professionals, we risk doing harm when we sit by, cowed by an expert's credentials or overwhelmed by unfamiliar words and overwhelming analyses peppered with Greek letters and mysterious coefficients.[18] We do harm when we allow bad science and bad scientists to ride roughshod over court process and the best interests of the child.
>
> The answer, of course, is to become educated and to be assertive within the limits of your role.
>
> To the expert who hides behind the alphabet soup that follows his name, whose parking permit is worth more than his gratuitous university title, who conceals meaning behind weighted means, alpha coefficients, and T-scores, who obfuscates via circumlocutious pronouncements and polysyllabic neologisms, who treats research like a holy text suited only for the eyes of an ordained few, who condescends to say, ipse dixit, "because I said so . . .," we say, simply, "where's the beef?"[19]

Research is the application of empirical methods to organize and measure phenomena of interest. The scientific method dictates how research should be conducted at every level of inquiry, from the cosmic to the subatomic, including and—for our purposes—especially at the level of family dynamics.

Because most research is captured quantitatively and communicated in the form of group means or averages, standard deviations and

18. *See* Kendall Coffey, *Inherent Judicial Authority and the Expert Disqualification Doctrine*, 56 Fla. L. Rev. 195, 195 (2004) ("With its explosion across America's litigation landscape, expert witnessing has become a foundation for decision-making in virtually all significant cases. Described by some courts as a 'cottage industry,' it has also become more lucrative than the usual day job for many professionals. With litigants and their counsel shopping relentlessly for key specialists, and the experts themselves pursuing engagements aggressively, the growth of expert consultations has spawned a proliferation of allegations concerning conflicts of interest.").

19. "Where's the beef?" originated in a 1984 television advertisement for Wendy's restaurants. It has since become an American cultural meme that challenges a speaker to disclose the substance of a claim.

variances, and in comparisons between distinct groups or in one group across time, research findings carry a certain mystical weight among non-researchers. When invoked in courts, research can have a shock-and-awe effect that threatens to overwhelm the judicial process and intimidate consumers. It is nonsensical but quite common to find that the experts with flow charts, laser pointers, and spreadsheets are more credible than others who present the same ideas in the vernacular. This effect tends to increase exponentially as the education of the listener declines, contributing to an essential epistemic injustice built into the legal process.

We urge you to become a well-informed and critical consumer of social science research. Start by reading John Ioannidis's masterpiece, "Why Most Published Research Findings Are False."[20] This no-holds-barred dissection of research methods continues to crash like a tidal wave against the pillars of institutions. Ioannidis's article demonstrates that most studies are so riddled with bias and methodological and statistical errors, that our lives are built around flawed beliefs and in desperate need of replication and generalization.

Ioannidis's observations are applied eloquently to family law matters in a recent must-read article on parental alienation:

> The argument that parental alienation has a direct "cause and effect" [A-B-C] is a tactical weapon with a devastating impact in the world of child custody litigation. One serious consequence of this A-B-C model, as it is argued by proponents, is the ability to confuse lawyers and judges by claiming that this causation is a series of direct connections easily explained as true by the observing "expert" without reference to any of the limits that scientists must ethically draw in social science research.[21]

The promise of this A-B-C linear causality is what many of today's so-called parental alienation "experts" are peddling in the form of theories, measurements, and statistics that purport to assign blame for a

20. John P.A. Ioannidis, *Why Most Published Research Findings Are False*, 2 PLoS Med. 696 (2005) (article e124), https://doi.org/10.1371/journal.pmed.0020124.

21. Kimberly Joyce, *Under the Microscope: The Admissibility of Parental Alienation Syndrome*, 32 J. Am. Acad. Matrimonial Law. 53, 54 (2019).

child's resistance of Parent B squarely on the shoulders of Parent A. All it takes is a little research savvy to discover the ipse dixit weakness of these findings. There is no *there* there. Without this underlying scheme, expert testimony would not be needed or helpful, and thus it would be inadmissible under decades of federal and state law.[22]

Theories and Conceptual Frameworks Are Not Data

The court wants to attend a play. It wants to understand the particular family's particular drama in context, complete with dialogue, free to inquire about the players, the set, and the stage as it will. Theory and conceptual frameworks set the stage but are seldom enough. The court wants to see the players in action. "[A] conceptual framework [is] a network, or 'a plane,' of interlinked concepts that together provide a comprehensive understanding of a phenomenon. The concepts that constitute a conceptual framework or theory may support one another, articulate their respective phenomena, and establish a framework-specific philosophy."[23]

More than simply educate the court, the expert who is able to apply abstract theory to the structures of the law is helping to narrow the G2i gap. The first two authors (Garber and Prescott) have done this, for example, by importing developmental psychology's familiar and long-validated concept of the transitional object into the frame of the best interests construct,[24] thereby giving family law professionals the opportunity to apply a rich history of developmental psychological research to specific courtroom dilemmas. This sort of application moves the family law expert from ipse dixit opinion onto the solid ground that can generate empirically based recommendations.

The first author (Garber) did the same in very different context by importing a wealth of data about attachment measurement procedures

22. *Id.* at 57 (footnote omitted).

23. Yosef Rafeq Jabareen, *Building a Conceptual Framework: Philosophy, Definitions, and Procedure*, 8 Int'l J. Qualitative Methods 49, 51 (2009).

24. *See generally* Benjamin D. Garber & Dana E. Prescott, *On the Value of Teddy Bears and Barbie Dolls: The Place of Children's Transitional Objects in Family Law*, 49 Sw. L. Rev. 189 (2020).

and interpretations into the child custody evaluation process.[25] This application creates a rich foundation upon which evaluators and experts can more easily bridge the G2i gap, generating empirically based hypotheses about children evaluated in specially designed custody evaluations. As one court stated:

> The problem is that the application was argued on a largely theoretical level, with the father arguing the theory that equal parenting is best and the mother arguing the theory that status quo is best, but with neither of them presenting evidence to support either theory as applied to these children.[26]

However much deference to an empirically sound body of research narrows the G2i gap, ultimately the problem of generalization to the individual remains. This frank reality does not, however, stop some experts from opining loud and long and entirely without hubris about the needs of 12-year-old, left-handed, red-headed, dyslexic Billy whom he has never met and—not incidentally—whose best interests are presently at stake. Cloaked in condescension and contaminated by unacknowledged biases, intuitions, emotions, morals, attitudes, and prejudices, this is still ipse dixit in all of its glory.

We implore readers to learn to pull back the curtain to challenge the ipse dixit expert, recognizing that this requires understanding research methodology from the nuts and bolts of subject selection, data collection, analysis, and interpretation, to generalization to the case at bar. To be shamed into silence by concepts like error rates, control groups, sampling, standard deviations, and variance is to do harm.[27] In support of this goal, we conclude this chapter with a very basic primer on several topics in social science research.

1. **Sampling and generalizability.** It is usually not possible to study an entire population. As a compromise, researchers collect data from a

---

25. Benjamin D. Garber, *Exploring a Process-Oriented Forensic Family Observation Protocol*, 54 Fam. Ct. Rev. 261 (2016).

26. Caharel v. Caharel, [2008] A.B.Q.B. 238 para. 28, https://canlii.ca/t/1wk43.

27. Numerous texts provide the novice a good place to start. For example, see AFCC Task Force, *supra* note 6; D.H. Kaye, *Statistics for Lawyers and Law for Statistics*, 89 Mich. L. Rev. 1520 (1991).

subset of that population believed to represent its critical variables. Conclusions about the sample are then be generalized to the whole with more-or-less caution.[28]

The representativeness and the generalizability of a sample increases as the number of members in the sample approaches the number of members in the population, and as the measured relevant characteristics of the sample approximate the measured characteristics of the population.[29] Thus, it might be relatively easy to characterize the population of Pitcairn Island, a tiny British territory in the South Pacific inhabited by 50 people. The members of this population are all easily identified and—at least because they live on an island—might all be accessible. As the size of a population increases, as the characteristics defining population membership become more diffuse, and as the accessibility of the population membership diminishes, sampling becomes more complex and generalizations from any sample to the population as a whole become weaker.

This is the case when one seeks to study highly conflicted, litigating families. The population is vast and ill-defined. They don't like to be studied at least because anything they disclose to researchers is vulnerable to disclosure in court. They're oddly not inclined to spend an hour or more completing interviews and questionnaires that will do them no good and, if discovered, may well be used against them by opposing counsel. As a result, we are left with weak generalizations colored by questionable theories and innumerable biases: "Family law-related research is of insufficient quality and quantity to be used to support specific recommendations on various

28. "Family justice practitioners should consider developmental, cultural, racial, socioeconomic, and other relevant factors when applying research findings to a specific family. Research is often based on 'convenience samples' using narrow social, racial, socioeconomic, or other groupings (e.g., white middle class), and the findings might not be applicable to persons of differing race/ethnicity, social class, or other social identifications or circumstances. Family justice practitioners should identify when research findings being presented might not apply to a specific family or group." AFCC Task Force, *supra* note 6, at 197.

29. Theory informs (and sometimes misleads) us to determine which variables are relevant. The theory of phrenology, for example, dictated which bumps on a subject's head mattered and how, but no sample was ever big enough to validate that theory. For an interesting argument related to phrenology and the law, see Pierre Schlag, *Law and Phrenology*, 110 Harv. L. Rev. 877 (1996).

issues, e.g., parenting time, effects of relocation, or quality of parent-child relationship maintained predominantly through technology."[30]

With this in mind, ask the next expert who cites research supporting her opinion how the research sample was gathered, how it represents the population in general, and how, if at all, it represents the population of high-conflict divorcing families.

2. **Reliability and validity.** These words each have simple meanings and tremendous authority.

Reliability asks whether data have been measured accurately. We answer this question by assuring that repeated measures across time or between researchers at the same time are consistent. Reliability coefficients are reported between 0.00 and 1.00 such that the higher the coefficient, the more reliable or accurate the measure is said to be.

Validity asks whether a reliable measurement is meaningful. Meaningfulness can be answered by studying any of a number of distinct questions such as: is the measurement congruent with other already established measurements of the same thing? Does the measurement accurately predict a specific future state? And does the measurement accurately describe other members of the same population who were not already assessed?

For example, in Chapter 15, we referred to survey results that found that many family law professionals surveyed endorsed a list of behaviors as constituting "parental alienation behaviors." This is inter-rater reliability. High agreement among respondents means that a majority of those queried identified the same behaviors as constituting alienation. Unfortunately, some uninformed or biased readers stopped there, without considering whether those agreed upon indices are valid. They are not. In this case, everyone applauded the king's new clothes, but it turned out that he wasn't wearing any. There are no data that connect these behaviors exclusively to polarizing dynamics and resist/refuse outcomes.

The problems of applying broad and reliable research findings to family law are matters of external validity.[31] This is why understanding sampling and methodology is so essential to relevance and admissibility.

---

30. AFCC Task Force, *supra* note 6, at 193.

31. Judith Cashmore & Patrick Parkinson, *The Use and Abuse of Social Science Research Evidence in Children's Cases*, 20 Psych. Pub. Pol'y & L. 239, 241 (2014).

When data are drawn from the population at large or, worse, from a self-selected sample (as when researchers solicit volunteers via Internet ads placed on websites that cater to one or another position), the resulting data may be reliable but are unlikely to be representative and valid for application to the family law population. This is why the attorney who attempted to defame the first author (Garber) in court by asking about his Yelp rating was grasping at straws. Raters are self-selected. Complaints are voiced far more often than compliments. One's Yelp rating is neither a reliable nor a valid source of data.[32]

3. **Transparency, and replication or reproducibility.** A decade ago, a pair of scientists announced that they had discovered a means of conducting cold fusion. Cold fusion is the holy grail of physics. In the rush of headlines and science that followed, no one was able to reproduce their finding. Their methods were a black box that they could not or would not disclose. The announcement was a sham. In 2004, the U.S. Department of Energy concluded:

> Ordinarily, new scientific discoveries are claimed to be consistent and reproducible; as a result, the discovery can usually be confirmed or disproved in a few months. The claims of cold fusion, however, are unusual in that even the strongest proponents of cold fusion assert that the experiments, for unknown reasons, are not consistent and reproducible at the present time. Internal inconsistencies and lack of predictability and reproducibility remain serious concerns.[33]

Science is not science unless its methods are transparent and its findings can be reproduced. Reproducibility means "the ability of a researcher to duplicate the results of a prior study using the same materials as were

32. These challenges to research and its generalizability are laid out in the various articles in the special issue of the *Family Court Review. See* Barbara Jo Fidler & Nicholas Bala, *Guest Editors' Introduction to the 2020 Special Issue on Parent-Child Contact Problems: Concepts, Controversies & Conundrums*, 58 FAM. CT. REV. 265 (2020).

33. ENERGY RESEARCH ADVISORY BOARD, U.S. DEPARTMENT OF ENERGY, COLD FUSION RESEARCH 36 (1989).

used by the original investigator."[34] This concept is as important to science as it is to expert testimony and admissibility in family court.[35]

Case in point: It is not sufficient for Dr. Brilliant to advertise that she can divine alienation by backward reasoning in counterintuitive ways using the special decoder ring that only she owns and refuses to share (i.e., ipse dixit). The reliability, validity, and admissibility of her claims are blind to the numbers of desperate parents who eagerly flock to her door ignorant and uncaring about the science if only they can have the cure. But the "cure," of course, is always hidden behind that next hurdle and the next bill and buried in polysyllabic psychobabble. This is not a scientist, this is a charlatan, lining her pockets at the cost of other people's health and happiness.

Peer Review and Sort-of-Kind-of "Peer" Review

Peer review is often identified as one among the criteria necessary to admit an expert's opinion. One might therefore imagine that peer review is a rigorous test of scientific principles, research methods, theoretical foundations, and the immutable, quantitative details of reliability, validity, and reproducibility. According to an Association of Family and Conciliation Courts (AFCC) Task Force:

> When using social science, family justice practitioners should rely on the best available research. Social science research relevant to family law can be found in a variety of sources and within a range of disciplines, including psychology, law, social

34. *Id.* (quoting Kenneth Bollen et al., Social, Behavioral, and Economic Sciences Perspectives on Robust and Reliable Science: Report of the Subcommittee on Replicability in Science Advisory Committee to the National Science Foundation Directorate for Social, Behavioral, and Economic Sciences 13 (2015)).

35. *See* Connie J.A. Beck et al., *Collaboration between Judges and Social Science Researchers in Family Law*, 47 Fam. Ct. Rev. 451, 457 (2009) ("Replication of findings of a study with an additional sample of subjects and by an independent research team is critical to being truly confident about whether a treatment works. Replication of results protects against drawing premature conclusions based on a particular set of researchers or therapists with a particular set of biases or from a subject sample that might be unusual.").

> work, family studies, sociology, and anthropology. High-quality research publications and reports are evaluated through a peer-review process, typically by experts in a specific area of research.[36]

Peer review in the physical sciences maintains these very high expectations. Unfortunately, peer review in the social sciences has eroded and been corrupted or at least co-opted within the family law community. In practice, peer review in family law often amounts to a blind critique by one expert in the field of another expert in the field, a process that is often more concerned with the breadth of citations and the clarity of prose than transparency of methods, the adequacy of samples, and the accuracy of statistics.[37] The process does not routinely or uniformly analyze methodology, sampling, data collection, analysis, interpretation, or application. Thus, peer review in the social sciences seldom guarantees that any particular scientific standard or ethic has been upheld.

In fact, social science peer reviewers are not themselves subject to review of any sort. There is no training, standards, best practices, or ethics specific to the process.[38] Indeed, in the rarified atmosphere of a scientific niche as specialized as divorce and resist/refuse dynamics, efforts to blind peer reviewers to an author's identity routinely fail. The professionals qualified to review a manuscript in this narrow niche are the same people most likely to submit a manuscript for review. Like living on Pitcairn Island, everyone in family law knows everyone else. Everyone recognizes their colleagues' idiosyncrasies and pet theories. There is thus little or nothing blind about the peer review process.

Thus, peer review becomes a myth despite its central role in science and as one criterion of admissibility in court:

> Publication in peer-reviewed journals is an essential step in the scientific process. It generates knowledge, influences future

36. AFCC Task Force, *supra* note 6, at 195.

37. *See* Mary Johanna McCurley et al., *Protecting Children from Incompetent Forensic Evaluations and Expert Testimony*, 19 J. Am. Acad. Matrimonial Law. 277, 286 (2004) ("Publication in a reputable, established, scientific journal and other forms of peer review increase the likelihood that substantive flaws in methodology will be detected.").

38. Tony Ross-Hellauer, *What Is Open Peer Review? A Systematic Review*, 6 F1000Research 3 (2017), https://www.ncbi.nlm.nih.gov/pmc/articles/PMC5437951.

experiments, and may impact clinical practice and public health. Ethically, research results must be reported completely, transparently, and accurately. However, publication is not simply the reporting of facts arising from a straightforward and objective analysis of those facts. When writing a manuscript reporting the results of an experiment, investigators usually have broad latitude in the choice, representation, and interpretation of the data. They may be tempted consciously or unconsciously to shape the impression that the results will have on readers and consequently "spin" their study results.[39]

---

39. Isabelle Boutron & Philippe Ravaud, *Misrepresentation and Distortion of Research in Biomedical Literature*, 115 Proc. Nat'l Acad. Sci. 2613, 2613 (2018).

Chapter 17
Remedies

"No parents are perfect. All have flaws of one kind or another. If families stay together, except in those rare circumstances in which a child is found to be in need of protection, the state and the courts allow imperfect parents to raise their children as best they can. The children, in most cases, are no worse for wear for the experience."[1]

"A court presiding over a child custody matter does not become a family czar with unlimited authority to order the parents to do anything that the court believes is in the best interests of the child."[2]

"[I]t seems to me that the primary purpose of therapeutic interventions should not be the restoration of the parent-child relationship, although that may be a byproduct of the intervention; the primary purpose should be restoring the child."[3]

Ubi Jus, Ibi Remedium

In law school, students may take a course on "remedies." By itself, that term may not mean much beyond acquiring the knowledge required to pass an exam. In the practice of law, however, remedies have a much deeper meaning.

---

1. N.R.G. v. G.R.G., [2015] B.C.S.C. 1062 para. 292, https://canlii.ca/t/gjmnn.
2. Allbright v. Allbright, 215 P.3d 472, 752, 756 (Idaho 2009).
3. John-Paul Boyd, *Therapeutic Interventions and the Alienated Child: Whose Interests Are We Serving, and How Are We Serving Them?*, Slaw, July 10, 2015, http://www.slaw.ca/2015/07/10/therapeutic-interventions-and-the-alienated-child-whose-interests-are-we-serving-and-how-are-we-serving-them.

Charles Alan Wright, a famous law professor, began a law review article in 1955 with the admonition that "[m]uch can be said about the law of remedies as a social institution."[4] In this context, he cited the "mouth-filling Latin maxim" *ubi jus, ibi remedium.*[5] The translation is rather well known: "*where this is a right, there is a remedy.*"

In legal parlance, "every litigated case, without exception, necessarily includes a question of remedy." There is a difference between remedies "dealt with in theory" and remedies that serve merely as "alternative weapons in the richly-stocked judicial arsenal."[6] Many family law advocates miss this point, as evident in the appellate courts' and trial judges' frequent refrain, "I know what you think happened, but what do you want me to do about that within the law?"

Plumbers have a very specific collection of tools with which they can attempt to fix pipe and drain problems. Carpenters carry saws and hammers so as to try to fix framing and trim. Dentists try to fix teeth. Auto mechanics try to fix cars. Courts similarly have a finite set of tools with which to try to fix a narrow range of problems. These remedies are the subject of this chapter.

Some readers may be surprised how often lawyers and their clients do not know what remedy they seek within the law. Because the family courts are to families like parents are to children, it's easy to turn to the court helpless and clueless simply wishing to be heard. That can mean anything from ordering a co-parent to give up a drug habit, to guaranteeing that child support will arrive on time, to protecting a victim from domestic violence, to dividing a child's time and affections like so much

4. Charles Alan Wright, *The Law of Remedies as a Social Institution*, 18 U. Det. L.J. 376, 376 (1955).

5. *Id.*; *see* Cleveland Indians Baseball Co., L.P. v. N.H. Ins. Co., 727 F.3d 633, 644 (6th Cir. 2013) (Clay, J., dissenting) ("Finally, the majority incomprehensibly cites the Latin maxim '*ubi jus, ibi remedium*' as if the existence of a remedy were an actual issue in this case. The more relevant Latin for this matter is '*restitutio ad integrum.*' That phrase refers to the idea that the damages awarded should restore the plaintiff to its original state."); Carlacci v. Mazaleski, 798 A.2d 186, 190 (Pa. 2002) ("This right is an adjunct of due process and Article I, Section 1 of the Pennsylvania Constitution and is not dependent upon express statutory authority. This matter is thus not controlled by the maxim *expressio unius es exclusio alterius*, but instead, by the maxim *ubi jus, ibi remedium.*").

6. Wright, *supra* note 4, at 376.

furniture. Some parents turn to the court for validation in the form of an official document or a statement from the bench punctuated by a dramatic bang of the gavel. Others litigate custody to win child support, residential responsibility, and decision-making authority. And still others turn to the court simply to win.

What Is a Remedy?

A remedy by a court is not a magic lantern or talisman. It is not an amulet or a voodoo doll that suddenly makes parenting or co-parenting or child development logical or sensible or easy, and it is certainly not a gold medal declaring one parent or litigator the victor. In the law, a remedy is a concrete intervention crafted within the scope of the court's authority and power. The legal definition is as follows:

> REMEDY. The means by which a right is enforced or the violation of a right is prevented, redressed, or compensated. Remedies are of four kinds:
>
> (1) By act of the party injured, the principal of which are defense, recaption, distress, entry, abatement, and seizure;
>
> (2) by operation of law, as in the case of retainer and remitter;
>
> (3) by agreement between the parties, *e.g.*, by accord and satisfaction and arbitration; and
>
> (4) by judicial remedy, *e.g.*, action or suit.[7]

A remedy is thus a specific and identifiable outcome that a court may lawfully enforce under authority granted by the legislature or established by case law precedent.[8] Contrary to many litigants' hopes and beliefs, judges are not omnipotent (and certainly are not omniscient). They

---

7. *Remedy*, Black's Law Dictionary (11th ed. 2019).

8. *See* Richards v. Thompson, 842 A.2d 1289, 1291–92, 1293 (Me. 2004) (affirming contempt order that modified a prior judgment by imposing, in its words, "more structured supervision" of the family by (1) adopting a specific visitation schedule with a designated supervisor for the parents' exchange of the child; (2) terminating the mother's right under the original judgment to approve the father's weekend visits in advance; and (3) scheduling a review hearing four months from the date of the order).

cannot make it up on the spot the way that you or I might beg a friendly waiter to deliver an entrée that's not on the menu even if well-replicated, empirical data, and a long list of impressive experts demonstrate the value of that meal. A remedy can be creative and thoughtful, but it must also be precise and enforceable. That latter point—the place where the law and science and common sense sometimes part ways—can be very difficult to explain to parents and concerned non-lawyer professionals.[9]

Trial as a Remedy in and of Itself

In the American adversarial legal system, trials are themselves a remedy. The opportunity to be heard by an impartial finder of fact may be the most common remedy in the judicial bag of tricks. Trial sets the stage for the adversarial process, intentionally working to sharpen the conflict "to ensure that issues in dispute are posed carefully and resolved fairly."[10] Yet the role of the judge requires great care to avoid being sucked into the morass of lingo and self-styled research that threaten to violate the cardinal rule of ethical science and judicial practice since the Nuremberg Convention in 1949: do no harm.[11]

---

9. Margaret M. Mahoney, *The Enforcement of Child Custody Orders by Contempt Remedies*, 68 U. Pitt. L. Rev. 835 (2006).

10. This point has fomented decades of criticism from the public to scholars and practitioners; some warranted, some bitter from experience. *See, e.g.*, Andrew Schepard, Children, Courts, and Custody: Interdisciplinary Models for Divorcing Families (2004); Barbara A. Babb, *Reevaluating Where We Stand: A Comprehensive Survey of America's Family Justice Systems*, 46 Fam. Ct. Rev. 230 (2008); Bernardine Dohrn, *Seize the Little Moment: Justice for the Child 20 Years at the Children and Family Justice Center*, 6 Nw. J.L. & Soc. Pol'y 334 (2011); Gerald W. Hardcastle, *Adversarialism and the Family Court: A Family Court Judge's Perspective*, 9 U.C. Davis J. Juv. L. & Pol'y 57 (2005).

11. *See* Allison M. Nichols, *Toward a Child-Centered Approach to Evaluating Claims of Alienation in High-Conflict Custody Disputes*, 112 Mich. L. Rev. 663, 679 (2014) ("Given the complex issues involved in these cases, it is understandable why judges might wish to rely on the advice of mental health professionals. Yet the law charges courts, not psychologists, with issuing custody orders, and Daubert and Frye stand for the proposition that judges may only call on experts to assist them in their duties if the testimony offered by those experts is valid. As testimony regarding [parental alienation syndrome] PAS cannot meet that standard under either test, it has no place in the courtroom.").

Science and Remedies?

The law speaks of remedies as a function of case precedent and court authority to act and allocate rights, resources, and responsibilities. By contrast, mental health professionals speak of remedies as evidence-based interventions, grounded in ethical and empirical research, statistical analysis, clinical experience, and tailored to fit the specific needs of an individual and family.[12]

There are those who defend mental health professionals' efforts to extrapolate from the general to the specific. In the interest of balance, we note the following:

> A sharp distinction between general and specific causation is alien to psychologists and most scientists. The ability to generalize to specific circumstances is probabilistic and applying knowledge in court is not different in principle from applying scientific evidence in other contexts. However, the confidence with which experts can generalize varies, depending on the state of available, relevant science. Like physicians' ability to diagnose a patient's physical symptoms, scientists' ability to link general and specific causation for the individual case crucially depends on the quality of available scientific evidence and the scientist's relevant expertise. Qualified social scientists who provide general, relevant knowledge and apply ordinary scientific reasoning may offer informed opinion about the individual case, but probabilistically. None of this usurps the triers of fact of their role, as they are capable of drawing their own conclusions, with scientific judgments as one input.[13]

12. Cindy Brooks Dollar, *Therapeutically (Un)Just Interactions in Family Court Proceedings*, 31 CRIM. JUST. POL'Y REV. 262 (2020); Laura Robertson & Karen Broadhurst, *Introducing Social Science Evidence in Family Court Decision-Making and Adjudication: Evidence from England and Wales*, 33 INT'L J.L. POL'Y & FAM. 181 (2019).

13. Susan T. Fiske & Eugene Borgida, *Standards for Using Social Psychological Evidence in Employment Discrimination Cases*, 83 TEMPLE L. REV. 867, 875–76 (2011) (footnotes omitted).

A great judge once told the second author (Prescott) in advance of a custody trial, "I can do this with a hatchet, or you can do it with a scalpel." By this, the judge meant that until the closing gavel sounds, the litigating parents retain the autonomy and authority to design their own nuanced remedy built upon their intimate and profound knowledge of their child and the family's unique dynamics, a knowledge that will always be far greater than that the court could ever acquire. Once the gavel sounds, however, the court imposes remedies by exercising its *parens patriae* authority, based on evidence tailored to the confines of the courtroom, its rules, and traditions, and limited by the skill of the lawyers and the time allotted to the case. This is despite the fact that the court may never meet the child, may never hear her thoughts and wishes and fears, and will certainly never tuck her in at night, teach her about the birds and the bees, or walk her down the aisle.

The Menu of Family Law Remedies

Building on the scaffolding set forth by a Canadian jurist,[14] we submit that the court is generally limited to remedies that fall into nine broad categories:

1. **Recursive investigative and evaluative processes.** The court can determine that the facts in evidence are insufficient and, on this basis, order further inquiry in any of a number of forms endorsed by jurisdiction and limited by available and affordable resources.[15] This includes, for example, parenting capacity evaluations,[16] individual psychological

14. N.R.G. v. G.R.G., [2015] B.C.S.C. 1062, https://canlii.ca/t/gjmnn.

15. Gary B. Melton et al., Psychological Evaluations for the Courts: A Handbook for Mental Health Professionals and Lawyers (2017).

16. Brigid Daniel, *Judgments about Parenting: What Do Social Workers Think They Are Doing?*, 9 Child Abuse Rev. 91 (2000); *see also* Angela White, NSW Dep't of Cmty. Servs., Literature Review: Assessment of Parenting Capacity (2005).

evaluations,[17] investigation of specific issues by a guardian ad litem,[18] or investigation by a child custody evaluator.[19] We refer to these as recursive because none of these are solutions on their own. Each is simply a means of gathering additional data so as to return to court in search of better-informed remedies.

Distinguishing among These Avenues of Further Inquiry

How these various services are defined, how they're implemented, when and how they can be ordered, who provides them, and how they're paid for all varies widely by jurisdiction. It's useful, nonetheless, to define several generic distinctions:

The court's responsibility before ordering further inquiry should be to refine and document the question(s) it hopes to have answered. "When judges fail to translate the issues in dispute into specific psycholegal questions that may be answered by child custody evaluators, they handicap their appointed experts."[20] Any reasonable family law

(continued on next page)

17. Steven Demby, *Interparent Hatred and Its Impact on Parenting: Assessment in Forensic Custody Evaluations*, 29 PSYCHOANALYTIC INQUIRY 477 (2009); Francisca Fariña et al., *A Meta-Analytic Review of the MMPI Validity Scales and Indexes to Detect Defensiveness in Custody Evaluations*, 17 INT'L J. CLINICAL & HEALTH PSYCH. 128 (2017); Douglas K. Symons, *A Review of the Practice and Science of Child Custody and Access Assessment in the United States and Canada*, 41 PRO. PSYCH.: RSCH. & PRAC. 267 (2010); Duk Soo Moon et al., *Custody Evaluation in High-Conflict Situations Focused on Domestic Violence and Parental Alienation Syndrome*, 31 J. KOREAN ACAD. CHILD & ADOLESCENT PSYCHIATRY 66 (2020).

18. Dana E. Prescott & Diane A. Tennies, *The Lawyer as Guardian Ad Litem: Should Status Make Expert Opinions All-In and Trump Gatekeeping Functions by Family Courts*, 30 J. AM. ACAD. MATRIMONIAL LAW. 379 (2017); Jon D. Phillips, *A Qualitative Study of Collaboration between Guardians Ad Litem and Caseworkers in the Child Welfare System*, 60 CHILD. & YOUTH SERVICES REV. 61 (2016).

19. Samir Patel & Laura Choate, *Conducting Child Custody Evaluations: Best Practices for Mental Health Counselors Who Are Court-Appointed as Child Custody Evaluators*, 36 J. MENTAL HEALTH COUNSELING 18 (2014).

20. Jonathan W. Gould & David A. Martindale, *Specific-Questions Guide to Child Custody Investigations*, LAW J. NEWSLETTERS, Apr. 2009, https://www.lawjournalnewsletters.com/sites/lawjournalnewsletters/2009/04/28/specific-questions-guide-to-child-custody-investigations.

professional should recognize a vague and generic order calling only for "Mr. Smith and Ms. Jones to submit to a child custody evaluation" as overly broad and an invitation to endure a licensing board complaint, if not civil actions.

We approach the question of psychological evaluation once again using the metaphor of an infinitely powerful orbiting telescope. Whether the focus of evaluation is on the individual, a dyad, or the whole system will depend on the nature of the question that the court seeks to have answered.

If the question to be answered concerns an individual's functioning, then an individual assessment may be most appropriate. The referral question sent to the evaluator may be, for example, "Determine whether Mr. Smith is psychotic and whether any such psychosis is likely to affect his parenting and co-parenting capacity." This referral calls for an individual adult psychometric evaluation and/or a parenting capacity evaluation. The latter is a request to document Mr. Smith's generic capacity to safely care for children.

The referral question, "Advise whether Billy has the psychological resources to be adjudicated as a mature minor," calls for a comprehensive psychological assessment of the child, likely including and integrating measures of intelligence, social, and emotional functioning, interpreting these outcomes in the content of any applicable "mature minor" statute.[21]

Questions about adult functioning raised in the context of contested child custody litigations are more difficult. They raise associated questions including whether assessing one of a pair of parents might adequately inform the legal process,[22] whether both parents should undergo individual psychometric assessments in the interest

(continued on next page)

---

21. Benjamin D. Garber, Keeping Kids Out of the Middle: Parenting Effectively in the Midst of Adult Conflict, Separation, and Divorce (2008).

22. Unless the psychologist is conducting a child custody evaluation, "[e]valuators shall endeavor to employ procedures that will create a sense of balance for those involved in the process. As one element of a balanced process, the evaluative criteria employed shall be the same for each parent-child combination." Association of Family and Conciliation Courts, Model Standards of Practice for Child Custody Evaluation 5.5(a) (2006).

of balance, and whether and how individual assessment of one or both bears on the family system questions at bar.[23] Given the nature of family law (and acknowledging our commitment to the systemic perspective), we believe that the family court's requests for further inquiry in contested custody and related matters (e.g., relocation, termination of parental rights) must focus on the quality of relationship fit, rather than on individual functioning. Thus, when the court seeks clarification about the adults' mutual ability to communicate constructively or the quality of Mom's relationship with her son, or more generally how best to understand and serve the best interests of a particular child, a child custody evaluation is likely the most appropriate next step.

2. **Detailed case management.**[24] Among the remedies available to most courts is the option to establish protocols that anticipate and seek to promptly defuse recurrent disputes. This includes within jurisdiction-specific prerogatives, as examples, (a) the court seizing itself of the case in the interest of continuity and time-efficiency, assuring that one jurist

23. Benjamin D. Garber & Robert A. Simon, *Individual Adult Psychometric Testing and Child Custody Evaluations: If the Shoe Doesn't Fit, Don't Wear It*, 30 J. Am. Acad. Matrimonial Law. 325 (2018).

24. Andrew Schepard, *The Evolving Judicial Role in Child Custody Disputes: From Fault Finder to Conflict Manager to Differential Case Management*, 22 U. Ark. Little Rock L. Rev. 395 (2000); Hogan v. Veno, 909 A.2d 638, 648 (Me. 2006) ("The court's decision to order reunification counseling as recommended by the guardian ad litem as one of the two alternative dispositions was also in opposition to its finding that, based on the testimony of the child's former counselor, 'forced counseling for [the child] with and about her father would be dangerous for [the child's] emotional health [and that o]rdering compliance with the earlier order or a similar substitute is too risky.'"); McClain v. McClain, 539 S.W.3d 170, 206 (Tenn. Ct. App. 2017) ("We determine that with such a focus, the trial court was, contrary to Father's argument, definitely considering the emotional needs and developmental levels of the Children (factor 7). In addition, the court had appointed a forensic psychologist to obtain insight into the reasons for the Children's psychiatric hospitalizations and, in light of Dr. Schacht's assessments, the mental and emotional fitness of each parent (factor 8).") (citation omitted).

will hear all subsequent motions whenever possible,[25] (b) alerting local first responders to the continuing need for vigilance,[26] (c) requiring that parties seek mediated outcomes,[27] and/or (d) requiring parties to seek arbitrated outcomes via alternative dispute resolution means (e.g., via parenting coordination[28]).

3. **Compliance contingencies.** The court can either (a) proactively require parties to take a specific action as a precondition to an identified and desired outcome (e.g., extending a period of parenting time), (b) proactively threaten to take action in response to a specific action or failure to act, or (c) retroactively hold parties in contempt for failing to

---

25. For example:

> It is imperative in high conflict family cases generally, and certainly in cases involving allegations of alienation like this one, that one member of the Court take charge of the case. . . . All proceedings in the court and all business arising from those proceedings, if practicable and convenient, must be heard, determined and disposed of before a single judge. . . . All proceedings subsequent to the hearing or trial including the final order, except as otherwise provided, and on a rehearing must, if practicable and convenient, be before the judge before whom the trial or hearing took place.

N.R.G. v. G.R.G., [2015] B.C.S.C. 1062 para. 49, https://canlii.ca/t/gjmnn (quoting A.A. v. S.N.A., [2009] B.C.S.C. 387 para. 77, https://canlii.ca/t/22vl8).

26. For example:

> A copy of this order will be provided to the Halton Regional Police, Ontario Provincial Police, and any police force in whose jurisdiction either of the parties lives, who will take all reasonable steps to assist in its enforcement if necessary. A copy of this order is also to be provided to the schools that the children attend.

X. v. Y., [2016] O.N.S.C. 545 para. 304(e), https://canlii.ca/t/gnlmn.

27. Jerome T. Barrett & Joseph Barrett, A History of Alternative Dispute Resolution: The Story of a Political, Social, and Cultural Movement (2004); Jessica J. Sauer, *Mediating Child Custody Disputes for High Conflict Couples: Structuring Mediation to Accommodate the Needs & Desires of Litigious Parents*, 7 Pepp. Disp. Resol. L.J. 501 (2007); Joan B. Kelly, *Family Mediation Research: Is There Empirical Support for the Field?*, 22 Conflict Resol. Q. 3 (2004); Alexandra Crampton, *Ethnographic Refusal as Research Method: Example from a Study of a Family Court Child Custody Mediation Program*, 14 Qualitative Soc. Work 453 (2015).

28. Robin M. Deutsch et al., *Critical Review of Research Evidence of Parenting Coordination's Effectiveness*, 56 Fam. Ct. Rev. 119 (2018); Steven L. Demby, *Parenting Coordination: Applying Critical Thinking to the Management and Resolution of Post-Divorce Conflict*, 72 J. Clinical Psych. 458 (2016).

comply with established protocols. With these options in mind, we recommend basic behavioral advice:

> [T]he threat of mild punishment imposed reliably and immediately is more effective than the threat of severe punishment that is delayed and uncertain. . . . Thus litigants who may breach court orders need to have a firm sense of what to expect from the court, and the certainty that the court will follow through on its threats. Swift, certain, uniform, and moderate consequences are most likely to be effective.[29]

The required or prohibited behaviors that these contingencies are built upon are as diverse as the litigants themselves. The menu of possible contingencies is, however, much more limited. They tend to (1) incur financial costs[30] including garnishment of wages, (2) require or restrict specific behaviors,[31] (3) cost parenting time, and/or (4) risk incarceration.[32]

---

29. Richard A. Warshak, *Parental Alienation: Overview, Management, Intervention, and Practice Tips*, 28 J. Am. Acad. Matrimonial Law. 181, 210 (2015) (footnote omitted). Note that this is precisely the same advice parents need to follow when concerns about child behavior management arise.

30. *See, e.g.*, Usack v. Usack, 17 A.D.3d 736, 740, 793 N.Y.S.2d 223 (N.Y. App. Div. 2005) (finding, in relevant part, that "defendant's support obligations are suspended pending further court order upon a showing that plaintiff has made good faith efforts to actively encourage and restore defendant's relationship with the children, and defendant's visitation with the children").

31. Some are very creative. For example:

> Mother shall immediately read *Divorce Poison: How to Protect Your Family from Bad-Mouthing and Brainwashing* and view *Welcome Back, Pluto* within one (1) month of her receipt of same. . . . Mother shall prepare *a written report* of what she learned from the book, movie and in counseling, including a list of a minimum of five (5) corrective measures she intends to take (or has taken) to facilitate reconciliation of children and Father's relationship. Mother's written report shall be submitted to Father, Dr. B. and the Attorney for the Children . . . .

Gregory S. v. Dana K., 52 Misc. ed 1211(A), 41 N.Y.S.3d 719 (table) (N.Y. Fam. Ct. July 1, 2016).

32. To illustrate:

> [T]the trial court sentenced the father to serve three days in jail for each adjudicated act of contumacy; however, it suspended the applicable sentences, placed the father on 24 months of unsupervised probation, and ordered that,

Behavioral contingencies can be particularly dramatic when parental relocation ("move away") is at issue. Whereas the court typically exercises its authority to adjust the parenting plan when one parent intends to relocate, the question arises as to whether the court can actually prohibit the parent from moving. "The issue is whether the magistrate court had authority to order that Mother live within a specific geographical location so that both parents could continue having frequent contact with and physical custody of their child."[33] In this particular case, the answer was no.

4. **Judicial exhortation.** As a remedy, judicial exhortation amounts to an exercise of the court's authoritarian voice to urge compliance and to protect the child. These exhortations often amount to a list of thou-shalt or thou-shalt-not commandments. The best example for the present purpose is the *non-denigration statement*, a clause forbidding parties (and their allies) from damning one another to or around their children because (ironically) *ipse dixit*: the court says so. One of the more exhaustive we've seen requires that

> [b]oth parents are restrained and enjoined from manifesting any form of conflict with each other, including, but not limited to assaulting, threatening, harassing, intimidating or arguing with the other parent in the presence of, or within the hearing of Anthony. Both parents are restrained and enjoined from disparaging each other, or their respective family members, friends or associates in the presence of, or within the hearing of Anthony. Both parents are enjoined from discussing the details of this litigation with Anthony, and from providing him with copies of documents from it for review. Both parents are restrained and enjoined from exercising undue influence over Anthony with

---

> during that 24-month period, the father was required to strictly comply with the orders of the judgment . . . .

O'Barr v. O'Barr, 163 So. 3d 1076, 1080 (Ala. Civ. App. 2014).

33. Allbright v. Allbright, 215 P.3d 472, 474 (Idaho 2009) ("During oral argument, Father asserted that if it was in the best interests of the child, a court could order the divorced parents to live next door to each other, or even to share the same residence. He stopped short, however, of stating that the court could order parents not to get divorced even if such order was in the child's best interests.").

> respect to this litigation or future litigation. Undue influence includes, but is not limited to, coaching Anthony as to what to say or orchestrating his actions with respect to the court or the other parent.[34]

5. **Court-ordered education and/or therapy.** Most courts can require one or both parties and/or their child(ren) to enroll in educational[35] and/or therapeutic interventions such as "reunification" therapy.[36] Perhaps the most common among these is some form of mandatory divorce education class.[37] For all of their potential value, these directives are frequently subject to the "lead a horse to water" criticism. For example:

> [T]his is a circumstance in which all three children must have therapy and both parents should actively participate to the extent the selected therapist deems appropriate. I will order the children to receive this therapy and I will encourage the parents to participate. However, no order levied against the parents will be successful if they are not willing to actively participate in the therapy.[38]

We note, however, scholarly opinions to the contrary:

> [T]he case law developed over more than 32 years provides ample authority for courts to exercise their power to compel parties to participate in psychotherapy and facilitate their children's participation . . . the combined evidence from the psychological literature and from other forensic arenas where legal institutions

---

34. Order on Plaintiff's Motion for Post-Judgment Relief, Andersen v. Prendergast, No. FM-11-684 (Me. Dec. 6, 2016).

35. Ellen P. Lukens & William R. McFarlane, *Psychoeducation as Evidence-Based Practice*, 291 Found. Evidence-Based Soc. Work Prac. 205 (2006).

36. Benjamin D. Garber, *Cognitive-Behavioral Methods in High Conflict Divorce: Systematic Desensitization Adapted to Parent-Child Reunification Interventions*, 53 Fam. Ct. Rev. 96 (2015); Linda S. Smith, *Family-Based Therapy for Parent-Child Reunification*, 72 J. Clinical Psych. 498 (2016); Toby Kleinman, *Family Court Ordered "Reunification Therapy:" Junk Science in the Guise of Helping Parent/Child Relationships?*, 14 J. Child Custody 295 (2017).

37. David G. Schramm & Emily H. Becher, *Common Practices for Divorce Education*, 69 Fam. Rel. 543 (2020).

38. L. M. v J. B., [2016] N.B.Q.B. 93 para. 143, https://canlii.ca/t/gt266.

and the mental health professions have successfully collaborated indicates that the conventional wisdom is wrong; that compulsory mental health intervention can be successful.[39]

Nevertheless, the legal question remains as to whether a court has the prerogative to require any individual to participate in therapy. Although a full exploration of this subject is far beyond the purview of this book,[40] we commend one court's resourceful work-around as follows:

> The judgment . . . does not directly order the child or the mother to participate in therapy. Rather, it sets participation in therapy as a prerequisite to the fixed date review of the change in custody. If the child or the mother refused to participate in the therapeutic process, they would lose the opportunity to have a fixed date review of the change in custody, without the need to show a change of circumstances. In that sense, the order made still left some scope for choice on their part as to participation in the therapy and the question of forcing treatment on an unwilling participant does not directly arise.[41]

6. **Court-ordered mediation services.** The court can try to assure that systemic conflicts are resolved promptly, efficiently, and in a less costly manner without court intervention by ordering parties to defer to a mutually trusted third party (e.g., a faith community leader), formal mediation, and/or co-parenting counseling,[42] noting that the court's willingness and ability to delegate its authority to others is often challenged.[43]

---

39. Elliot Wiener & Sara Weiss, *Court-Ordered Psychotherapy in Custody Disputes*, N.Y.L.J., July 30, 2007.

40. Interested readers are referred to the discussion of court-ordered therapy in criminal matters: Jessica Wilen Berg, *Give Me Liberty or Give Me Silence: Taking a Stand on Fifth Amendment Implications for Court-Ordered Therapy Programs*, 79 Cornell L. Rev. 700 (1994).

41. A.M. v. C.H., [2019] O.N.C.A. 764 para. 45, https://canlii.ca/t/j2nf4.

42. Benjamin D. Garber, *Directed Co-Parenting Intervention: Conducting Child-Centered Interventions in Parallel with Highly Conflicted Co-Parents*, 35 Pro. Psych.: Rsch. & Prac. 55 (2004); Jay Lebow & Kathleen Newcomb Rekart, *Integrative Family Therapy for High-Conflict Divorce with Disputes over Child Custody and Visitation*, 46 Fam. Process 79 (2007).

43. *See, e.g.*, *In re* Kamil, 242 A.3d 801, 812–13 (N.H. 2020).

7. **Limiting and/or supervising parenting time.** Concerns about a child's safety in the care of a parent are often addressed by limiting the duration, frequency, timing (e.g., daylight hours only), conditions, and/or location (e.g., public places only) of parent-child contact. This includes the court's discretion to require that contact be supervised either by a family member or an impartial professional. For example:

> Supervised visitation is often court-ordered to minimize and prevent child maltreatment, to reduce the risk of harm to both parents and children, to improve and facilitate positive parent-child relationships, and to provide written accounts of the factual observations of the visit to the court, if required. In addition, supervised contact can help to prevent children from feeling abandoned, while providing opportunities for positive interactions with non-custodial parents, thereby minimizing further re-traumatization.[44]

8. **Transferring custody.** Also known as *custody reversal*, this controversial and extreme remedy is most often discussed when a child's resist/refuse behaviors are linked (usually via the court's endorsement of expert opinion) to Parent A's intransigent alienating behaviors (Chapter 15), and then only after serial intrusive psychotherapeutic interventions and the court's exhortations have failed.[45] The court's necessary and unenviable calculus in these situations weighs the child's likely long-term benefits remaining in the alienating parent's care against the expectable

---

44. Michael Saini & Rachel Birnbaum, *The Supervised Visitation Checklist: Validation with Lawyers, Mental Health Professionals, and Judges*, 49 Fam. L.Q. 449 (2015); *see also* Karen Oehme & Kelly O'Rourke, *Protecting Victims and Their Children through Supervised Visitation: A Study of Domestic Violence Injunctions*, 3 Faulkner L. Rev. 261 (2012).

45. "The trial judge concluded that the child's long-term best interests favoured a reversal of custody and a suspension of access, intended to be time-limited, to the mother and her allies, in the hopes that the father and son could achieve some rapprochement. Accordingly, by judgment dated October 30, 2018, the trial judge ordered an immediate custody reversal and prohibited contact between the child and his mother and siblings for six months, with custody and access to be reviewed at the end of the six-month period, subject to certain conditions. In his reasons on motion dated January 18, 2019, the trial judge further ordered no contact between the child and the mother's extended family." A.M. v. C.H., [2019] O.N.C.A. 764 para. 2, https://canlii.ca/t/j2nf4.

emotional trauma and social displacement of custody reversal.[46] There is no single clear means of balancing this equation, noting many cases with very serious negative outcomes.[47] We note, however, one court's very positive follow-up to a very dramatic custody reversal:

> That case seems to have had a very happy ending. In a subsequent hearing Hebner J. observed that: "On the evidence as a whole, I find that a change in custody has made a remarkable difference in the relationship these three girls have with their father. In fact, I can safely say that the change in custody has saved that relationship. Were it not for the change in custody, I have no doubt whatsoever that the children would not have any sort of relationship with their father": 2016 ONSC 3678 at para. 32.[48]

9. **Terminating parental rights (TPR).** Although TPR may seem odd or threatening to include among remedies, it is neither. It is included under the law as a remedy encompassed within the scope of the court's constitutional authority.[49]

TPR is parentectomy: "[an] extreme action initiated by the state to irrevocably sever the legal bond between parent and child."[50] In many respects for family systems, particularly with race and poverty as factors, TPR has an intergenerational finality that Justice Ruth Bader Ginsberg

---

46. "Given the evidence in this case regarding the daughters' 'dismissing, disrespectful and at times rude manner' toward the father, and Doris's 'intense separation anxiety' and her stated fears (whether real or imagined), an immediate custody reversal in this case would pose risks of trauma to one or both daughters, and would not be in their best interests. An immediate custody reversal in this case could be a recipe for failure and long-term resentment." Luo v. Le, [2016] O.N.S.C. 202 para. 41, https://canlii.ca/t/gmzdr.

47. Joyanna Silberg & Stephanie Dallam, *Abusers Gaining Custody in Family Courts: A Case Series of Over Turned Decisions*, 16(2) J. Child Custody 140 (2019).

48. A.M. v. C.H., [2019] O.N.C.A. 764 para. 35 n.1.

49. For an historical review of this point, see Susan B. Hershkowitz, *Due Process and the Termination of Parental Rights*, 19 Fam. L.Q. 245 (1985). The disparate impact of this "remedy" is thoroughly explored in Mario L. Barnes & Erwin Chemerinsky, *The Disparate Treatment of Race and Class in Constitutional Jurisprudence*, 72 Law & Contemp. Probs. 109 (2009).

50. Esther Wattenberg et al., *When the Rehabilitation Ideal Fails: A Study of Parental Rights Termination*, 80 Child Welfare 405 (2001).

described as the "destruction of . . . family bonds" and a "devastatingly adverse action."[51]

This most-extreme remedy is supposed to be exercised when all other means of facilitating a child's opportunity to enjoy a safe and healthy relationship with a parent have been exhausted. As such, TPR occurs far more often in child protection (e.g., abuse and neglect) matters than in family law, per se. However, given the co-occurrence of allegations of alienation and allegations of abuse and neglect (Chapter 15), TPR falls not only within the purview of the family court's authority but also on the short menu of available family law remedies.

In the United States, child protection cases are, in many respects, child custody cases for the poor or disadvantaged.[52] Millions of children find themselves caught in the child protection system every year. In 2016, for example, one in every 100 U.S. children under age 18 experienced the termination of a parent's rights. The risk is highest for the youngest, most socially, emotionally, and economically deprived, for Native American and African American children,[53] and for children whose mothers suffer from mental illness.[54]

---

51. M.L.B. v. S.L.J., 519 U.S. 102, 125 (1996).

52. Paul Chill, *Burden of Proof Begone: The Pernicious Effect of Emergency Removal in Child Protective Proceedings*, 42 Fam. Ct. Rev. 540 (2004); Children's Bureau, U.S. Department of Health and Human Services, Child Maltreatment 2017 tbls. 3.1–3.8 (2019), https://www.acf.hhs.gov/sites/default/files/documents/cb/cm2017.pdf; Janet L. Wallace & Lisa R. Pruitt, *Judging Parents, Judging Place: Poverty, Rurality, and Termination of Parental Rights*, 77 Mo. L. Rev. 95 (2012).

53. Christopher Wildeman et al., *The Cumulative Prevalence of Termination of Parental Rights for U.S. Children, 2000–2016*, 25 Child Maltreatment 32 (2020).

54. *See* Dana E. Prescott, *The AAML and a New Paradigm for Thinking about Child Custody Litigation: The Next Half Century*, 24 J. Am. Acad. Matrimonial Law. 107 (2011); *see also* Corina Benjet et al., *Evaluating the Parental Fitness of Psychiatrically Diagnosed Individuals: Advocating a Functional-Contextual Analysis of Parenting*, 17 J. Fam. Psych. 238, 238, 240 (2003); Jana B. Singer, *Dispute Resolution and the Postdivorce Family: Implications of a Paradigm Shift*, 47 Fam. Ct. Rev. 363, 364 (2009) ("A second element of the paradigm shift in family dispute resolution is the belief that most family disputes are not discrete legal events, but ongoing social and emotional processes."); Nancy Darling & Laurence Steinberg, *Parenting Style as Context: An Integrative Model*, 113 Psych. Bull. 487, 488 (1993) ("The model we offer defines parenting style as a constellation of attitudes toward the child that are communicated to the child and that, taken together, create an emotional climate in which the parent's behaviors are expressed.").

The courts' frequent failure to consider behavior in context (i.e., how do history and exigencies of the moment compel any particular act?) and routine inability to predict future acts (no matter what experts might say to the contrary) means that the least culturally and linguistically literate, the least well-represented, the least healthy, and the most needy and disturbed families get the least justice. We've referred to this throughout this volume and elsewhere as epistemic inequity. In response, Benjet and her colleagues recommend a functional/contextual model for child custody determinations and associated remedies:

1. An emphasis on "good enough" or minimally acceptable parenting[55]
2. Specific steps to maximize respect for cultural and linguistic diversity
3. A contextual or ecological rather than a fault-finding, individual understanding of parenting capacity accounting, for example, for each parent's social network and each child's developmental or special needs
4. Incorporating factors that complement behavioral health such as physical healthcare (e.g., sanitation, hygiene, safety in the home environment including a history of violence) and home and social network stability
5. Actively considering the child's larger social network (e.g., coparental communication, a parent's new partners, sibling and stepsibling relationships) "as is"[56]

55. In this regard see Joseph Goldstein et al., The Best Interests of the Child: The Least Detrimental Alternative (1996).

56. *See* Benjet et al., *supra* note 54, at 246.

Why should family law and child protection remedies take such a broad view?

In 1996, Congress passed the Adoption and Safe Families Act (ASFA), designed to promote more timely permanent placements for children in the child welfare system.[57] Viewed as landmark child protection legislation, the ASFA was enacted as a response to growing concerns about "foster care drift"—that is, "children experiencing multiple, unstable foster care placements over extended periods, children virtually lost within the child welfare system."[58]

Should the interminable and destructive "custody drift" common to so many high-conflict custody litigating families be subject to similar policies and procedures? It's easy to wonder what would happen if parents in private custody matters were subject to the same legally mandated time lines (months instead of years), interventions, and criteria for change, and faced with the same ultimate threat of TPR.

If we are genuinely invested in serving the best interests of the child, then certainly custody matters are deserving of the same level of scrutiny as child protection matters. This means minimizing the erosion of the child's security, safety, and nurturance while their parents' litigation drags on. We must recognize and act to prevent harm no matter the child's race, religion, gender, privilege, or zip code. After all, professional burnout and compassion fatigue in chronic conflict child custody cases (Chapter 18) is nothing compared to what the children subject to these actions must endure.[59]

---

57. Anna Rockhill et al., *Is the Adoption and Safe Families Act Influencing Child Welfare Outcomes for Families with Substance Abuse Issues?*, 12 Child Maltreatment 7 (2007).

58. *Id.* at 8.

59. Ann M. Ordway et al., *Understanding Vicarious Trauma, Burnout, and Compassion Fatigue in High-Conflict Divorce*, 28 Fam. J. 187 (2020).

Evidence-Based Medicine

Every mental health code of ethics requires its adherents to administer assessment instruments[60] and prescribe treatments or interventions on the basis of empirical efficacy.[61] In today's healthcare environment, this means greater and greater deference to evidence-based medicine (EBM).[62] EBM is intended "to develop and promote an explicit and rational process for clinical decision making that deemphasized intuition and unsystematic clinical expertise while emphasizing the importance of incorporating the best research findings into clinical care," or more simply as "the conscientious and judicious use of current best evidence from clinical care research in the management of individual patients."[63] EBM now dictates a great deal of decision making (not to mention third-party reimbursement heuristics) across much of healthcare. For better or worse, psychology and social work have been relatively slow to join the EBM crowd, and we family law professionals have barely dipped our metaphorical toes in the water.[64] "The challenges associated with translational science and interprofessional practice are substantial and call for more unified practice models, a common language, and unifying goals. Because the training of practitioners in the health professions differs,

---

60. "Psychologists administer, adapt, score, interpret, or use assessment techniques, interviews, tests, or instruments in a manner and for purposes that are appropriate in light of the research on or evidence of the usefulness and proper application of the techniques." American Psychological Association, Ethical Principles of Psychologists and Code of Conduct 9.02(a) (2017).

61. "When obtaining informed consent for treatment for which generally recognized techniques and procedures have not been established, psychologists inform their clients/patients of the developing nature of the treatment, the potential risks involved, alternative treatments that may be available, and the voluntary nature of their participation." *Id.* 10.01(b).

62. Jason M. Satterfield et al., *Toward a Transdisciplinary Model of Evidence-Based Practice*, 87 Milbank Q. 368 (2009).

63. *Id.*

64. Leonard Gibbs & Eileen Gambrill, *Evidence-Based Practice: Counterarguments to Objections*, 12 Rsch. Soc. Work Prac. 452 (2002).

their vocabulary, conceptual frameworks, and research methods often differ as well, thereby impeding cross-disciplinary translation."[65]

The problem is as simple to state as it is difficult to correct: there are very few or no empirical studies that can inform us whether and under what circumstances any of the nine legal remedies summarized above (or others not adequately captured here) are likely to be effective. Part of the problem is the pervasive and essential injustice of our justice system.[66] Another is the many difficulties associated with data collection within such a high-stress population (Chapter 16). A third and perhaps the most basic impediment is the fact that one can't worry about generalizability when there is no normative group data to begin with.

Unless and until we understand the population of high-conflict divorcing parents, our observations about them amount to little more than anecdotes. In fact, we know little or nothing about what custody-contending adults share in common above and beyond the fact that they are contending their children's future custody. Talking about evidence-based interventions best suited for an unstudied population is like trying to buy shoes for a person about whom you know nothing at all. Thus, although psychometricians have amassed terabytes of data about their pet assessment instruments, the validity of these instruments—that is, the descriptive and predictive value generalized from research with non-custody litigating samples—among high-conflict and divorcing families remains a matter of serious concern and much professional debate.[67]

This is not to say that the field of family law is not moving in the right direction, albeit perhaps at a glacial pace. We note, for example, surveys summarizing child custody evaluators' practices[68] particularly

---

65. *Id.*; *see* Allen Rubin & Jennifer Bellamy, Practitioner's Guide to Using Research for Evidence-Based Practice (2012).

66. Dana E. Prescott, *Bending the Light of Social Science in Family Court: Epistemic Injustice and Epistemic Exceptionalism Matter*, 33 J. Am. Acad. Matrimonial Law. 99 (2020).

67. Garber & Simon, *supra* note 23.

68. Cassandra Valerio & Connie Beck, *Testing in Child Custody Evaluations: An Overview of Issues and Uses*, 14 J. Child Custody 260 (2017).

when questions of intimate partner violence arise.[69] We note efforts to characterize some of the dynamics that we have set out to describe here,[70] even while we remain highly critical of the methodology and, therefore, the conclusions of some of these studies.

Finally, we note with some pride and hope for the future newly published guidelines for how and when family law professionals should defer to empirical data, allowing nonetheless that many professionals maintain that "family law-related research is of insufficient quality and quantity to be used to support specific recommendations on various issues, e.g., parenting time, effects of relocation, or quality of parent-child relationship maintained predominantly through technology."[71] With this in mind, we close this chapter with another Latin phrase that must always guide our work: *primum non nocere.*

Above all, do no harm.[72]

69. Daniel G. Saunders, *Research Based Recommendations for Child Custody Evaluation Practices and Policies in Cases of Intimate Partner Violence*, 12 J. Child Custody 71 (2015); *see also* Carla Smith Stover et al., *Interventions for Intimate Partner Violence: Review and Implications for Evidence-Based Practice*, 40 Pro. Psych.: Rsch. & Prac. 223 (1990).

70. *E.g.*, Amy J.L. Baker & Douglas C. Damall, *A Construct Study of the Eight Symptoms of Severe Parental Alienation Syndrome: A Survey of Parental Experiences*, 47 J. Divorce & Remarriage 55 (2007).

71. AFCC Task Force, *Guidelines for the Use of Social Science Research in Family Law*, 57 Fam. Ct. Rev. 193 (2019).

72. Cedric M. Smith, *Origin and Uses of Primum Non Nocere—Above All, Do No Harm!*, 45 J. Clinical Pharmacology 371 (2005); *see* A.B. v. Y.Z., 878 A.2d 807, 813 (N.J. 2005) (Rivera-Soto, J., concurring in result) ("In this instance in particular, we are well instructed by the maxim primum non nocere (first do no harm), or that we 'make a habit of two things—to help, or at least, do no harm.' Hippocrates, *Epidemics*, bk. 1, ch. 11. Both our own limitations on expert testimony as well as plain common sense tell us that there is no need for expert proofs to reach the self-evident conclusion that requiring a child sexual abuse victim to confront his abuser in open court will be traumatic for the victim.").

Chapter 18
Where Metaphors Fail

"As narratives and metaphors influence our cognition and help us reason about [the] abstract and ideas (a large part of our work as jurists) we would be wise to pay closer attention to them."[1]

"Family law is the legal system's metaphor, the crucible where so much else in law intersects. It offers some of the most dynamic layers through which to examine the role of law generally, and the role of those professionals who function on its behalf."[2]

"There but for the grace of god go I."

Metaphor is a writer's tool no less than pencil and paper. It's used to help readers share a point of view. Metaphorically speaking, a metaphor is an invitation to join a party. It's an opportunity to understand another person's idea or experience or perspective. But a metaphor can never capture the full breadth and depth of the thing that it's intended to communicate. Corners are rounded and edges are shaved and colors are enhanced or dulled or shifted altogether in the translation from *thing* to an attractive, relatable, but shadowy representation of that thing.

This book has invited you to share our perspective on family systems by way of metaphor. In Section I, we invited you to imagine looking down on planet Earth through an infinitely powerful telescope, shifting focus from the subatomic to the super-cosmic. We've argued that patterns repeat across every level of inquiry, creating a nested hierarchy of

1. Étienne Cloutier, *A Tale of Two Metaphors: A Narrative Take on the Canadian Constitution*, 64 McGill L.J. 447, 447 (2019), https://canlii.ca/t/t0bb.
2. Rosalie Silberman Abella, *The Law of the Family in the Year of the Family*, 26 Ottawa L. Rev. 533, 533 (1994), https://canlii.ca/t/29bp.

fractal systems. At the level of family, we spoke of child development in terms of a drip emerging from a cup of water. Both processes move from an undifferentiated state toward a state of bounded coherence.

We've often referred back to a metaphorical coffee cup filled with complementary amounts of emotion and reason. As emotion fills this cup, the opportunity to think clearly and draw reasoned conclusions diminishes until, overcome with rage or grief or fear or even joy, we are reduced to a primitive state of fight-or-flight, freeze-or-flock reflexes.

In Section II, we offered an Audubon-like taxonomy—an analogy if not precisely another metaphor—of the dynamics that often emerge within conflicted family systems. Whereas Audubon was able to distinguish phyla based on distinct and mutually exclusive features, our distinctions are based on how relationship boundaries emerge and are defined and redefined across time, variously enabling and inhibiting healthy child development. Unlike Audubon, our types are mutable and mutually compatible, thereby requiring the evaluator to consider all possible hypotheses as they might bear on serving the best interests of the child.

Here in Section III, we've begun to examine how those same dynamics are recapitulated when the telescope's focus is broadened to take in the family system interacting with allied and superordinate systems, particularly the legal system. In particular, we've highlighted the parallels between the remedies that the court can impose on the family and the remedies that the parents can impose on their children.

As authors, we've succeeded if we've communicated these nonlinear and chaotic, Escher-like ideas clearly.[3] Our metaphors have served their intended purposes if we've broadened your thinking and informed your professional practice even a little, no matter how much you might agree or disagree with any particular position. But in the interest of fairness and transparency, we cannot end this book without first admitting that this is where our metaphors fail.

3. "Escher-like" being a simile, not an analogy or a metaphor.

Etic versus Emic

These terms are mainstays of cultural anthropology and social psychology,[4] but are sadly absent from the family law literature. *Etic* describes an observer's perspective from outside of the system being studied. *Emic* describes the subject's perspective on the inside of the system. The difference between the two is about boundaries.

The *etic* looks in on a system from outside of its boundaries without bias or alliance, inviting a balanced and objective assessment. Because the etic point of view is anchored outside of the system that it studies, it can yield valid and meaningful comparisons and contrasts between systems and of their constituent members. "The etic approach realizes that members of a culture often are too involved in what they are doing . . . to interpret their cultures impartially."[5]

The *emic* looks at the system from within, embedded in the experience and immersed in its reality. The emic validates personal experience but has no baseline that might allow comparison or analysis. Where the etic is objective, the emic is subjective. Where the etic is scientific, the emic is phenomenological. Where the etic foster emotional distance, the emic foster rapport. And where the etic categorize and quantify, the emic empathize.

Medicine traditionally promotes an etic approach, in part as a means of protecting the physician: "The image of the technically skillful, rational, and emotionally detached doctor dominates the profession, and inhibits physicians from engaging emotionally with their patients and their own feelings . . . ."[6] The etic medical model is cast in sharp relief

---

4. *E.g.*, Nina Hansen & Luzia Heu, *All Human, Yet Different: An Emic-Etic Approach to Cross-Cultural Replication in Social Psychology*, 51 Soc. Psych. 361 (2020); Andrew Lindridge, *Etic-Emic Dilemma*, *in* Wiley Encyclopedia of Management (Carey Cooper et al. eds., 2015).

5. Conrad Kotta, Mirror for Humanity 47 (2006).

6. Angeliki Kerasidou & Ruth Horn, *Making Space for Empathy: Supporting Doctors in the Emotional Labour of Clinical Care*, 17 BMC Med. Ethics article 8 (2016), https://doi.org/10.1186/s12910-016-0091-7. For a dramatic counterexample, see *Gesundheit: Good Health Is a Laughing Matter* by Patch Adams and Maureen Mylander, known more universally as "Patch Adams" (Universal Pictures 1998).

when compared to other professions' emic approaches. For example, "psychiatrists have translated folk models into diagnostic categories whereas anthropologists have emphasized culture-specific meanings of illness."[7]

Many types of psychotherapy promote an emic approach, explicitly promoting the client's experience of the therapist-client relationship as practice for relating to others, capitalizing on transference and countertransference as tools that can yield insight and behavior change: "The therapeutic alliance remains a key component of creating successful outcomes in psychotherapy. Empathy also continues to be an integral factor to not only forming the alliance, but also increasing a client's ability to feel validated and understood."[8]

Our telescope metaphor is etic. It artificially casts us outside of the boundaries of human experience, looking down upon the relationships that we have endeavored to describe even as we live them ourselves. The metaphor affords us perspective and promotes the objectification that Audubon needed in order to classify his subjects,[9] even while it creates a wholly contrived and unrealistic *not-me* perspective.

This objective, *not-me* etic approach is necessary. It removes us from the equation to the extent that that is ever fully possible. It allows us to think in terms of norms and baselines so as to more objectively evaluate that which we study. Standing outside the system and looking in helps to defuse the otherwise toxic emotions inherent in conflicted family systems and child custody litigation. We would be remiss, however, having surveyed our subject from a distance like alien visitors to the human zoo, not to finally acknowledge what you've known all along to be true: we are whom we study.

Tell the truth: More than once while reading this book you found yourself thinking, unbidden, of a close family member. Maybe you

7. Britt Dahlberg et al., *Bridging Psychiatric and Anthropological Approaches: The Case of "Nerves" in the United States*, 37 Ethos 282 (2009).

8. Margaret McCoy Lynch, Factors Influencing Successful Psychotherapy Outcomes (2012) (Master of Social Work Clinical Research Paper, St. Catherine University), https://sophia.stkate.edu/msw_papers/57.

9. On the other hand, consider Jane Goodall's emic perspective, living months at a time amidst the chimpanzees that she studied. Learn more at Jane Goodall Institute, *About Jane*, https://www.janegoodall.org/our-story/about-jane (last visited July 24, 2021).

paused while reading, wondering if your relationships are enmeshed, if you and your partner have triangulated your son, if your daughter is keeping her distance because she's been estranged, or if your rash words have alienated your kids from their other parent. We'd be surprised if you haven't, at some point, intentionally spoken or acted differently in your personal life while reading this book, hypersensitized to the mechanics of relationship dynamics. Perhaps you even startled, the way that every medical student does when first learning about diseases, certain that we'd been peeking in your window and writing about your family system.

How Should You Use This Book?

The answer is as simple to state as it is difficult to do: Use this book to anchor your professional perspective outside of the families that you study. Use this book to reinforce the boundary that sets you apart, as a shield to deflect the powerful relationship pressures that constantly threaten to suck you into each conflicted family's destructive dynamics. Use this book as a buoy to keep you afloat in the flood of pleading, raging, terrifying emotion that characterizes our work. All metaphors aside, use this book to maintain an etic perspective on your work in family law.

We intend this book to be used as a field guide, a reference that will help you to more accurately identify each family's unique constellation of relationship pressures. We have gone to great lengths to help you to better recognize and minimize bias, to critically digest research, to listen carefully for the expert's ipse dixit weakness, and to accept that a statistical analysis does not in and of itself produce truth. We have purposefully (and sometimes painfully) seeded our descriptions of family dynamics with illustrative quotes, case law, commentary, and further resources in order to help you shore up your observations, consider additional hypotheses, and be better able to defend your conclusions.

Our purpose is to anchor your professional point of view in the etic, to reinforce the boundary that separates the superordinate legal system from the subordinate family system. We strongly believe that this position is both required by all relevant ethical standards, professional guidelines, and best practices, and—more simply—is necessary to your health and well-being.

On Self-Care

We are aware that an etic approach to family law can sound cold or heartless or even selfish. We're also well aware that some professions and some professionals eschew the etic in favor of the emic, blurring boundaries, becoming enmeshed with their clients, mistaking objectivity for the opposite of compassion. These mental health providers and evaluators, guardians ad litem, lawyers, experts, and even judges immerse themselves not only in their work, but in the emotions and relationships of those with whom they work.

We certainly credit these professionals for their dedication, commitment, and generosity, even as anxiety bubbles up over their relative lack of boundaries. Among these are countless first responders, disaster aid workers, and warriors who abandon the comfort of their own homes for weeks or months at a time to protect peace, fight forest fires, rebuild dams, fill sandbags, construct homes or schools, and provide medicine and education to those without. The world is a better place for the efforts of these selfless people, but the social and emotional costs that they endure can be horrific: "Monitoring one's own feelings and reactions comes with a price: controlled empathy is the most stressful and dangerous type of empathy. This process of restricting one's emotions, feelings, and reactions to hearing traumatic stories on a continuous basis can be quite distressing."[10]

The risk of the emic is burnout, compassion fatigue, and vicarious trauma.[11] These are among the social and emotional scars that professionals incur when one's etic shield is lowered. When the emotional insulation afforded by psychological resilience fails (Chapter 3). When the profession requires and/or the professional chooses to immerse herself in others' pain. "[T]ry as we might, we cannot divorce ourselves from our own personal interests and perceptions that shape the questions we ask, the theoretical filters and methods we choose, and the conclusions we

10. Alexis Resnick et al., *Surviving Bench Stress*, 49 Fam. Ct. Rev. 610, 613 (2011).

11. Jay L. Lebow, Treating the Difficult Divorce: A Practical Guide for Psychotherapists (2019).

make."[12] The emic immersion in others' pain is among the reasons that first responders are among the most vulnerable professionals to suicide.[13]

What Are Burnout, Compassion Fatigue, and Vicarious Trauma?

These three interwoven terms capture the human experience of emotional overload. Together, they describe an acquired numbness to the human condition, an erosion of empathy often accompanied by "emotional exhaustion, depersonalization, and reduced personal accomplishment."[14] Professional burnout, compassion fatigue, and vicarious trauma can become a self-perpetuating downward spiral of depression and anxiety with tremendous costs not only to the professional himself, but to his loved ones and to those whom he is supposed to serve. For example:

> [W]orking with traumatized young children can take its toll because it often is very difficult to witness hardship and human suffering, and at the same time, as professionals, be required to maintain boundaries and professional roles, to

(continued on next page)

12. Emma Calgaro, *If You Are Vulnerable and You Know It Raise Your Hand: Experiences from Working in Post-Tsunami Thailand*, 17 Emotion Space & Soc'y 45 (2015).

13. "It is estimated that 30 percent of first responders develop behavioral health conditions including, but not limited to, depression and posttraumatic stress disorder (PTSD), as compared with 20 percent in the general population. In a study about suicidality, firefighters were reported to have higher attempt and ideation rates than the general population. In law enforcement, the estimates suggest between 125 and 300 police officers commit suicide every year." Substance Abuse and Mental Health Services Administration, Disaster Technical Assistance Center Supplemental Research Bulletin—First Responders: Behavioral Health Concerns, Emergency Response, and Trauma 3 (2018) (citations omitted), https://www.samhsa.gov/sites/default/files/dtac/supplementalresearchbulletin-firstresponders-may2018.pdf.

14. David B. King & Anita DeLongis, *When Couples Disconnect: Rumination and Withdrawal as Maladaptive Responses to Everyday Stress*, 28 J. Fam. Psych. 460 (2014).

> make decisions about children's lives, and to take actions to help vulnerable young children and their families.[15]

Vicarious trauma (also known as secondary traumatic stress) is characterized by "reactions to the emotional demands on therapists and social network members from exposure to trauma survivors' terrifying, horrifying, and shocking images; strong, chaotic affect; and intrusive traumatic memories."[16] The concept was renamed compassion fatigue once studies began to recognize it as a "normative occupational hazard for trauma workers and mental health professionals."[17]

Vicarious trauma is often experienced as a reliving or personalization of the traumatic experience endured by another, avoidance of triggers associated with the trauma and/or the victim, uncharacteristic or ego-dystonic emotional numbness, and/or persistent arousal in the form of hypervigilance and hyperreactivity.[18]

Burnout is classically described as

> emotional exhaustion, depersonalization, and reduced personal accomplishment that can occur among individuals who do people-work of some kind . . . [a] response to the chronic emotional strain of dealing extensively with other human beings, particularly when they are troubled or having problems. . . . A pattern of emotional overload and subsequent emotional exhaustion is at the heart of the burnout syndrome. A person gets overly involved emotionally, overextends himself or herself, and feels overwhelmed by the emotional demands imposed by other people.[19]

---

15. Joy D. Osofsky, *Vicarious Traumatization and the Need for Self-Care in Working with Traumatized Young Children*, *in* Clinical Work with Traumatized Young Children 336 (Joy D. Osofsky ed., 2011).

16. Sharon Rae Jenkins & Stephanie Baird, *Secondary Traumatic Stress and Vicarious Trauma: A Validational Study*, 15 J. Traumatic Stress 423 (2002).

17. Charles R. Figley, *Compassion Fatigue as Secondary Traumatic Stress Disorder: An Overview*, *in* Compassion Fatigue: Coping with Secondary Traumatic Stress Disorder in Those Who Treat the Traumatized 1 (Charles R. Figley ed., 1995).

18. See Chapter 14 regarding estrangement and how a child's vicarious experience of Parent B's behavior is associated with contact resistance and refusal.

19. Christina Maslach, Burnout: The Cost of Caring 3 (1982).

As family law professionals, we run the same risks. The families that seek our help often come to us already traumatized.[20] Frontline health-care workers (e.g., therapists,[21] social workers,[22] child protective services workers[23]) are easily and often swept under the tide of their clients' emotional pain.[24] Guardians ad litem endure the same or worse.[25] These risks are amplified across professions and roles due to the constant flood of violent and sexual images available via the Internet[26] and as a function of client psychopathology: "The odds of facing false accusations are multiplied when dealing with families in which a parent suffers from a personality disorder."[27]

Attorneys sometimes argue that their fact-based role working with high-conflict families protects them from their toxic emotions. While there may be some truth in this for lawyers in other fields and for those who stay far away from the courtroom, family law attorneys are at very high risk of burnout, compassion fatigue, and vicarious trauma:

---

20. Rebecca M. Stahl, *Responding Effectively to Trauma Manifestations in Child Welfare Cases*, 58 FAM. CT. REV. 920 (2020).

21. "Over half of sampled psychotherapists reported moderate-high levels of burnout. . . . Younger age, having less work experience, and being overinvolved in client problems were the most common personal risk factors for moderate-high levels of stress and burnout among psychotherapists." Gabrielle K. Simionato & Susan Simpson, *Personal Risk Factors Associated with Burnout among Psychotherapists: A Systematic Review of the Literature*, 74 J. CLINICAL PSYCH. 1431 (2018).

22. Ricky Finzi-Dottan & Michal Berckovitch Kormosh, *The Spillover of Compassion Fatigue into Marital Quality: A Mediation Model*, 24 TRAUMATOLOGY 113 (2018).

23. "Sixty-two percent of participants scored in the high range on Emotional Exhaustion, the aspect some researchers consider to be the heart of Burnout." Dina G. Anderson, *Coping Strategies and Burnout among Veteran Child Protection Workers*, 24 CHILD ABUSE & NEGLECT 839 (2000).

24. Drew D. Kiraly, *Health Professionals and Suicidal Behavior*, *in* FORENSIC PSYCHIATRY: A PUBLIC HEALTH PERSPECTIVE 193 (Leo Sher & Joav Merrick eds., 2015).

25. William Halikias, *The Guardian ad Litem for Children in Divorce: Conceptualizing Duties, Roles, and Consultative Services*, 32 FAM. & CONCILIATION CTS. REV. 490 (1994).

26. Shely Polak et al., *Secondary Traumatic Stress in the Courtroom: Suggestions for Preventing Vicarious Trauma Resulting from Child Sexual Abuse Imagery*, JUV. & FAM. CT. J., Summer 2019, at 69.

27. Richard A. Warshak, *Risks to Professionals Who Work with Troubled and Alienated Parent-Child Relationships*, 44 AM. J. FAM. THERAPY 111 (2016).

> Survey results demonstrated that attorneys experience more symptoms of secondary trauma and burnout compared with mental health providers and social service workers. The attorneys demonstrated higher levels of intrusive recollection of trauma material; avoidance of reminders of the material; diminished pleasure and interest in activities; and difficulties with sleep, irritability, and concentration.[28]

Judges are no less vulnerable.[29] "Some of the daily stressors endured by judges include endless caseloads, severe time limitations, social isolation, lack of privacy, and the weight of deciding the fates of others."[30] In one study:

> The majority of judges (63%) reported one or more symptoms that they identified as work-related vicarious trauma experiences. Female judges reported more symptoms, as did judges with seven or more years of experience. In addition, female judges were more likely to report internalizing difficulties, while judges with more experience reported higher levels of externalizing/hostility symptoms.[31]

Self-care is both the best prophylaxis and remedy for burnout, compassion fatigue, and vicarious trauma. Self-care means routinely and intentionally refueling oneself. Rebuilding and fortifying the social, emotional, and physical boundaries that separate systems. It means constantly renewing the emotional insulation that protects personal from professional. It means using this book to anchor oneself outside and apart from the trauma that we invite in the door every workday. Self-care means, in essence, eschewing the emic in favor of the etic.

---

28. Lisa Morgillo, Student Note, *Do Not Make Their Trauma Your Trauma: Coping with Burnout as a Family Law Attorney*, 53 Fam. Ct. Rev. 456, 468 (2015).

29. Charles P. Edwards & Monica K. Miller, *An Assessment of Judges' Self-Reported Experiences of Secondary Traumatic Stress*, Juv. & Fam. Ct. J., Summer 2019, at 7.

30. Resnick et al., *supra* note 10, at 610.

31. Peter G. Jaffe et al., *Vicarious Trauma in Judges: The Personal Challenge of Dispensing Justice*, Juv. & Fam. Ct. J., Fall 2003, at 1.

Self-care is a constant, conscious, and purposeful act as important as (and including) diet, sleep, and exercise. It means making choices that replenish resilience very much the same way that we must make choices to stop to refuel our vehicles.

> Self-care includes participating in a professional support network (e.g., an attorney, a peer consultation group, colleague assistance programs) . . . developing and activating policies and procedures for managing unexpected adverse events (e.g., obtaining liability insurance, developing a professional will, responding to a subpoena or a notice of a malpractice claim, managing social media, responding to a patient suicide), and participating in activities that build and sustain emotional and physical well-being (e.g., mindfulness, volunteer work).[32]

The American Bar Association (the publisher of this book) actively promotes lawyers' self-care in terms of "a healthy work-life balance."[33] How? One attorney author recommends, "wake up earlier . . . take the long way . . . always take a lunch break . . . stay hydrated, [and] call a loved one or family member daily."[34]

Social workers are similarly advised to make self-care a priority by focusing on physical rest and nourishment, emotional rest and nourishment, and sustenance modulation: "Every helper must utilize self-restraint with regard to what and how much they consume (e.g., food, drink, drugs, stimulation) since it can compromise their competence as a helper."[35]

---

32. Janet L. Sonne, PsycEssentials: A Pocket Resource for Mental Health Practitioners 287 (2012).

33. Chanell Autrey, *Be Kind to Yourself: Don't Lose Track of Your Self-Care Goals*, A.B.A., https://www.americanbar.org/groups/young_lawyers/projects/no-limits/dont-lose-track-of-your-self-care-goals/ (last visited July 24, 2021).

34. Theresa Austin, *Easy Ways to Integrate Self-Care into Your Daily Life*, A.B.A. https://www.americanbar.org/groups/young_lawyers/publications/after-the-bar/personal-life/easy-ways-to-integrate-self-care-into-your-life (last visited July 24, 2021).

35. Charlene Richard, *The Standards of Self-Care (Part 1 of 3)*, SWHelper, Aug. 6, 2013, https://swhelper.org/2013/08/06/the-standards-of-self-care-part-1-of-3; *see also* Substance Abuse and Mental Health Services Administration, Trauma-Informed Care in Behavioral Health Services (2014) (Treatment Improvement Protocol (TIP) Series, No. 57).

We read these and similar professional self-care guidelines as calling for an etic approach, creating and maintaining boundaries that reinforce the coherence of systems. Our ethical guidelines and best practice standards demand that we stand outside the families that we serve with good reason. We hope that this book safely anchors you there, guides your inquiry, and promotes your personal well-being.

B.D. Garber, Ph.D.
D.E. Prescott, J.D., Ph.D.
C. Mulchay, Ph.D.

Your feedback, questions, and contributions are always welcome at DynamicsNotDiagnoses@gmail.com.

Chapter 19
Resources

Select additional citations and resources by topic

Types of Parenting and Their Dynamic and Developmental Outcomes across Cultures

Dorit Alt, *First-Year Female College Students' Academic Motivation as a Function of Perceived Parenting Styles: A Contextual Perspective*, 22 J. ADULT DEV. 63 (2015).

Diana Baumrind, *Is a Pejorative View of Power Assertion in the Socialization Process Justified?*, 17(4) REV. GEN. PSYCH. 420 (2013).

Diana Baumrind, *Current Patterns of Parental Authority*, 4 (1, Pt.2) DEVELOPMENTAL PSYCH. 1 (1971).

Diana H. Baumrind, *The Influence of Parenting Style on Adolescent Competence and Substance Use*, 11 J. Early Adolescence 56 (1991).

Diana H. Baumrind, *Authoritarian vs. Authoritative Parental Control*, 3(11) Adolescence 255 (1968).

Diana H. Baumrind, *Effects of Authoritative Parental Control on Child Behavior*, 37(4) Child Dev. 887 (1966).

Elisardo Becoña et al., *Parental Permissiveness, Control, and Affect and Drug Use among Adolescents*, 25(3) Psicothema 292 (2013).

Dell E. Bednar & Terri D. Fisher, *Peer Referencing in Adolescent Decision Making as a Function of Perceived Parenting Style*, 38(152) Adolescence 607 (2003).

Mariëlle D. Beijersbergen et al., *Remaining or Becoming Secure: Parental Sensitive Support Predicts Attachment Continuity from Infancy to Adolescence in a Longitudinal Adoption Study*, 48 Developmental Psych. 1277 (2012).

Gitu Bhatia & Michael Saini, *Cultural Dynamics of Divorce and Parenting*, *in* Parenting Plan Evaluations: Applied Research for the Family Court 463 (Leslie Drozd et al. eds., 2016).

M.J. De la Torre-Cruz et al., *Relationship between Parenting Styles and Aggressiveness in Adolescents*, 12(1) Electronic J. Rsch. Educ. Psych. 147 (2014).

Philippa M. Eve et al., *What Is Good Parenting? The Perspectives of Different Professionals*, 52(1) Fam. Ct. Rev. 114 (2014).

Benjamin D. Garber, Developmental Psychology for Family Law Professionals: Theory, Application, and the Best Interests of the Child (2009).

Stelios N. Georgiou et al., *Cultural Value Orientation and Authoritarian Parenting as Parameters of Bullying and Victimization at School*, 48(1) Int'l J. Psych. 69 (2013).

David R. Hibbard & Gail E. Walton, *Exploring the Development of Perfectionism: The Influence of Parenting Style and Gender*, 42(2) Soc. Behav. & Personality 269 (2014).

John P. Hoffmann & Stephen J. Bahr, *Parenting Style, Religiosity, Peer Alcohol Use, and Adolescent Heavy Drinking*, 75(2) J. Stud. on Alcohol & Drugs 222 (2014).

Koen Luyckx et al., *Parenting and Trajectories of Children's Maladaptive Behaviors: A 12-Year Prospective Community Study*, 40(3) J. Clinical Child & Adolescent Psych. 468 (2011).

Angie L. Miller et al., *Parenting Style, Perfectionism, and Creativity in High-Ability and High-Achieving Young Adults*, 35 J. for Educ. Gifted 344 (2012).

David A. Nelson et al., *Parenting, Relational Aggression, and Borderline Personality Features: Associations over Time in a Russian Longitudinal Sample*, 26(3) Dev. & Psychopathology 773 (2014).

Renee B. Patrick & John C. Gibbs, *Maternal Acceptance: Its Contribution to Children's Favorable Perceptions of Discipline and Moral Identity*, 177(3) J. Genetic Psych. 73 (2016).

Martin Pinquart & Rubina Kauser, *Do the Associations of Parenting Styles with Behavior Problems and Academic Achievement Vary by Culture? Results from a Meta-Analysis*, 24(1) Cultural Diversity & Ethnic Minority Psych. 75 (2018).

L. Alan Sroufe et al., The Development of the Person: The Minnesota Study of Risk and Adaptation from Birth to Adulthood (2009).

Tatiana Alina Trifan et al., *Have Authoritarian Parenting Practices and Roles Changed in the Last 50 Years?*, 76(4) J. Marriage & Fam. 744 (2014).

Masayo Uji et al., *The Impact of Authoritative, Authoritarian, and Permissive Parenting Styles on Children's Later Mental Health in Japan: Focusing on Parent and Child Gender*, 23(2) J. Child & Fam. Stud. 293 (2014).

Lindsey Varvil-Weld et al., *Hurting, Helping, or Neutral? The Effects of Parental Permissiveness toward Adolescent Drinking on College Student Alcohol Use and Problems*, 15(5) Prevention Sci. 716 (2014).

Akiko Watabe & David R. Hibbard, *The Influence of Authoritarian and Authoritative Parenting on Children's Academic Achievement Motivation: A Comparison between the United States and Japan*, 16(2) N. Am. J. Psych. 359 (2014).

Parenting Capacity Evaluations

Sandar T. Azar et al., *The Evaluation of Parental Fitness in Termination of Parental Rights Cases: A Functional-Contextual Perspective*, 1 Clinical Child & Fam. Psych. Rev. 77 (1998), DOI: 10.1023/A:1021883611965.

Corina Benjet et al., *Evaluating The Parental Fitness of Psychiatrically Diagnosed Individuals: Advocating a Functional-Contextual Analysis of Parenting*, 17(2) J. Fam. Psych. 238 (2003).

Karen S. Budd & Rachael E. Springman, *Empirical Analysis of Referral Issues and "Ultimate Issue" Recommendations for Parents in Child Protection Cases*, 49 Fam. Ct. Rev. 34 (2011), DOI: 10.1111/j.1744-1617.2010.01351.

Karen S. Budd, *Assessing Parenting Competence in Child Protection Cases: A Clinical Practice Model*, 4 Clinical Child & Fam. Psych. Rev. 1 (2001), DOI: 10.1023/A:1009548509598.

KAREN S. BUDD ET AL., EVALUATION OF PARENTING CAPACITY IN CHILD PROTECTION (2011).

Karen S. Budd & Michelle J. Holdsworth, *Issues in Clinical Assessment of Minimal Parenting Competence*, 25 J. CLINICAL CHILD PSYCH. 2 (1996), DOI: 10.1207/s15374424jccp2501_1.

Geoffrey D. Carr et al., *Evaluating Parenting Capacity: Validity Problems with the MMPI-2, PAI, CAPI, and Ratings of Child Adjustment*, 36(2) PRO. PSYCH.: RSCH. & PRAC. 188 (2005), DOI: 10.1037/0735-7028.36.2.188.

Kari S. Carstairs, *Rorschach Assessment of Parenting Capacity: A Case Study*, 32(1) RORSCHACHIANA 91 (2011).

PETER W. CHOATE, PARENTING CAPACITY ASSESSMENTS: THE GOOD, THE BAD, AND THE UGLY: PAPER PREPARED IN SUPPORT OF A WORKSHOP TO THE NATIONAL JUSTICE INSTITUTE (2013), http://www.academia.edu/3893605/Parenting.

Christopher Conley, *A Review of Parenting Capacity Assessment Reports*, 47 ONTARIO ASS'N CHILDREN'S AID SOCIETIES J. 16 (2003), http://www.oacas.org/pubs/oacas/journal/2003_2004winter/2003_2004winter.pdf.

Terry Donald & Jon Jureidini, *Parenting Capacity*, 13 CHILD ABUSE REV. 5 (2004), DOI: 10.1002/car.827.

Steve Farnfield, *A Theoretical Model for the Comprehensive Assessment of Parenting*, 38 BRIT. J. SOC. WORK 1076 (2008), DOI: 10.1093/bjsw/bcl395.

Paul H. Harnett, *A Procedure for Assessing Parents' Capacity for Change in Child Protection Cases*, 29 CHILD. & YOUTH SERVICES REV. 1179 (2007), DOI: 10.1016/j.childyouth.2007.04.005.

Kristin D. Hurley et al., *Assessing Parenting Skills and Attitudes: A Review of the Psychometrics of Parenting Measures*, 23 J. CHILD & FAM. STUD. 812 (2014), DOI: 10.1007/s10826-013-9733-2.

Brian D. Johnson et al., *A Parenting Competency Model*, 14 PARENTING: SCI. & PRAC. 92 (2014), http://dx.doi.org/10.1080/15295192.2014.914361.

Danielle J. Key et al., *The MMPI-2 in Parenting Capacity Evaluations: Scale Elevations and Effects of Underreporting*, 51(6) PRO. PSYCH.: RSCH. & PRAC. 630 (2020).

Fred Schmidt et al., *Assessing the Parent-Child Relationship in Parenting Capacity Evaluations: Clinical Applications of Attachment Research*, 45(2) FAM. CT. REV. 247 (2007).

Anne-Fleur W.K. Vischer et al., *Assessing Parenting in the Context of Reunification of Infant/Toddlers and Their Families: How to Face the Challenges?*, 38 INFANT MENTAL HEALTH J. 406 (2017), DOI: 10.1002/imhj.21646.

Harriet Ward et al., UK Department for Education, Assessing Parental Capacity to Change When Children Are on the Edge of Care: An Overview of Current Research Evidence (2014).

Angela White, NSW Department of Community Services, Assessment of Parenting Capacity: Literature Review (2005).

Johanna Woodcock, *The Social Work Assessment of Parenting: An Exploration*, 33 Brit. J. Soc. Work 87 (2003), DOI: 10.1093/bjsw/33.1.87.

Child Custody Evaluations

Geri S.W. Fuhrmann & Robert A. Zibbell, Evaluation for Child Custody (2011).

Jonathan W. Gould & David A. Martindale, *Child Custody Evaluations: Current Literature and Practical Applications*, *in* 11 Handbook of Psychology 101 (Irving B. Weiner & Randy K. Otto eds., 2d ed. 2012).

Jonathan W. Gould & David A. Martindale, The Art and Science of Child Custody Evaluations (2007).

Daniel J. Hynan, Child Custody Evaluation: New Theoretical Applications and Research (2015).

Michael E. Lamb, *Critical Analysis of Research on Parenting Plans and Children's Well-Being*, *in* Parenting Plan Evaluations: Applied Research for the Family Court 170 (Leslie Drozd et al. eds., 2d ed. 2016).

David A. Martindale et al., *Model Standards of Practice for Child Custody Evaluation*, 70 Fam. Ct. Rev. 45 (2007).

Parenting Plan Evaluations: Applied Research for the Family Court (Leslie Drozd et al. eds., 2016).

Philip M. Stahl, Conducting Child Custody Evaluations: From Basic to Complex Issues (2010).

Intimate Partner Violence

William G. Austin & Leslie M. Drozd, *Judge's Bench Book for Application of the Integrated Framework for the Assessment of Intimate Partner Violence in Child Custody Disputes*, 10(2) J. Child Custody 99 (2013).

James N. Bow & Paul Boxer, *Assessing Allegations of Domestic Violence in Child Custody Evaluations*, 18(12) J. Interpersonal Violence 1394 (2003).

Leslie M. Drozd et al., *Parenting Coordination in Cases Involving Intimate Partner Violence*, 58(3) Fam. Ct. Rev. 774 (2020).

Peter G. Jaffe et al., *Custody Disputes Involving Allegations of Domestic Violence: Toward a Differentiated Approach to Parenting Plans*, 46(3) Fam. Ct. Rev. 500 (2008).

Fernanda S. Rossi et al., *Intimate Partner Violence and Child Custody*, *in* Parenting Plan Evaluations: Applied Research for the Family Court 346 (Leslie Drozd et al. eds., 2d ed. 2016).

Michael A. Saini et al., *Treating Children Exposed to Intimate Partner Violence within the Context of Child Custody Disputes*, *in* Evidence-Informed Interventions for Court-Involved Families: Promoting Healthy Coping and Development 303 (Lyn R. Greenberg et al. eds., 2019).

Epistemic Injustice and Bias Risks and Research in Family Court

Miguel Clemente & Zara Diaz, *Machiavellianism and the Manipulation of Children as a Tactic in Child Custody Disputes: The MMS Scale*, 21(2) J. Forensic Psych. Rsch. & Prac. 171 (2021).

Francisca Fariña et al., *A Meta-Analytic Review of the MMPI Validity Scales and Indexes to Detect Defensiveness in Custody Evaluations*, 17(2) Int'l J. Clinical & Health Psych. 128 (2017).

Miranda Fricker, Epistemic Injustice: Power and the Ethics of Knowing (2007).

Emily Haney-Caron & Kirk Heilbrun, *Lesbian and Gay Parents and Determination of Child Custody: The Changing Legal Landscape and Implications for Policy and Practice*, 1(1) Psych. Sexual Orientation & Gender Diversity 19 (2014).

Jerry Kang et al., *Implicit Bias in the Courtroom*, 59 UCLA L. Rev. 1124 (2011).

Madison McGowan, *Forensics' Fight: A Need for Aggressive Strategies against Confirmation Bias*, 5(1) Themis: Rsch. J. Just. Stud. & Forensic Sci. 11 (2017).

Tess Neal & Stanley L. Brodsky, *Forensic Psychologists' Perceptions of Bias and Potential Correction Strategies in Forensic Mental Health Evaluations*, 22(1) Psych. Pub. Pol'y & L. 58 (2016).

Jennifer H. Peck & Wesley G. Jennings, *A Critical Examination of "Being Black" in the Juvenile Justice System*, 40(3) Law & Hum. Behav. 219 (2016).

Dana E. Prescott, *Bending the Light of Social Science in Family Court: Epistemic Injustice and Epistemic Exceptionalism Matter*, 33 J. Am. Acad. Matrimonial Law. 99 (2020).

Dana E. Prescott & Diane A. Tennies, *Bias Is a Reciprocal Relationship: Forensic Mental Health Professionals and Lawyers in the Family Court Bottle*, 31 J. Am. Acad. Matrimonial Law. 427 (2018).

Aaron Robb, *Methodological Challenges in Social Science: Making Sense of Polarized and Competing Research Claims*, 58(2) Fam. Ct. Rev. 308 (2020).

Irwin Sandler et al., *Convenient and Inconvenient Truths in Family Law: Preventing Scholar-Advocacy Bias in the Use of Social Science Research for Public Policy*, 54(2) Fam. Ct. Rev. 150 (2016).

Jennifer Saul, *Implicit Bias, Stereotype Threat, and Epistemic Injustice*, *in* The Routledge Handbook of Epistemic Injustice 235 (Ian James Kidd et al. eds., 2017).

Anke Snoek & Dorothee Horstkötter, *Ethical Issues in Research on Substance-Dependent Parents: The Risk of Implicit Normative Judgements by Researchers*, 32(9) Bioethics 620 (2018).

Rachel Treloar, *High-Conflict Divorce Involving Children: Parents' Meaning-Making and Agency*, 40(3) J. Soc. Welfare & Fam. L. 340 (2018).

Rebecca Tsosie, *Indigenous Peoples and Epistemic Injustice: Science, Ethics, and Human Rights*, 87 Wash. L. Rev. 1133 (2012).

Stephanie N. Webb et al., *Attitudes toward Same-Sex Parenting: An Effect of Gender*, 64(11) J. Homosexuality 1583 (2017).

Child Abuse

Child Sexual Abuse: Disclosure, Delay, and Denial (Margaret-Ellen Pipe et al. eds., 2013).

Leslie Drozd et al., *Trauma and Child Custody Disputes: Screening, Assessment, and Interventions*, *in* Evidence-Informed Interventions for Court-Involved Families: Promoting Healthy Coping and Development 260 (Lyn R. Greenberg et al. eds., 2019).

Kathryn Kuehnle, Assessing Allegations of Child Sexual Abuse (1996).

Kathryn Kuehnle & Mary Connell, The Evaluation of Child Sexual Abuse Allegations: A Comprehensive Guide to Assessment and Testimony (2008).

Infantilization

Ellen B. Bogolub, *Symbiotic Mothers and Infantilized Only Children: A Subtype of Single-Parent Family*, 1 Child & Adolescent Soc. Work J. 89 (1984).

Robert Kinscherff & Catherine C. Ayoub, *Legal Aspects of Munchausen by Proxy*, *in* TREATMENT OF CHILD ABUSE 242 (Robert M. Reece ed., 2000).

Mary W. Lindahl, *Beyond Munchausen by Proxy: A Proposed Conceptualization for Cases of Recurring, Unsubstantiated Sexual Abuse Allegations*, 18 J. CHILD SEXUAL ABUSE 206 (2009).

Adultification and Parentification

Caveat lector: The term "parentification" is used very differently across authors and studies, often confounding efforts to draw broad conclusions.

Jenna H. Beffel & Amy K. Nuttall, *Influences of Parentification and Benefit Finding on Prosocial Behavior among Typically Developing Siblings of Individuals with Autism Spectrum Disorder*, 104 RSCH. DEVELOPMENTAL DISABILITIES article 103694 (2020).

Judyta Borchet et al., *We Are in This Together: Retrospective Parentification, Sibling Relationships, and Self-Esteem*, 29(10) J. CHILD & FAM. STUD. 2982 (2020).

BURDENED CHILDREN: THEORY, RESEARCH, AND TREATMENT OF PARENTIFICATION (Nancy D. Chase ed., 1999).

Linda Burton, *Childhood Adultification in Economically Disadvantaged Families: A Conceptual Model*, 56 FAM. REL. 329 (2007).

John Byng-Hall, *The Significance of Children Fulfilling Parental Roles: Implications for Family Therapy*, 30 J. FAM. THERAPY 147 (2008).

Nancy D. Chase, *Parentification: An Overview of Theory, Research, and Society Issues*, *in* BURDENED CHILDREN: THEORY, RESEARCH, AND TREATMENT OF PARENTIFICATION 3 (Nancy D. Chase ed., 1999).

Louise Earley & Delia Cushway, *The Parentified Child*, 7 CLINICAL CHILD PSYCH. & PSYCHIATRY 163 (2002).

Benjamin D. Garber, *Parental Alienation and the Dynamics of the Enmeshed Parent-Child Dyad: Adultification, Parentification, and Infantilization*, 49(2) FAM. CT. REV. 322 (2011).

Robert E. Godsall et al., *Why Some Kids Do Well in Bad Situations: Relation of Parental Alcohol Misuse and Parentification to Children's Self-Concept*, 39(5) SUBSTANCE USE & MISUSE 789 (2004).

Linda R. Goglia et al., *Generational Boundary Distortions by Adult Children of Alcoholics: Child-as-Parent and Child-as-Mate*, 20(4) AM. J. FAM. THERAPY 291 (1992).

Lisa M. Hooper et al., *Characterizing the Magnitude of the Relation between Parentification and Psychopathology: A Meta-Analysis*, 67 J. Clinical Psych. 1028 (2011).

Lisa M. Hooper et al., *Predictors of Growth and Distress Following Childhood Parentification: A Retrospective Exploratory Study*, 17 J. Child & Fam. Stud. 693 (2008).

Gregory J. Jurkovic et al., *Parentification in the Lives of High-Profile Individuals and Their Families: A Hidden Source of Strength and Distress*, *in* The Family Psychology and Counseling Series. High-Performing Families: Causes, Consequences, and Clinical Solutions 129 (Bryan E. Robinson & Nancy D. Chase eds., 2001).

Gregory J. Jurkovic et al., *Parentification of Adult Children of Divorce: A Multidimensional Analysis*, 30(2) J. Youth & Adolescence 245 (2001).

Gregory J. Jurkovic et al., *Assessing Childhood Parentification: Guidelines for Researchers and Clinicians*, *in* Burdened Children: Theory, Research, and Treatment of Parentification 92 (Nancy D. Chase ed., 1999).

Gregory J. Jurkovic, Lost Childhoods: The Plight of the Parentified Child (1997).

Jennifer Katz et al., *A Retrospective Study of Daughters' Emotional Role Reversal with Parents, Attachment Anxiety, Excessive Reassurance-Seeking, and Depressive Symptoms*, 37 Am. J. Fam. Therapy 185 (2009).

Jenny Macfie et al., *Pathways from Infant Exposure to Marital Conflict to Parent-Toddler Role Reversal*, 29 Infant Mental Health J. 297 (2008).

Ofra Mayseless et al., *"I Was More Her Mom Than She Was Mine": Role Reversal in a Community Sample*, 53 Fam. Rel.: Interdisc. J. Applied Fam. Stud. 78 (2004).

Olga Oznobishin & Jenny Kurman, *Parent-Child Role Reversal and Psychological Adjustment among Immigrant Youth in Israel*, 23 J. Fam. Psych. 405 (2009).

Molly P. Valleau et al., *Parentification and Caretaker Syndrome: An Empirical Investigation*, 22 Fam. Therapy 157 (1995).

Sophie Walsh et al., *The Role of Parentification and Family Climate in Adaptation among Immigrant Adolescents in Israel*, 16 J. Rsch. on Adolescence 321 (2006).

Robert S. Weiss, *Growing Up a Little Faster: The Experience of Growing Up in a Single-Parent Household*, 35(4) J. Soc. Issues 97 (1979).

Chester A. Winton, Children as Caregivers: Parental and Parentified Children (2003).

Intensive "Residential" Treatment Programs

Joan B. Kelly, *Commentary on "Family Bridges: Using Insights from Social Science to Reconnect Parents and Alienated Children" (Warshak, 2010)*, 48(1) Fam. Ct. Rev. 81 (2010), https://doi.org/10.1111/j.1744-1617.2009.01289.x.

Jean Mercer, *Arē Intensive Parental Alienation Treatments Effective and Safe for Children and Adolescents?*, 16(1) J. Child Custody: Rsch. Issues & Pracs. 67 (2019), https://doi.org/10.1080/15379418.2018.1557578.

Overcoming Parent-Child Contact Problems: Family-Based Interventions for Resistance, Rejection, and Alienation (Abigail Judge & Robin M. Deutsch eds., 2016).

Kathleen M. Reay, *Family Reflections: A Promising Therapeutic Program Designed to Treat Severely Alienated Children and Their Family System*, 43(2) Am. J. Fam. Therapy 197 (2015).

Michael Saini & Robin Deutsch, *Training, Dissemination, and Evaluation*, *in* The Overcoming Barriers Approach to Children's Resistance, Rejection, Alienation: A Family-Based Intervention (Abigail Judge & Robin Deutsch eds., in press).

Matthew J. Sullivan, *Overcoming Barriers Family Camp: A Program for High-Conflict Divorced Families Where a Child Is Resisting Contact with a Parent*, 48(1) Fam. Ct. Rev. 116 (2010), https://doi.org/10.1111/j.1744-1617.2009.01293.x.

Peggie Ward et al., *Overview of the Overcoming Barriers Approach*, *in* Overcoming Parent-Child Contact Problems: Family-Based Interventions for Resistance, Rejection, and Alienation 131 (Abigail M. Judge & Robin M. Deutsch eds., 2017).

Richard A. Warshak, *Reclaiming Parent-Child Relationships: Outcomes of Family Bridges with Alienated Children*, 60 J. Divorce & Remarriage 645 (2019), https://doi.org/10.1080/10502556.2018.1529505.

Richard A. Warshak, *Family Bridges: Using Insights from Social Science to Reconnect Parents and Alienated Children*, 48(1) Fam. Ct. Rev. 48 (2010).

Alienation Treatment Alternatives

Stephanie Dallam & Joyanna L. Silberg, *Recommended Treatments for "Parental Alienation Syndrome" (PAS) May Cause Children Foreseeable and Lasting Psychological Harm*, 13(2/3) J. Child Custody: Rsch. Issues & Pracs. 134 (2016).

Barbara Jo Fidler et al., American Psychology-Law Society Series. Children Who Resist Postseparation Parental Contact: A Differential Approach for Legal and Mental Health Professionals (2013).

Steven Friedlander & Marjorie Gans Walters, *When a Child Rejects a Parent: Tailoring the Intervention to Fit the Problem*, 48(1) Fam. Ct. Rev. 98 (2010), https://doi.org/10.1111/j.1744-1617.2009.01291.x.

Benjamin D. Garber, *Cognitive-Behavioral Methods in High-Conflict Divorce: Systematic Desensitization Adapted to Parent-Child Reunification Interventions*, 53(1) Fam. Ct. Rev. 96 (2015), https://doi.org/10.1111/fcre.12133.

Abigail M. Judge & Rebecca Bailey, *More Than Words: The Use of Experiential Therapies in the Treatment of Families with Parent-Child Contact Problems and Parental Alienation*, *in* Overcoming Parent-Child Contact Problems: Family-Based Interventions for Resistance, Rejection, and Alienation 91 (Abigail M. Judge & Robin M. Deutsch eds., 2017).

Shely Polak & John A. Moran, *The Current Status of Outpatient Approaches to Parent-Child Contact Problems*, *in* Overcoming Parent-Child Contact Problems: Family-Based Interventions for Resistance, Rejection, and Alienation 63 (Abigail M. Judge & Robin M. Deutsch eds., 2017).

Richard A. Warshak, *Ten Parental Alienation Fallacies That Compromise Decisions in Court and in Therapy*, 46(4) Pro. Psych.: Rsch. & Prac. 235 (2015), https://doi.org/10.1037/pro0000031.

Additional Alienation Citations of Note

Nicholas Bala et al., *Differentiated Case Management for Family Cases: "One Judge for One Family,"* 26 Canadian J. Fam. L. 339 (2011).

Nicholas Bala et al., *Parental Alienation: Canadian Court Cases 1989–2008*, 48 Fam. Ct. 162 (2010).

Nicholas Bala et al., *Alienated Children and Parental Separation: Legal Responses in Canada's Family Courts*, 38 Queen's L.J. 79 (2007).

John-Paul E. Boyd, Canadian Research Institute for Law and the Family, Alienated Children in Family Law Disputes in British Columbia (2015) (2015 CanLIIDocs 321), http://canlii.ca/t/2863 (last visited July 24, 2021).

Douglas Darnall & Barbara F. Steinberg, *Motivational Models for Spontaneous Reunification with the Alienated Child*, 36 Am. J. Fam. Therapy 107 and 253 (2008).

Robin Deutsch et al., *Trauma-Informed Interventions in Parent-Child Contact Cases*, 58(2) FAM. CT. REV. 470 (2020).

Leslie M. Drozd & Nancy Williams Olesen, *Is It Abuse, Alienation, and/or Estrangement? A Decision Tree*, 1(3) J. CHILD CUSTODY 65 (2004).

Barbara Fidler & Nicholas Bala, *Children Resisting Post-Separation Contact with a Parent: Concepts, Controversies, and Conundrums*, 48 FAM. CT. REV. 10 (2010).

BARBARA JO FIDLER ET AL., CHALLENGING ISSUES IN CHILD CUSTODY ASSESSMENTS: A GUIDE FOR LEGAL AND MENTAL HEALTH PROFESSIONALS (2008).

Janet R. Johnston & Joan B. Kelly, *Rejoinder to Gardner's "Commentary on Kelly and Johnston's 'The Alienated Child: A Reformulation of Parental Alienation Syndrome,'"* 42(4) FAM. CT. REV. 622 (2004).

Kimberley J. Joyce, *Under the Microscope: The Admissibility of Parental Alienation Syndrome*, 32 J. AM. ACAD. MATRIMONIAL LAW. 53 (2019).

Michael Saini et al., *Empirical Studies of Alienation*, *in* PARENTING PLAN EVALUATIONS: APPLIED RESEARCH FOR THE FAMILY COURT 374 (Leslie Drozd et al. eds., 2016).

Holly Smith, *Parental Alienation Syndrome: Fact or Fiction? The Problem with Its Use in Child Custody Cases*, 11(1) U. MASS. L. REV. article 5 (2016), https://scholarship.law.umassd.edu/umlr/vol11/iss1/5.

Marjorie Gans Walters & Steven Friedlander, *When a Child Rejects a Parent: Working with the Intractable Resist/Refuse Dynamic*, 54(3) FAM. CT. REV. 424 (2016).

Integrated Dyadic Assessment

Sylvia J. Ansay & Daniel F. Perkins, *Integrating Family Visitation and Risk Evaluation: A Practical Bonding Model for Decision Makers*, 50 FAM. REL. 220 (2001), https://doi.org/10.1111/j.1741-3729.2001.00220.x.

Evaluation of Domestic Violence and Child Abuse Relevant to Determinations of Estrangement

ASSESSING DANGEROUSNESS: DOMESTIC VIOLENCE OFFENDERS AND CHILD ABUSERS (Jacquelyn C. Campbell & Jill Messing eds., 3d ed. 2017).

Marion Bailhache et al., *Is Early Detection of Abused Children Possible?: A Systematic Review of the Diagnostic Accuracy of the Identification of Abused Children*, 13(1) BMC PEDIATRICS 202 (2013).

David P. Bernstein et al., *Validity of the Childhood Trauma Questionnaire in an Adolescent Psychiatric Population*, 36(3) J. Am. Acad. Child & Adolescent Psychiatry 340 (1997).

Mark Chaffin & Linda Anne Valle, *Dynamic Prediction Characteristics of the Child Abuse Potential Inventory*, 27(5) Child Abuse & Neglect 463 (2003), https://doi.org/10.1016/S0145-2134(03)00036-X.

Ko Ling Chan, *Evaluating the Risk of Child Abuse: The Child Abuse Risk Assessment Scale (CARAS)*, 27(5) J. Interpersonal Violence 951 (2012).

Corine de Ruiter et al., *The Child Abuse Risk Evaluation Dutch Version (CARE-NL): A Retrospective Validation Study*, 17(1) J. Fam. Trauma Child Custody & Child Dev. 37 (2020), https://doi.org/10.1080/15379418.2019.1699488.

Kerry M. Drach et al., *The Diagnostic Utility of Sexual Behavior Problems in Diagnosing Sexual Abuse in a Forensic Child Abuse Evaluation Clinic*, 25(4) Child Abuse & Neglect 489 (2001).

Joeli Hettler & David S. Greenes, *Can the Initial History Predict Whether a Child with a Head Injury Has Been Abused?*, 111(3) Pediatrics 602 (2003).

Charles Kodner & Angela Wetherton, *Diagnosis and Management of Physical Abuse in Children*, 88(10) Am. Fam. Physician 669 (2013).

Kathryn Kuehnle & Mary Connell, *Child Sexual Abuse Evaluations*, *in* 11 Handbook of Psychology 579 (Irving B. Weiner & Randy K. Otto eds., 2d ed. 2012).

F. Lindblad, *Evaluation of Child Sexual Abuse—What Should Be Evaluated?*, 4 Scandinavian J. Soc. Welfare 55 (1995).

Jill R. McTavish et al., *Identifying Children Exposed to Maltreatment: A Systematic Review Update*, 20 BMC Pediatrics 113 (2020), https://doi.org/10.1186/s12887-020-2015-4.

Jill R. McTavish et al., *Children's Exposure to Intimate Partner Violence: An Overview*, 28(5) Int'l Rev. Psychiatry 504 (2016), https://doi.org/10.1080/09540261.2016.1205001.

Joel S. Milner, *Physical Child Abuse Perpetrator Screening and Evaluation*, 18(1) Crim. Just. & Behav. 47 (2016), https://doi.org/10.1177/0093854891018001005.

Joel S. Milner, *Applications of the Child Abuse Potential Inventory*, 45 J. Clinical Psych. 450 (1989).

National Institute for Health and Care Excellence, Child Maltreatment: When to Suspect Maltreatment in Under 18s (2017 update), https://www.nice.org.uk/guidance/cg89/resources/child-maltreatment-when-to-suspect-maltreatment-in-under-18s-pdf-975697287109.

Aideen M. Naughton et al., *Emotional, Behavioral, and Developmental Features Indicative of Neglect or Emotional Abuse in Preschool Children: A Systematic Review*, 167(8) JAMA PEDIATRICS 769 (2013).

William O'Donohue & April R. Bradley, *Conceptual and Empirical Issues in Child Custody Evaluations*, 6(3) CLINICAL PSYCH.: SCI. & PRAC. 310 (2006), https://doi.org/10.1093/clipsy.6.3.310.

Oregon Office for Services to Children and Families, Child Abuse and Neglect Risk Factor Checklist (2000), https://apps.state.or.us/Forms/Served/ce0955a.pdf.

Suriati M. Saini et al., *Systematic Review and Critical Appraisal of Child Abuse Measurement Instruments*, 272 PSYCHIATRY RSCH. 106 (2019).

Arianne H. Teeuw et al., *Screening for Child Abuse Using a Checklist and Physical Examinations in the Emergency Department Led to the Detection of More Cases*, 108(2) ACTA PAEDIATRICA 300 (2019).

Robert Wells et al., *A Validational Study of the Structured Interview of Symptoms Associated with Sexual Abuse (SASA) Using Three Samples of Sexually Abused, Allegedly Abused, and Nonabused Boys*, 21(12) CHILD ABUSE & NEGLECT 1159 (1997).

Factitious Disorder Imposed on Another and Related Citations

For an excellent overview start here: ANNE LAZENBATT & JULIE TAYLOR, NATIONAL SOCIETY FOR THE PREVENTION OF CRUELTY TO CHILDREN, FABRICATED OR INDUCED ILLNESS IN CHILDREN: A RARE FORM OF CHILD ABUSE? (2011), https://www.pure.ed.ac.uk/ws/portalfiles/portal/12941026/K201118.pdf.

Catherine C. Ayoub, *Munchausen by Proxy*, *in* THE CAMBRIDGE HANDBOOK OF FORENSIC PSYCHOLOGY 690 (Jennifer M. Brown & Elizabeth A. Campbell eds., 2010).

Catherine C. Ayoub et al., *Munchausen by Proxy: Presentations in Special Education*, 7(2) CHILD MALTREATMENT 149 (2002).

Brenda Bursch et al., *Evaluation and Management of Factitious Disorder Imposed on Another*, 28 J. CLINICAL PSYCH. IN MED. SETTINGS 67 (2019), https://doi.org/10.1007/s10880-019-09668-6.

Camky v. Colvin, No. 6: 12-cv-01973-BR (D. Or. Dec. 2, 2013).

Pietro Ferrara et al., *Factitious Disorders and Munchausen Syndrome: The Tip of the Iceberg*, 17(4) J. CHILD HEALTH CARE 366 (2013).

Danya Glaser, *Fabricated or Induced Illness: From "Munchausen by Proxy" to Child and Family-Oriented Action*, 108 CHILD ABUSE & NEGLECT article 104649 (2020), https://doi.org/10.1016/j.chiabu.2020.104649.

James C. Hamilton & Kathryn A.K. Kouchi, *Factitious Disorders and the Adjudication of Claims of Physical and Mental Injury*, 11(1) PSYCH. INJ. & L. 9 (2018), https://doi.org/10.1007/s12207-017-9310-x.

In Interest of DH, No. 15-1865 (Iowa Ct. App. Apr. 27, 2016).

In re LD, No. 2015-283 (Vt. Nov. 19, 2015).

Lane v. Colvin, Civil No. 2: 14-cv-02188-MEF (W.D. Ark. Dec. 30, 2015).

Judith A. Libow, *Beyond Collusion: Active Illness Falsification*, 26(5) CHILD ABUSE & NEGLECT 525 (2002).

Rodriguez v. Colvin, No. 8: 12-cv-1592-T-33EAJ (M.D. Fla. Aug. 20, 2013).

Mary J. Sanders & Brenda Bursch, *Psychological Treatment of Factitious Disorder Imposed on Another/Munchausen by Proxy Abuse*, 27 J. CLINICAL PSYCH. IN MED. SETTINGS 139 (2019), https://doi.org/10.1007/s10880-019-09630-6.

John T. Stutts et al., *Malingering by Proxy: A Form of Pediatric Condition Falsification*, 24(4) J. DEV. & BEHAV. PEDIATRICS 276 (2003).

Gregory P. Yates & Marc D. Feldman, *Factitious Disorder: A Systematic Review of 455 Cases in the Professional Literature*, 41 GEN. HOSP. PSYCHIATRY 20 (2016).

Index

A

J

L

M

N

O

P

Q

R

S